Dear Merv

MERV HUGHES

Dear Merv

A SUE HINES BOOK
ALLEN & UNWIN

First published in 2001

A Sue Hines Book
Allen & Unwin
83 Alexander Street
Crows Nest NSW 2065
Australia
Phone: (61 2) 8425 0100
Fax: (61 2) 9906 2218
Email: info@allenandunwin.com
Web: www.allenandunwin.com

National Library of Australia
Cataloguing-in-Publication entry:

Merv Hughes : dear Merv.

   ISBN 1 86508 620 7.

   1. Hughes, Merv - Correspondence. 2. Cricket players –

   Australia – Correspondence.

   796.358092

Designed by Andrew Cunningham – Studio Pazzo
Typeset by Pauline Haas – Girl's Own Graphics
Printed by Griffin Press, South Australia

10 9 8 7 6 5 4 3 2 1

Contents

	Opening Stand	1
Chapter 1	Growing Up	11
Chapter 2	Life in Werribee, Part I	31
Chapter 3	Life in Werribee, Part II	63
Chapter 4	Life in Werribee, Part III	85
Chapter 5	A Mother's Letters to Home	107
Chapter 6	Life in Essex	121
Chapter 7	Mum's Advice Pays Off	145
Chapter 8	My First Test	169
Chapter 9	Another Test Match	195
Chapter 10	The Hat Trick	217
Chapter 11	The Struggle Continues	241
Chapter 12	The Ashes Tour, 1989	255
Chapter 13	London, Sydney, Hyderabad, Sharjah and Los Angeles	279
Chapter 14	Life in Werribee, epilogue	305
Chapter 15	Everybody's Mate	317
Chapter 16	Merv Hughes Personals	345
Chapter 17	The End	353
	Acknowledgements	367

Opening Stand

Gladesville
NSW.

Merv Hughes,

you're an overweight, disgusting prick and a disgrace to the Australian cricket tradition. You've been getting away with that sort of behaviour for far too long. You don't deserve to be included in any national team and you have made all Australians cringe.

Ian G.

Nice handwriting. Good use of the word 'cringe', which in my opinion, doesn't get a run as often as it should. A letter written by an obviously intelligent fellow.

People write letters for all sorts of reasons, and often it's to get something off their chest. Ian wrote this letter in response to some footage of me bowling in a Test match against the Kiwis, in New Zealand in 1993, where I was having a less than friendly discussion with Mark Greatbatch. I have always rated Mark as a batsman and he doesn't mind a beer after the game, so we get on pretty well. The television camera was over his shoulder, pointing at me, and the telescopic lens made it look like we were about two metres away from each other. In fact, he was behind the batting crease and I was more than half a pitch away from him. When I'm getting hit around like I was that day, I don't like wasting energy by walking too far up the batsman's end. As we stood there discussing how good a batsman I thought he was, waiting for the ball to be retrieved from the grandstand roof, I spat on the pitch. Absent-mindedly, unconsciously, without intent. I just don't spit on or at people. On the television it looked awful, but neither of the two umpires, nor the match referee, thought it warranted any action. Greatbatch made 29 off 30 balls before I bowled him.

Of course the incident was replayed all day in New Zealand and Australia, and the Australian team management thought I should be more aware of the image I was portraying, so I was fined $500. Happy days. Ian was sitting in his lounge room in Gladesville, saw the footage without understanding the effect of telephoto lenses, and not knowing my motivations, thought he should let me know how he felt. But I think Ian just wanted to write down how upset he was, to make himself feel better. I don't think he meant me to get the letter, because despite all the care he took in writing his name and address at the top of the page, and again on the back of the envelope, this is what he wrote on the front:

You can imagine the shock Ian got when the phone rang at his local pub.

'Hello, this is Ian.'

'Hello, Ian. Merv Hughes here.'

'Hah, hah good one. Who is it?'

'Ian, it's Merv Hughes.'

'Yeah, sure mate. Who is it?'

'"You're an overweight, disgusting prick and a disgrace to the Australian cricket tradition." You don't think you can write a letter like that, put your name and address on it, and expect not to hear from me, do you?'

'Oh, shit.'

'That's about right, Ian.'

By the end of the conversation, Ian understood what had happened that day, and was asking me to join him at the pub to meet him and his mates.

When I was on tour, I loved getting letters from home. Hearing about the everyday aspects of life has always been pretty important to me. And I seem to be surrounded by friends and family who are enthusiastic letter-writers. No matter where I was or how my cricket was going, it was amazing how positive I felt after getting a letter from home. It always struck me how lucky I was to have people close to me who would make the effort to write just because they wanted to let me know I hadn't been forgotten. Of course, Mum wrote to me every week from the time I left for England in April 1983, until she and Dad returned from country Victoria at the end of 1986. When I re-read what my family and my mates thought it was important for me to know over the years, I can see why I turned out the way I have. That's my excuse anyway.

Many of the letters from family and friends discussed what was happening in cricket. There is something special about cricket that urges people to put pen to paper, as though the game itself creates a poetry and a rhythm that needs to be recorded. When I was seventeen, I got this from my young cousin Sean.

Sorrento

16 October 1978

Dear Mervyn,

How are you. I am great. Last Saturday was the second day of our first cricket match, we play two-day matches. The Saturday before we batted. I made 12 in about 1½ hours. I really opened the innings because one of our openers went out halfway through the first over. After about another three overs the other opener went out. Then Richard King our captain came in he and I made a partnership of 39. Richard would hit the ball and there would be

3 in it, so Richard would call there's 3 in this and we would run 3
without calling. I went out run out. After another couple of overs
Richard had to retire at 43 (you have to retire once you make 40).
Then Christie and Darren Sullivan came in. They battled great.
We batted all day and made 4–156. We bowled the next Saturday.
In their first innings I took 5–0. And in their second innings I took
3–26, I bowl leg spin. We won by an innings and 123 runs. It's
taken me one week to write this letter, and we have started
another match against Boneo and we are in a pretty good
position. We bowled and I took 4–2 off 3 overs. We are batting at
the moment. I am 3 n.o. We are 3–28 chasing their score of all out
for 33. I hope your cricket is going well.

FROM
SEAN

P.S. Another week later I made 23 n.o. in 2½ hours.

Many of the letters are from fans. You might think fan mail is exactly
that, with people writing to tell you how good you are. But often people
write to express their opinion, which is not always complimentary, or
they offer advice. Of course, everyone's entitled to their opinion, it's just
that sometimes that opinion is wrong.

Most of the critical letters I have received were from Australians.
Usually, criticism comes from those who don't understand the context of
an incident. Or they have seen something that I have done that has irritated
them and because I was representing Australia, as Australians they feel
entitled to let me know they disapprove. I reckon that's great because it
means they are passionate about being Australian, and that they think
what I do as a cricketer is important. Otherwise they wouldn't get so upset.
Or perhaps they're just cranky bastards who want to have a whinge.

Surprisingly to some, I haven't received a lot of negative letters. A fan
asking for an autograph is the type of letter I get most frequently. I have
always tried to respond to those requests, as they usually include a piece
of paper or some piece of memorabilia, such as a collector's card or a
photograph, to be signed. Early on I worked out that the only way to stay
out of the poorhouse was to reply to those who sent a stamped, self-

addressed envelope. Sometimes, I got the stamp but not the address. So sorry if you think I owe you an autograph (and a stamp). I tried.

It always gave me a thrill to think that young fans of cricket would put some value in receiving my signature on a card or piece of paper. Sifting through the thousands of letters I have received over the years, I came across this one:

> Michael B.
> Thornbury
> Victoria
>
> Dear Mr Merv Hughes
> My name is Michael. I am a young fan of yours. You were my Favourite cricketer in Australia when you were playing cricket for the Vics and Australia. I would go to all the games to see you play here in Melbourne. I Really admire all of your sporting achevements in cricket. I had these cards at home and I was hoping that you could Sign them please. Best of Luck For the Future.
> > Yours ThankFully
> > Michael B.

And in the same handwriting as Michael B:

> Michael L.
> Port Melbourne
> Vic
>
> Dear Mr hughes
> My name is Michael. I am a young fan of yours. You were my favourite cricketer to play for Vics and Australia. I would go to all the games to see you play here in Melbourne. I Really admire all of your sporting achevements in cricket. I had these cards at home and I was hoping that you could Sign them please. Best wishes to you and your family For the future.
> > Yours Thankfully
> > Michael L.

And then, from the same address as Michael L:

> Matthew F.
> Port Melbourne
> Victoria
>
> Dear Mr Hughes
> My name is Matthew. I am a young Fan of yours. You were my
> Favourite cricket of all time. I Really admire all of your sporting
> achivements in cricket. I had these THREE cards at home and I
> was hoping that you could PLEASE sign them IF possible thank
> you. Best wishes to you and your Family for the Future.
> > Yours Thankfully
> > Matthew F.

Finally, from a different address in Thornbury:

> Matthew G.
> Thornbury
> Vic
>
> Dear Mr Hughes
> My names Matthew. Im a young fan of yours. You are my all time
> favourite cricketer to play for Vics and Australia. It was honour to
> see you play. I had these cards at home and I was hoping that you
> could Sign them please best of luck for the future.
> > Yours Thankfully
> > Matthew G.

It wasn't until I looked at these together, so willingly responded to over a number of years, that I was struck by the similarities in paper, hand-writing and punctuation. They are identical.

Apparently, autographed cards can be sold for a reasonable amount of money, but I always took the view that if a young cricket enthusiast wanted an autograph for himself, then it was an honour to help them out, and I would never put a price on my signature. I tried to track down

Michael B, Michael F, Matthew F and Matthew G, to help them with their punctuation, but he is living on a Mediterranean Island off the coast of his Swiss bank account.

All of these letters are printed as they were written. Occasionally, I have been forced to censor some letters, either in the interests of good taste, or to protect the guilty. Names have been disguised, so if you think you recognise yourself, you don't. Unless you've lived in Werribee during the last 25 years. If that's the case, then you are probably in this book somewhere, and I thank you.

Even after censoring, some of the language in the letters is not suitable for all eyes. So I have prepared a system of ratings to be used as 'Guidance for Children'. Each letter has a symbol that will give some indication of content.

(G) **Gee** this is interesting, I'll discuss this at dinner.

(PG) **Parents** may need **Guidance** with some of the words in this one.

(M) **Maternal** advice follows.

(R) **Really**, you shouldn't let your mum catch you reading this one.

CHAPTER ONE

Growing Up

North Eastern District Cricket Cup Competition
U/16 Inter-Zone Fixture – Sunday, 29 January 1978

The following players will represent North East (Zone 8) against Upper Goulburn & Port Phillip (Zone 9) at Yea Recreation Reserve on the abovementioned date.

Shane Robertson	(Wangaratta) (c)
Adrian Black	(Ovens & Kiewa) (vc)
Mark Ash	(Rutherglen)
John Clohessy	(Rutherglen)
Stewart Feldtmann	(Benalla)
Simon Hore	(Albury & Border)
Gregory Hoysted	(Wangaratta)
Mervyn Hughes	(Ovens & Kiewa)
Trevor McDonald	(Wangaratta)
Stephen Marks	(Mansfield)
Noel Shepherd	(Albury & Border)
Anthony Taraville	(Albury & Border)

Scorer – Aileen Gough   (Euroa)

Time of assembly – 11.15am

Players to provide own bat, pads, gloves etc., seek co-operation from personal club in this direction, if necessary.

Association secretaries to ensure players have transport to Yea.

Parents are invited to attend this fixture.

All concerned to make own arrangements for luncheon prior to commencement of play.

Where necessary try to arrange for a loan of North East Zone 8 Green & Gold representative cap from former players in your association area.

Hours of play – 12 noon – 6.30pm – batting time – maximum 3.05 hrs.

Each team will bat 12 players and field 11 (alternating).

Keith Sherwill
Team Manager

MERV: My first invitation to play representative cricket. I also played Under 21 in the rep side for the North East in Zone 8, against the Upper Goulburn and all the zones in North Eastern Victoria. It would have been my first match wearing the Green and Gold if I'd been able to borrow a cap. Unfortunately, it rained all day, so not a ball was bowled.

The Hughes family was living in Myrtleford, where Dad was teaching at the Primary School. We were there for two years, 1976 and 1977, and I played Under 16 cricket for Myrtleford and senior cricket for Buffalo, in the same team as my father. I was fourteen years old. If I had gone up there and played junior cricket I wouldn't have developed as quickly as I did. I made my first century in senior cricket at Buffalo.

 30 August 1978

SYDNEY

CONGRATULATIONS ON REPRESENTING WERRIBEE 1STS IN FOOTBALL. HOPE YOU REMEMBER ALL YOUR MATES AND YOUR DAD'S MATES WHEN YOU HIT THE BIG TIME IN GEELONG
GRAHAM EDGAR

MERV: Graham Edgar is a very good friend of my father's. We've been back in Werribee since January, and I started playing in the VFA in the Under 19s. The new coach has decided to give some young blokes a go, so I've made it to the seniors for the Lightning Premiership.

G WERRIBEE FOOTBALL CLUB
12 October 1978

Dear Player,
On Monday October 23rd, a Players' Night will be held in the
Club Rooms at Chirnside Park commencing at about 7.30 PM.
The main purpose of the evening is to finalise match payments for
the season 1978.

We will also be showing the Video Tape of the televised part of
the Lightning Premiership Grand Final. Those players involved in
the Lightning Premiership games are asked to bring their gear
with them for a team photo.

The evening will also give the opportunity to the Trip Away
organisers to fill you in on any last-minute details.

Yours faithfully,
T. Edwards
Secretary

MERV: The VFA has two divisions and Werribee was a Second Division
team. We ended up winning the Lightning Premiership, knocking over
first division clubs Coburg and Sandringham to take out the title. I can't
remember too much about the night but we are on about $40 a win – so
I am the richest kid at school.

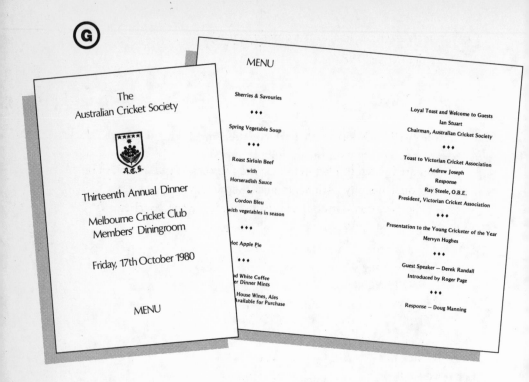

MERV: I have been playing District cricket at Footscray this year. In 1979–80 we won a premiership in my first year in the First XI. I've also been invited into the Victorian State Squad and I was picked in a couple of the Victorian Under 23, Under 21 and Under 19 squads. I have just played my first game for Victoria in the Under 23 team as an eighteen-year-old.

The members of the Australian Cricket Society are enthusiastic supporters of cricket, but I didn't know too much about it. Every year they try to spot a young cricketer that will make it to the Test team. I got to the night and the guest speaker was Derek Randall, a wonderful English Test batsman who was known for his idiosyncratic approach to the game. He is playing District cricket for Prahran. To hear him speak about the game and be awarded the Young Cricketer of the Year at the MCG was a big deal for me. Mum and Dad and my sister Peta went and I had my first big adventure in my HT Holden station wagon, The Green Hornet. I had got my licence just before this and I drove Snappa and Katy (his girlfriend) and took a girl by the name of Marie Squires to the do.

VICTORIAN CRICKET ASSOCIATION
21 September 1981

Dear Merv,

Victorian State Squad 1981–82 – Trial Match

You are invited to play in the second pre-season trial match to be held on Thursday 24th September (Show Day).

The previously announced teams to play in the match are as follows:

R. ROBINSON'S XI	G. YALLOP'S XI
R. Robinson (Capt.)	G. Yallop (Capt.)
P. Davies	M. Hughes
J. Higgs	M. McCarthy
S. McCooke	G. McBurney
R. McCurdy	G. Matthews
M. Walker	P. Newton
G. Watts	J. O'Keefe
G. Webb	G. Ross
D. Whatmore	P. Sacristani
J. Wiener	S. Small
A. Wildsmith	P. Young

The match will be played at Oakleigh Technical School situated on the corner of North Road and Poath Road, Oakleigh.

Hours of play will be 10.30 a.m. to 5.30 p.m. and the match will be of 50 overs per innings. Lunch will be provided.

If you are unable or unwilling to accept this invitation, please advise me immediately.

With best wishes,
Yours sincerely,
K. W. Jacobs
Secretary

MERV: This letter means I am getting closer to selection for Victoria. I am in the pretenders team, and have Max Walker, Rod McCurdy, Alan

Hurst and Ian Callen ahead of me. So basically I am no chance for a year or two.

 VICTORIAN CRICKET ASSOCIATION
30 December 1981

Dear Merv,

**McDonald's Cup First Round Match – S.A. v. Victoria
1 January 1982**

You are invited to play for Victoria in the above match. The previously announced team is:

J. Scholes (Capt.)	M. Hughes
J. Moss (V-Capt.)	D. Jones
L. Balcam	I. Maddocks
S. Graf	G. Watts
B. Green	J. Wiener
J. Higgs	G. Yallop

12th man to be announced on the morning of the match.

Manager for this match will be Mr Bert Numa.
Travel – Travel to Adelaide will be on Ansett Flt 202 departing Melbourne at 9.20 a.m. on Thursday 31st December, 1981. The return flight to Melbourne will be on Ansett Flt 203 departing Adelaide at 10.00 a.m., and scheduled to arrive in Melbourne at 11.35 a.m. on 2nd January, 1982.
    Would you please report to the Tullamarine check-in counter on Thursday no later than 8.45 a.m.
Accommodation – Adelaide Highrise.
Hours of Play – Hours of play will be from 10.00 a.m. to 5.45 p.m.; with a lunch break being taken from 1.30 p.m. to 2.15 p.m. .

Pale blue pads will be supplied in Adelaide, which are required to be worn by all batsmen.

Allowances – Daily allowance for the tour will be $32.50 gross per day with a general expense allowance of $48. Each player will receive the general expense allowance and a total daily allowance (net of tax) of $44.20.

Prizemoney – Prizemoney will be $1,200 to the winning team, $600 to the losing team and an award for the man of the match of $200.

As usual, the contents of the Players' Handbook and Code of Behaviour (as previously circulated) will apply to this match.

Should you be unable or unwilling to accept this invitation, please advise me immediately.

With best wishes,

Yours sincerely

K. W. Jacobs

Secretary

MERV: This is it: my first invitation to play for Victoria. And don't you love the request to advise the VCA Secretary if I am unwilling to accept the invitation. Try to keep me away!

Although I did nearly miss it. State training was on the Wednesday night, 30 December and I was down at the beach – Ocean Grove – with Snapper and Burnsy and the usual suspects. Burnsy had a holiday house down at Ocean Grove and it is a great place to unwind. No radio, no television and we don't read the newspapers when we are there. Exercise is a swim then a walk to the Barwon Heads pub for dinner. One night we got home and Snappa, Burnsy and I were sitting there looking at each other, pretty pleased with life. Three young blokes with a fridge full of beer just sitting in a lounge room with no TV. Snappa looked around and said, 'You know what we need here right now?'

And I just nodded my head, knowing what he was thinking, that three young ladies wouldn't go astray, and we looked at Burnsy and there he was shaking his head, 'Yeah, a colour TV'd be fantastic wouldn't it?'

Burnsy suffered for years over that, whenever we were at the BHP, it was, 'Hey, Burnsy, let's make it a big night and pick up a couple of colour tellies and take them back to your place!'

I was planning to skip training that night and ran into Geoff Billman and his wife, who I knew from the Werribee Cricket Club, at lunchtime in Ocean Grove. She congratulated me and I had no idea what she was on about. I bought the first newspaper I could find, then had to borrow Snappa's car and get the hundred kilometres up the highway, stopping at Werribee for my gear, in an hour and a half to be at training on time. If I hadn't made it I probably would never have played!

I was given the letter at training and we travelled to Adelaide the next day. I was going to skip training, because I didn't think that I was going to be looked at. Ian Callen and Rod McCurdy were injured and Alan Hurst and Max Walker retired that week so they'd just lost four fast bowlers from the team in seven days.

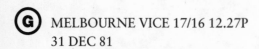

(G) MELBOURNE VICE 17/16 12.27P
31 DEC 81

MR MERV HUGHES
ADELAIDE OVAL
NORTH ADELAIDE

BEST WISHES MERV
PRESIDENT COMMITTEE AND PLAYERS FOOTSCRAY
CRICKET CLUB

MERV: My second telegram.

Victoria 4 for 253 from 49.5 overs defeated
South Australia 5 for 249 from 50 overs.
M. Hughes 2 for 59 from 10 overs.
Dean Jones 2 for 40 from 10 overs.

MERV: How badly did I go, out-bowled by Dean Jones! John Inverarity played First Class cricket for about 20 years and never hit a six . . . but he got me. Interesting match payments in a game that we won. But that is not what you play sport for.

The number of letters and telegrams that I have received for my first game for Victoria really surprised me. It is a little daunting that so many people are following my career.

4 January 1982

Dear Merv,

We were all so pleased to read of your selection in the Victorian XI and really got a kick out of you doing well.

I bet you got a real thrill when you rolled Rick Darling. May try and get down to watch you in one of the games in Melbourne.

Good wishes and best of luck in your future matches.

Harry, Lou & Kim

MERV: Harry Alexander is the only bloke from Euroa to play Test cricket. He was involved with football and cricket and very good friends with Dad. We lived just down the road from them and it was just a block away from the footy and cricket ground.

 WERRIBEE CRICKET CLUB
President I. Hughes

Dear Merve,

On behalf of the Committee of Management, Members and Players of the Werribee Cricket Club, I wish to congratulate you on your recent inclusion into the Victorian Cricket Team.

I hope that your recent match against South Australia will be the first of many for Victoria and on behalf of all at the Werribee Cricket Club, I wish you continued success.

Regards,

Jim Cann

(Secretary)

MERV: I was down at Werribee for a couple of years before I shifted to Footscray to play District cricket. I reckon the President must have had a talk to the Secretary and said that it would be a good idea to send a letter off as the President would never write to me himself. But Jimmy Cann was a long time servant of the Werribee Cricket Club and it's great to get that support from a team that I used to play with.

(G) VICTORIAN CRICKET ASSOCIATION
13 January 1982

Dear Merv,

**Victoria v. South Australia at Kardinia Park, Geelong
15–18 January 1982**

You are invited to play for Victoria in the above match. The invitation, as usual, is conditional upon your acceptance of the previously distributed regulations and policies of the Victorian Players' Handbook.

The previously announced team to play in the match is as follows:

J. Scholes (Capt.)	M. Hughes
J. Moss (Vice-Capt.)	D. Jones
R. Bright	I. Maddocks
I. Callen	G. Watts
B. Green	J. Wiener
J. Higgs	G. Yallop

12th man to be announced on the morning of the match.

Travel – Travel to Geelong will be by private vehicle for which an allowance will be paid for a maximum of 5 motor vehicles.
Accommodation – Geelong Travelodge, Cnr Myer and Heringhap Sts, Geelong.
Allowances – Daily allowance for the match will be $32.50 gross per day with a general expense allowance of $85.00.
Each player will receive a general expense allowance and a total daily allowance of $88.40.
Practice – Practice has been arranged for 4.00 p.m. Thursday 14th January, at Kardinia Park.

Should you be unable or unwilling to accept this invitation please advise me immediately.

With best wishes for a successful match,

Yours sincerely
K. W. Jacobs
Secretary

MERV: Perhaps I have done something right. The selectors have decided on a youth policy for the bowlers, so they have given me the nod for my debut First Class match, at the centre of the cricket universe.

Victoria 160 and 6 for 252 drew with
South Australia, 244 and 6 declared for 279.
M. Hughes 3/53 and 0/52, 1 not out first inns.

MERV: I had been doing pre-season football training at Kardinia Park with the Geelong Football Club before Christmas. At least I was able to drop in on the coach of Geelong, Billy Goggin, to tell him I was busy with cricket. He said he didn't think the club should interrupt me while I was playing for Victoria, and that he would get back in touch with me when the cricket season was over. I'm still waiting to hear from him.

 WERRIBEE FOOTBALL CLUB
19 January 1982

Dear Merv,
On behalf of all your friends in the Werribee Football Club, I congratulate you on being selected for Victoria in the Sheffield Shield matches.

I am sure that this is only the start of a long career in interstate, and hopefully, international cricket.

Yours sincerely,
P. D. Mullaney
(President)

(G) VICTORIAN CRICKET ASSOCIATION
25 January 1982

Dear Merv,

Western Australia v. Victoria
29 January – 1 February 1982

You are invited to play for Victoria in the above match. The previously announced team is:

J. Scholes (Capt.)	D. Jones
R. Bright	S. O'Donnell
I. Callen.	P. Sacristani
B. Green	G. Watts
J. Higgs	J. Wiener
M. Hughes	G. Yallop

12th man to be announced on the morning of the match.

Would you please report to the Tullamarine check in counter on Wednesday *no later than 8.45 a.m.*
Accommodation: Perth Sheraton.
Allowances: Daily allowance for the tour will be $32.50 gross per day with a general expense allowance of $160. Each player will receive the general expense allowance and a total daily allowance of $132.60 . . .

MERV: A Perth match, so the money is huge: $292.60 for the game, including expenses, after tax.

Western Australia 307 and 263 drew with
Victoria 316 and 6 for 120.
M. Hughes 2/60 and 0/41, 4 runs in first inns.

VICTORIAN CRICKET ASSOCIATION
9 February 1982

Dear Merv,

Victoria v. Queensland at Kardinia Park, Geelong
12–15 February 1982

You are invited to play for Victoria in the above match. The invitation, as usual, is conditional upon your acceptance of the previously distributed regulations and policies of the Victorian Players Handbook.

The previously announced team to play in the match is as follows:

J. Scholes (Capt.)	M. Hughes
J. Higgs (Vice-Capt.)	D. Jones
I. Callen	P. Sacristani
P. Davies	G. Watts
S. Graf	J. Wiener
B. Green	G. Yallop

12th man to be announced on the morning of the match . . .

MERV: Back to my favourite ground.

 Victoria 536 and 3 for 57 drew with
Queensland 282 and 340.
M. Hughes 4/69 and 2/73, did not bat.

ROTARY CLUB OF MYRTLEFORD
10 February 1982

Dear Merv,
This letter is to extend on behalf of the Rotary Club of Myrtleford
congratulations from Members on your recent selection in the
Victorian Sheffield Shield Cricket Team. You can be rest assured
you have the best wishes and support of Myrtleford and we look
forward to seeing a successful career.

> Yours faithfully,
> G. Nevin
> Secretary

 VICTORIAN CRICKET ASSOCIATION
16 February 1982

Dear Merv,

**Victoria v. New South Wales at Junction Oval, St Kilda
19–22 February 1982**

You are invited to play for Victoria in the above match. The
previously announced team is:

J. Scholes (Capt.)	M. Hughes
J. Higgs	D. Jones
I. Callen	P. Sacristani
P. Davies	G. Watts
S. Graf	J. Wiener
B. Green	G. Yallop

12th man to be announced on the morning of the match . . .

New South Wales 8 dec. for 305 and 2 for 93 defeated
Victoria 161 and 235.
M. Hughes 4/71 and 1/19, 17 runs first inns.

MERV: My first defeat in Sheffield Shield cricket.

VICTORIAN CRICKET ASSOCIATION
24 February 1982

Dear Merv,

South Australia v. Victoria
26 February – 1 March 1982

You are invited to play for Victoria in the above match. The
previously announced team is:

J. Scholes (Captain)	M. Hughes
J. Higgs (Vice-Captain)	D. Jones
I. Callen	P. Sacristani
P. Davies	J. Wiener
S. Graf	A. Wildsmith
B. Green	G. Watts

12th man to be announced on the morning of the match . . .

South Australia 423 and 1 for 161 defeated
Victoria 297 and 286.
M. Hughes 2/97 and 0/32, 0 and 1 not out.

(G) AUSTRALIAN CRICKET BOARD
12 February 1982

Dear Merv,

1982 Esso Australia Cricket Scholars

You have been nominated by your State Association/Council for consideration by the Australian Selection Committee as one of four Esso Australia Cricket Scholars. The final selection will be made soon and the four successful players' names will be announced either late February/early March.

In case you don't know, the Board in conjunction with Esso Australia, are providing four scholarships to England for 1982. Each player will be allocated to a County for a period of 12 weeks for the purpose of intensive cricket development. Living, accommodation and equipment allowances and return air travel are provided from the Esso sponsorship. It is likely that the players will go in mid-April to end June, and are not permitted to have any other playing commitment in England during the period of the Scholarship.

Would you immediately contact your State Association office or, if on a Sheffield Shield tour, the local office and advise whether or not you would be available to accept a Scholarship, if selected. That office will then telex your reply to the Board office.

If you have any queries, please do not hesitate to ring either Graham Halbish or myself.

> Yours sincerely,
> D. J. Richards
> Executive Director

c.c. Australian Selection Committee
State Secretaries/General Manager

MERV: A letter with the green and gold coat of arms shining out from the top. This is a great moment. To be under consideration means that the

Victorian selectors think I have a future, and that my performances for the state will be considered by the Australian selectors. The Esso Scholarships are seen as the development scheme for future Test players.

 20 February 1982

Dear Merv,
I support Victoria in the Sheffield Shield and congratulations on taking 6 wickets against Queensland last week.

Could you please autograph the enclosed photo and return it to me in the SAE?

Yours sincerely,
Ian C.

MERV: My first written request for an autograph. Even if he hadn't mentioned my six wickets, I would have let him have it.

 Dear Merv,
Just a note to congratulate you on your fine Cricket Season this year.

It was a proud moment for me to see you on T.V. from my set in Sydney. Well done! Next move is the Test Team.

Hope to see you soon.
Graham Edgar

CHAPTER TWO

Life in Werribee

PART I

Werribee considers itself a country town. Just off the Princes Highway between Melbourne and Geelong, it is surrounded by flat agricultural land. Twenty-five minutes up the road is Melbourne's Westgate Bridge, which leads into the city centre. So it is closer in time to the centre of Melbourne than most of the eastern suburbs.

After another winter playing football with Werribee, mid-week basketball with Panels and pre-season training with the Victorian squad, the summer started early with a game against a Country XI.

(G) VICTORIAN CRICKET ASSOCIATION
15 September 1982

Dear Merv,

Victoria v. A Country XI – Rochester
18–19 September 1982

You are invited to play for Victoria in the above match. The Squad of players selected for this match is as follows –

G. Yallop (Captain)	M. Hughes
P. Cox	J. Moss
P. Davies	R. McCurdy
S. Graf	P. Sacristani
B. Green	M. Taylor
J. Higgs	G. Watts
	J. Wiener

. . .

MERV: The summer almost ended as well. I ruptured my hamstring in this game and then did a 'grunt' muscle in my chest in a Footscray District match. I was pretty relieved to be selected for a One Day game on New Year's Day: two New Year's Eves in a row without a drink.

(G) VICTORIAN CRICKET ASSOCIATION
23 December 1982

Dear Merv,

**Victoria v. Queensland – McDonald's Cup First Round Match
1 January 1983 at the M.C.G.**

You are invited to play for Victoria in the above match. The previously announced Team is –

G. Yallop – Captain	D. Jones
J. Wiener – Vice-Captain	R. McCurdy
L. Balcam	G. Miles
I. Callen	G. Richardson
S. Graf	M. Taylor
M. Hughes	D. Whatmore

12th man to be announced on the morning of the match . . .

N.B.: Please note that the coloured clothing as worn in the McDonald's Cup match in Hobart, should again be worn for this match.

MERV: What the selectors didn't tell me until I got to the ground was that I would be twelfth man for the day. What a waste. And the Vics got done, so it was a long day. Mind you, it wasn't a complete loss, because if you played in a McDonald's Cup game they used to give you vouchers and no-one else would take them. So I'd collect them all and use them on the way back from Ocean Grove with Snappa – Big Mac: buy one, get one free – I think we bought about ten each one day . . .

Short of match practice, I was given a run in my first Victorian Second XI match. And it was a pretty good team, with Tony Dodemaide and Simon Davis both eventually playing Test matches for Australia.

G VICTORIAN CRICKET ASSOCIATION
23 December 1982

Dear Merv,

South Australian 2nd XI v. Victorian 2nd XI
4, 5 & 6 January 1983 at the Adelaide Oval

You are invited to play for Victoria in the above match. The previously announced Team is –

B. Green – Captain	P. King
P. Davies	R. Templeton
S. Davis	D. Shepherd
A. Dodemaide	G. Watts
M. Hughes	W. Whiteside
P. Jackson	A. Wildsmith

Manager for this Tour will be Mr Bert Numa . . .

MERV: I played four Shield matches for the season taking eleven wickets, plus another One Dayer and a four-day game against Sri Lanka. Instead of establishing myself at state level, I feel like I am only just hanging on. I think I need more cricket, so I am considering giving footy a miss for the winter and trying to find a team in Leagues cricket in England. I am not sure how I am going to pay for it all, or even if I can persuade a club to give me a game.

(G) AUSTRALIAN CRICKET BOARD
14 March 1983

Dear Merv,

Esso Australia Cricket Scholarships – 1983

I am writing to confirm that you have been conditionally selected
by the Australian Selection Committee, as one of four players
from throughout Australia to receive an Esso Australia Cricket
Scholarship for 1983. On behalf of the Board, may I extend our
congratulation to you.

The four players selected and the Counties to which they have
been allocated are:

Mike Haysman – Leicestershire
Merv Hughes – Essex
Rob Kerr – Nottinghamshire
Greg Matthews – Worcestershire

The purpose of this scholarship is to provide promising young
Australian players with the opportunity to play and improve their
game under English conditions and the Board expects you, as a
recipient, to take full advantage of this unique opportunity.

Your scholarship will operate for twelve weeks from your
arrival in London. For this period you will be attached to the
Essex County Cricket Club where arrangements will be made for
your involvement in playing, coaching and associated activities. It
is hoped that the opportunity will arise for you to participate in
some County Second XI matches, or matches of a like nature.

The terms of the sponsorship from Esso Australia Limited
provide for return Australia/England airfares (this will be on
Qantas); $500 towards the provision of proper cricket kit and
equipment (which may be purchased in either Australia or
England); an allowance of $AUS25 per day for the full twelve
weeks to cover meals away from home and incidental expenses
such as fares; a subsidy to your host or billet to cover
accommodation and meals. Your host club in England will make

the necessary arrangements for your accommodation, hopefully in a family environment.

As this is the third year of the Scholarship, we look to you to ensure the scheme's continued success in 1983. Your host Club will be asked to submit a report on your cricket and general experience gained. It is of paramount importance both to the Board and to Esso Australia Limited that you uphold the highest ideals of behaviour and sportsmanship, and co-operate with your hosts throughout the twelve-week period of the scholarship.

The terms of the scholarship also preclude you from accepting any professional engagement or fee (cricket or otherwise) during the period of your scholarship visit to England. However, if you are invited to participate in any extra matches for which you are offered travel expenses, this is acceptable, subject to it being acceptable to your host Club.

The Board requires your written acceptance of the terms and conditions of the scholarship as set out above. Please sign the attached agreement and return it to me as soon as possible. Upon receipt of your acceptance, a cheque for $500 will be forwarded immediately to assist with the purchase of whatever equipment you might require to be properly outfitted for the trip.

Esso Australia will be providing you with a blazer, slacks, shirt etc. This outfit is an important part of the image of the Esso Australia cricket scholarships, and should be worn by you on all appropriate occasions.

I shall contact you again shortly in regard to more details of your travel arrangements and your involvement with your English Club. Please ensure that you have a current Australian passport which will remain valid throughout the period of your visit. I would anticipate you leaving Australia late April.

Should you have any queries on any of the above matters, or on any other aspect of the scheme, please do not hesitate to contact me (ring reverse charges if you wish).

Yours sincerely,
D.L. Richards
Executive Director

MERV: The Esso Scholarship. It is a big part of the development of young Australian cricketers. Esso and the ACB sends four players a year to England to play in the Second XI at a County Club. Players are also assigned to play with a club in the local league, so it is four months of pretty much non-stop cricket. In the four years that the scheme ran, some handy cricketers were given scholarships. Esso Scholarships are a sign that as a young bloke I have at least been noticed by the national selectors. And with a $500 cheque about to arrive for advance purchase of gear, Snappa and Burnsy are odds-on to have a very big 'no-shout' night with the compliments of the ACB!

As for my cricket development, to be picked to go to Essex is a huge bonus for me. When I first got down to Footscray, Ken Eastwood, who played Test cricket, was captain of the seconds, and I learned a lot playing under him for just over twelve months. The Essex County Second XI is led by Mike Denness – who captained England – and my time there will be filled with cricket lessons. As players, the club has John Lever and Neil Foster to talk to about bowling and Keith Fletcher and Graham Gooch to bowl at in the nets.

(G) CITY OF FOOTSCRAY
22 March 1983

Dear Mr Hughes
At its meeting on Monday evening, 21 March 1983, Council's attention was drawn to your outstanding achievement in receiving an 'Esso' sponsorship to play with the English County Team of Essex during the forthcoming English Cricket season.

As one of only four (4) cricketers throughout Australia, and the only Victorian, to receive such prestigious sponsorship, it is a sure indication that you are within reach of achieving National honours as an Australian Test Cricketer.

On behalf of the Council of the City of Footscray, please accept our heartiest congratulations and best wishes for the future.
Yours sincerely,
[signatures illegible] Mayor, Councillor, Town Clerk

MERV: I am 21 years old, I've never been overseas, and now the council is writing to me to tell me I am about to play Test cricket. I am feeling no pressure, as I just want to establish myself at state level at this stage and I know how difficult a task that is proving to be. So the accolades are nice and I am beginning to realise that I might have a future in the game. But I have to survive four and a half months in England first, and I know I am going to miss life in Werribee.

 27 April 1983

Dear Mervyn,
Thank you for ringing this morning – hope things worked out O.K. with your luggage. Let's know if we have to send money (for excess baggage) to anyone. Also, how was your trip & did you stop anywhere and what do you think of England at this early stage?

Melanie had lunch here today. Both she and Gary had Toastmaker sandwiches. Next week at kinder there is a farewell kid's party for Sonya who leaves next Thursday. Hope Gary likes his new teacher as much as he likes her.

Last night Daddy thought we might have been missing you so he put on his impression of lots of your ways! (Gave us coaches speeches and Peta and I hugs, and then went through all the sayings you were using Monday – 'Get off me back', & something about a dummy.) [That'd be 'spit the dummy', Mum, not 'where the hell is my dummy, I want to pack it for England'.]

Today in the mail there was a card from Auntie Greta wishing you all the best also Uncle Eric rang to speak to you last night & said to pass on his best wishes too & Aunty Frieda did likewise in a letter to me today.

Collingwood had a great win in the night footy last nite – Daddy was pleased. Daddy also got your car keys back yesterday. Gary said to tell you lots of things!!! He liked the aeroplane you went on yesterday (how were the hosties?)

This says MERVYN [lots of scribble by Gary]. Peta won her b'ball last nite at Albert Park – Plays again at 5.50 tonite. Will go now, no more space – Lots of love from all of us
Freda

MERV: Then again, given the detail in the first letter from Mum – written the day after I left Melbourne – there isn't too much I am going to miss out on. I hope I don't have to read about little brother Gary's lunches for the next four months.

GEELONG 14.11 95 def. CARLTON 12.13 85
C'WOOD 19.16 130 def. NTH MELB 15.18 108
FITZROY 22.11 143 def. ST KILDA 15.12. 102
RICHMOND 15.16 106 def. HAWKS 12.16 88
MELB 18.18 126 def. SWANS 12.21 93
Do you get Footy Scores from here??

Monday 2 May 1983

Hi Mervy,
How are you and did you enjoy your first weekend in England? We went to Woodend on Sat – Geoff, his girls, Pop & Gary went mushrooming & then Geoff drove us around Mt Macedon & Macedon. Quite unbelievable! Our friends, the Elderfields, look as though they are at her Mum's home in two big caravans. Their home was just burnt right out – No sign of any garden at all, & it was a lovely garden, & no chimneys left standing. [The Mt Macedon area was devastated during the Ash Wednesday bushfires in February 1983.]

Guess what? Dean Chiron made St Kilda's 20; although he started on the bench he was mentioned in the best players in one of the Sunday papers, got quite a mention on World of Sport & was just pipped (by a F'scray player – Sewell?) (I think) for goal of the day.

Lindsay James rang the day you left Aust, to wish you all the best – didn't realize you were going so soon. He said Bill Tyson is in for a job with Rothmans.

Hope Sweeney rang this morning (to catch you before you left) with your boots. I rang Elaine at VCA to see if any more cricketers going to England & after talking at the office she thinks Graham Yallop may be the best bet IF he makes the Aus. team. The Australians arrived back from Sri Lanka & the team for England is being selected now.

Poor old Footscray fell in a heap on Sat & were trounced by Essendon 27.19 (181) to 7.7 (49). Eastcoast has just announced they are going to sponsor them & on teli Fri nite they showed the players putting on Blue jumpers.

Werribee had a good win against Dandenong 18.13 (121) – 16.14 (110). Catts, Paul Smith & Wise were dropped for Douglas, & Simmons & Egg were on the bench.

Macedon 2nds were defeated by Romsey 22.26 to 0.0 so your father (STUPIDLY) thinks he may give them a ring to see if they want him to play.

Don't know anything of the W'bee game as we went to Blairos yest arvo. Haven't seen or heard of Gavin, Kate, or Robyn & things are quiet at the shop. It was quiet in all the shops on Thurs – don't know where all the people were. Must go, love from all of us
       Fre

MERV: Mum looks like she's getting into a good rhythm early, with the second letter in five days. She hasn't settled on her opening as yet, and has abandoned the formality of 'Dear Mervyn' for a far too casual approach.

I suppose I should introduce you to my family. Mum, who refers to herself as Freda or Fre at the sign-off, but Mummy elsewhere. Sister Peta is about eleven months older than me, and Gary is my brother, born just after I turned seventeen. So in 1983, scribble was all he could manage. Dad, who appears as Ian, Daddy or Pop, was a primary school teacher and ultimately a Principal. That's why we moved around a lot when I was younger. A good way to meet the locals in any country town is to play sport, so Dad was always involved in cricket and football wherever we lived and Mum played a lot of tennis. In 1983 they were still very competitive and very active, which probably explains Gary.

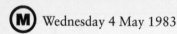 Wednesday 4 May 1983

P.S. Gavin, Katy & Deb came & had their lunch here on Tues.

Hi Merv,
How are you? Hope you are settling in O.K. How's the English weather? It's been raining here for days now and the drought is well & truly broken. Because of the rain, Queensland has been declared a State of Disaster. Yarram, too, was on the news again tonight all flooded. Robyn told me when I rang her earlier that the school kids would be happy as the school is one of the 1st places to flood. Robyn went to the Skyhooks concert on Monday & said it was great.

Finches played with four players & were beaten by Wyndham. Robyn had her bag stolen at Chris Squires 18th birthday & was most upset as the bag came from Bali & she also lost her good leather wallet & key chain & a good bit of money and her licence. She does not expect to get anything back.

Hookesy has decided to stay in S.A. & has signed a contract with them for next three years. As Yallop has resigned as captain, Ray Bright has been tipped to captain the Vics. No sign of a coach as yet.

Last night St Kilda played Richmond so we got a pretty good look at this one. It was a great match & Richmond finished up winning by a couple of goals.

Bartlett looks like missing a few games – he's got an injury similar to your cheek bone injury & done by a teammate. He's played 380 games & is trying to reach 400.

A 61 year old potato farmer & a few others ran from Sydney to Melbourne. The potato farmer cut almost 2 days off the record – he hardly slept during the run – and won almost $10,000 for his great effort.

Best go now, shopping day tomorrow – school holidays start Friday. Gary & I will probably go to Euroa for the second week.

Bye for now, Love from all of us
Freda

MERV: The great Cliff Young, a potato farmer from Colac in western Victoria, was competing in the Sydney to Melbourne Ultra Marathon. The scores at the top of Mum's earlier letter are those of the Victorian Football League. This is Australia's major football competition, although you can see that South Melbourne had just been transferred to Sydney and renamed the Sydney Swans, while the other eleven teams are based in Victoria. Mum's missing me.

 5 May 1983

To Dear Mervie,

How's it going – I hope you're not too tired to read this after all (3) of Mum's letters. Everyone has been asking how you are, have we heard from you & when do you start playing? By everyone I mean all different customers at the bank; everyone I work with, Panels, Careys, Les Wright in particular wanted to know all about things. He has done his hamstring *again* (third time & is back to square one again). Jeff Hughes wants to know if you had enough money & how much did the others take. He got cleaned up at footy last Saturday. Lara lost & Jeff got concussed & carried off. His neck's in a brace & he's got this week off work. The doctor said he was lucky not to break it, so it must be pretty bad. Panels came a draw last week with Mossfield – Naz wasn't playing either – Burnsie was their big recruit for the night. How's the family you're staying with – I hope everything's going well for you. I was worried about how you'll go with the different currency! We see your car around town, so often think of you. Chris had his first exam at school today – don't know how he went. We're still winning basketball Mondays. I play on Wednesdays too now with Preston Devils. It's 5th Division but it's good. I see Naz & the boys & Tricia – although I haven't spoken to her. Jamie Swann was asking about you too – I thought it was really nice, but he only wanted to order a pair of Puma basketball boots off you – he didn't even know you'd left! Did Mum tell you there was an article in the Banner about you? Have you met up with Mrs

Cullen yet? Or seen anyone else from Aust. It's really quiet at home & work just isn't the same anymore – according to Nancy – she really misses you & Gav playing hide & seek with her. Kathy at work (the junior) sends her love – she misses her smile in the green shop! Jeff isn't allowed to play footy for a month at least. This weekend we will probably watch F'scray & C'wood. F'scray have finally fired up – when you're not here to watch them. Lots of love – miss you heaps – so does about half of W'bee. Panels definitely do too.

Peta XXXXX

 10 May 1983

Hilly

How ya groing ya pommy bastard. It's TUESDAY THE TENTH, and I am at home because I've got no work. We lost basketball to Chevrons last night. We played a shocker. Burnsy played his first game for us last week. We came a draw 37–37 against Duran Duran's team.

Went to the footy on Sunday at Sandringham. Werribee won by about six goals. They were 13 goals up at 3/4 time. They played really well. The seconds won too. Lara aren't going too well. We lost to Bell Post Hill by two goals. Pat, Robbie & I got the money, they played well but I played average, gave a few shirt-fronts though.

We beat Belmont by 1 point on Saturday, I hardly got a kick, played back pocket.

Centrals played Hoppers last Saturday and won by about 10 goals. Everyone's missing you and your shit-stirring but I am number one shit-stirrer while your away, and doing it well. I've been hanging shit on everyone at Werribee's football.

I'm thinking about selling my car. If I fix it up I should get 2½ grand. I think I will buy Robbies car for 3½.

Hope your getting plenty of wickets and strays over there . . .

What's the food like over there. Do the pickles out of the Big

Macs stick to the roof? I did a bewdy at McDonalds the other night. Must have got sprung cause they told us to leave.

I haven't seen much of Katie but she's coming over for dinner today and we're going over to Crossa's for Steve's birthday tonight. They are both well. Snozza started work today with Mick The Skip Grotto. Don't see Snozza much cause he's still in love. Boonga's coming home soon but no-one's heard from Kevin. Greeny hasn't been playing cause he's got the flu. We miss him on the field.

My arm's getting tired, that's why the writings getting worse. (Good excuse). We haven't been going out much. Went to Cats on Saturday night which wasn't bad. We went out to a Pub on the way home from Sandringham which was all right. Some bad news, Duddo made a comeback and wore the infamous no. 9. I thought you'd be spewing. (He only wore it for one game).

Had lunch at Freda's the other day, she said she was missing you. She has already wrote three letters to you. Better go now, getting cramps in the hand. I got your letter yesterday make the next one a bit longer ya scab. Everyone's missing you and says Hello. Look after yourself.

From SNAPPA

P.S. (Don't Bring no Herpes Back).

Gavin Whiting
(free autograph)

P.S.S. Gavin hadn't sealed the envelope so I thought I'd say hello! I had a counter lunch last Friday with some girls from work (WOW!!). I've been out and about that's why Gavin hasn't seen much of me. I'm playing softball in Melbourne on Sundays its tough work.

See ya Mervie. Kato!!

I'll only tell you this once, so sit up and pay attention, otherwise you'll lose the plot and miss all the important parts of life in Werribee. The cast is as follows:

Andrew Barlow plays football with me at Werribee.

Barry the window dresser is the window dresser at the sports store that I have worked at for years and I think his name was Barry Walsh.

Becky is Darren Wise – plays basketball in my number two side which is called Chevron.

Bluey is Snappa's Mum, Patricia.

Bluey is also Darren Goodwin, also known as Duran Duran. You'll have to work it out.

Bracken is the Leipers' Red Setter.

Bruno, Smiley, Hynesy, Goady, Andy Van Gamett and **Goody** are all blokes that play footy at Lara.

Centrals is the Werribee Centrals football team – they play in the Western Suburban League. My father used to play for them back in the 1940s (well, 1970s).

Chironee is Dean Chiron, son of a mate of Dad's. Dean played VFL with St Kilda.

Chocky Chock is Robert Hancock, commonly known as Chock, a friend of mine from Myrtleford.

Chooka was Richard Leftchook who I think at one stage coached Werribee seconds but I work with him in Dove's sports store in Werribee and he played football with Dad at Werribee Centrals.

Chris is Chris Pedigrew who is Pete's boyfriend.

The Cole twins were recruited from Lara to Geelong to play in the VFL.

Crossa is Steve Crossley who plays cricket with us at Werribee. He's married to Jan.

Damien Christiansen was also recruited to Geelong from Lara.

Danny (Burnsy) Burns plays football at Werribee and he plays basketball with us occasionally.

Daisy is Steven Day – I play footy with him at Werribee.

Deb & Robbie Barker – Robbie Barker plays with the infamous Panels basketball team and Debbie is Kato's sister.

Duddo no idea, obviously someone who Snappa doesn't rate very highly. And what's worse, he wore my number 9 jumper for Werribee!

Dungy is Dungy Dover who is Kevin Dover's brother.

Basically anyone who has one of those puffed-up sort of haircuts is **Duran Duran.**

Garry is one of Pete's workmates.

Gavvy is Gavin Whiting – Snappa.

Gillian McLean is Andrew Barlow's girlfriend.

Goady is Andrew Goat.

Goody is Darren Goodwin.

Greeny is Terry Green – he is the gun full forward at Lara and also plays indoor cricket with us.

Hynesy is Steven Hynes.

Hilly is me: when I played my first game for Victoria, the captain told the scoreboard attendant that my name was Merv Hill, so Mum would think I wasn't playing.

Ivo works at the sports store I work at.

Jeff is Jeff Hughes who plays footy with Lara and works in the bank with Peta.

Joanne and George – Joanne Whiting – Snappa's sister and George is her boyfriend, he is a kick boxer and a very scary man.

Katie or Kato Hughes is no relation, and is Snappa's long-time girlfriend.

Kevin Dover plays footy and indoor cricket with us.

Lara is playing in the GDFL, which is the Geelong District Football League, and Snappa is playing with them. Lara is the next town down the highway towards Geelong.

The Larabee's is the indoor cricket side – half Lara, half Werribee – hence Larabee.

The Leifers are the family I stay with in England.

Livvy and Wiggy are my aunt and uncle, Brian Wiggins and Elizabeth Wiggins, parents of Shaun Wiggins, my cousin.

Marie is Marie Squires, Terry's sister and Becky's girlfriend.

Mick the Skip Grotto. A mate from Werribee.

Mick Bignall. I played junior football with him. He played cricket at Werribee then went to Essendon.

Nanna Noonan is my father's mother.

Nazar is Nazar Chapdjian – plays basketball.

Nicky Condon is a bloke who I used to go to school with in about Grade 2 and he plays at Werribee Footy Club.

Nozza or **Snozza** is the same person.

Panels – Werribee Panels is the basketball side I play for. Werribee Panel Beaters is owned by Snappa's Dad (Gavin Whiting's father) and he is our sponsor – so we are just known as the Panels. Snappa & I play for Panels.

Paul Smith and **Rod Harrington** – play for the Larabee indoor cricket side and play football and cricket at Werribee.

Prissa and **Whitey** are Clint Prismall and Sharon White.

Richo is Alan Richardson who plays football at Werribee.

Robyn Pickering is my most recent former girlfriend.

Ronnie Nipples is Ron Nichols who was a very good cricketer. I think he played at Footscray for some time but ended up coaching in the Western Suburban sub-district mainly at Yarraville, and then at Werribee.

Smiley is John someone.

Sniffy is our dog – little black and white border collie/kelpie cross.

Snozza is Phil Cullen. He trains footy at Werribee, but plays down at Lara, plays indoor cricket and a little bit of basketball.

Terry is Terry Squires, he plays for Panels.

Trish Cockrem made the Australian Basketball team – she's from Ayr in Queensland and I used to go out with her many years ago.

Trish and **Graham** are Debbie & Kate's younger brother and sister.

Thursday 12 May 1983

(Bill $186 from Panels arrived last week. They overlooked it when you went to settle up.)

Hi Mervyn,
Thanks a lot for your letter – so pleased to hear that you seem to be settling into things O.K.

Please thank Jill for her letter – Gary tells everyone about Bracken taking the socks. He thinks that's a great joke.

Shopping day today & lots of people (as usual) were asking after you . . . Today I bought a little pocket book on 'Cricket' written by Peter Smith – so I hope to learn a bit about County Cricket from it.

Ivo is back at the shop – Deanne misses you a lot. Her deb ball is Fri week & she's getting very nervous.

Centrals thrashed Hoppers last week – they were both undefeated going into that game. Ivo said he got a lot of rubbishing from Centrals spectators. Pop went up to the game but left at ½ time because the game was so one-sided.

Footscray & C'wood had a great game last Sat & although Footscray had a great last quarter, they were beaten by 1 goal. They were thrashed in Tuesday night's game against Norwood. Dean Chiron was in the best players again but Melb. defeated St Kilda. Werribee won well at Sandringham (up by 13 goals at ½ time but only winning by 5). They hope to win again against Waverley on Sunday so Nicky Comben told me this morning (only out of the four on percentage). Robyn called around on Monday after her game – she hasn't heard anything of her bag.

School holidays are on; Gary & I hope to go to Euroa next Thurs for a couple of days. Daddy MIGHT go.

Last Sunday was Mothers Day & with that money that I didn't pay back to you I bought myself a nice red shirt. Ian gave me a fry pan, Sniffy $20, Gary a lovely plate from Home (which I picked out) & Pete a nightie & a mug with Mother on.

Will say goodbye now, Love from all of us & Nanna Noonan (who said to 'Behave Yourself')

G 17 May 1983

Dear Merv,

2½ of us are fine, so is Rajah. Good to hear you're having fun. Kate and I are going to see your mum some lunch times. Gary shows us things from Kinder. It's school holidays at the moment so your pop is home too. Your mum was a bit upset on Mothers Day. She was hoping for a phone call.

Mrs Cullen is home safely. Phillip blew her car up so she has nothing to drive for a while.

Marie's wrist is still in plaster and isn't healing properly. She isn't allowed to go to work and is not getting paid. She's very sad at the moment.

Panels 1 beat Panels 2 last night thank God. David Cations was playing fool as usual. Lakers only beat us by 10, we are picking up a bit at last. How's the weather? Have you seen much T.V.? Have you lost any weight?

Danny Burns is playing for Panels 1. Last night he nearly got a goal for Panels 2. We all think of you quite a bit, hoping you are playing well. Robbie is rapped about the Top. [A Tottenham Hotspurs shirt.] Naz, Terry, Beakie and a few others are coming to watch FA Cup Sat. night. I think they're sleeping in the back room so I hope its not too cold. Marie and I will stay inside I think. It's getting very much like winter now. Kate and Gav are going to Daisy's 21st this week.

Running out of room.

See You Later

Love Deb & Robbie

19 May 1983

Dear Merv,

HI, how are you? I'm fine. Rhonda's fine, still very crazy but fine. I just received a letter from Colin and Margie they said hello! Gav's looking well. He recently got a hair cut, looks great real short.

Hello to your new family up there. What are they like? Have they got good accents?

What's new, eh! you always ask!

Basketball's yukko. Peta beat us again last Monday (16th) only by 10 though. Panels I beat Panels II hollow, great game, poor Danny was absolutely wrecked. He'd partied the night before till about 5am (Gav said) because his parents were away and got up for work at 7.30am by 7pm he looked like a zombie. He also put up a great rebound for Panels II, so funny that Gavin was rolling on the floor laughing, well! it wasn't that funny.

We won our first softball game in Melb, last week, 3–8. They were wrapped. Mustn't win often up there.

How's your weight? [It was even an issue then! Get off me back!]

They keeping you fit and healthy? I'm still stumpy and overweight my family say. Who cares! Ken Fletcher does. We saw him last Friday night (13th) he looks great. He stirs about overweight people but was happy to see me and the other volleyball girls. We went to a Tullamarine pub for 2 ? hrs and then after we got kicked out at 10.30 we stood outside & yakked till 11.30pm. Great night.

Had a counter lunch with Deb, Michelle Foote & Chris Lancaster the other day. Great gossip session. We talked about you, Gavin, footy, disco's etc . . .

Everyone misses you, you lucky devil. Marie's arm still isn't out of plaster. Trish & Grae, back to school Monday. Boy they're lucky kids, don't do anything but get everything they want. Deb's looking well. Jan's due 1 week and a half. DON'T FORGET!! She's huge (for Jan anyway). Always looks lovely. Whitings have booked for HONKERS again $1300 each or so. Bloody unreal they are.

Gavin took me to Empress for tea last Sunday night (15th).

Daisy 21 this Saturday (21st). Haven't seen Ang, Paul, Gil or Bails in ages so we'll have big gossip on that night. I'll give Daisy a kiss from you O.K.

What else, oh works OK. Ivo's back at Doves. Says you probably won't get your job back, but I think if you make a name for yourself over there everyone will want you. Just look at the Royals (only joking). Well Merv, as you said before you left, Look after yourself, don't go over board, and please don't get anyone into trouble if you can help it.

Love ya!

Kato

 19 May 1983

Dear Mervie,

How's it going. Really pleasing that you wrote to us & everyone else. Robyn was really rapt – she was like me. We didn't think you'd write. Tricia made the Aust. team if you're interested (?) Jeff's neck is getting better – he had a week off work & came back wearing a neck brace but it seems ok. He's starting to practice again & can play in a few weeks.

Five million people ask about you all the time. You'd be pleased to know Danny Maher said to say hello to you from him. Last week we as in Lakers had an exciting game against Finches. We won, but it was close & Francis got reported. His tribunal is next week & Dad's on it! I got my hair cut last night – I thought you'd be thrilled to know – really short. Dad was selling raffle tickets for a car – so I bought you one. I hope you win so that you don't have to worry about buying a car when you come home.

Have you seen many Australians around? . . . Mum & Gaz have gone to Euroa so it's just Pop and I. He is looking around for a new car. Mrs Whiting was cut with Gav because he wouldn't show them his letter. Hmm, what have you been up to??? So make sure you write hello Mrs Whiting on the envelope or something.

Hope cricket & practice is going well. The only results we get are Essex 1STS. You're in the 2nds aren't you? Any chance of the firsts? Rapt to hear you sound happy & settled. Jeff was pleased you found a drongo like yourself & Gav to muck around with. He reckons you'd feel more at home. W'bee are going ok in the footy too – winning a few games. We don't go now that you're not playing. Haven't even watched Port play yet. Centrals & Port Colts played & Port caused a big upset by winning by 20pts. Chooka was not very happy. He went straight home after the game.

Panels got beaten by Chevron – unreal hey? Steve Pinzone watches us play Thursday nights at Albert Park & might be helping to coach which will be really good. He's pretty nice hey . . .

Say hello to your new family. Just make sure you don't forget us 'cos we all miss you. Dad especially even though he doesn't say anything. He thinks Mum & I are dull & boring!

Lots of Love
Peta XXX

 24 May 1983

Hillman,

How ya growing? Sorry I am a bit late with the letter but we've been reasonably busy. (Not really, just lazy). Had the day off today because it looked like it might rain, and I was a bit stuffed from the weekend. There's a new disco in W/Bee, at the footy club called the underground. What a joke. More like a blue light disco. My writing is up to standard again. (I can't even read it properly). We've got a bye tonite so I might go out to Crossa's for a change.

Went to Daisy's 21st at Sunshine last Saturday night, then to Richo's 21st. Daisy's was quiet but Richo's was all right. I stayed at Katies with a mongrel all night (they're the breaks) . . .

Lara is going real bad, got shit on last Saturday. I am not going too bad. Not as good as I used to be because I'm too slow and I've lost most of my leap. (So everyone tells me.) You might have to become a roof tiler when you get back because Ivo is back at Doves full-time. Bit rough but they're the breaks. Early in July Danny, Britto, Smily, Hynsey, Goaty, Andy Van Gamett, Goody and I are going to the snow at Buller for a week. We are staying at a chalet in the snow . . . It's pretty expensive $360 for five days but you get accommodation, 2 meals a day, ski lifts and lessons.

Boonga is back in Lara. He came back with Dungie, who belted the new publican at the Lara pub. So he had to leave Lara that night because the cops were after him. Snozza has got a Duran Duran haircut and we give him heaps.

Burnsie said to say Gedday. He is playing well at football, should be pressing for the firsts. He is still playing basketball for us. The other night against Panels 2 he nearly shot 2 points for the other side. He put the shot up then he realised that we were going the other way. We all call him wrong way now. The oldies are booked in for Hong Kong again in August for 25 days, so I hope the pool is finished by then. Could have a few orgys at my house. Got your letter today, it was good. Bad luck about the knock backs, but it happens to the best of us. I've spun enough shit so I better go now. Keep enjoying yourself, everyone's missing you back here. Check ya later.

> from
> SNAPPA

P.S. Keep writing.

---

 24 May 1983

Hi Mervyn,
Good to hear from you yesterday & pleased that you are able to play some cricket. We heard Sunday that it has rained in England 36 days on end & we didn't think you'd be playing at all. Guess it must be soft to run up to bowl. Your batting seems O.K. Keep it up!

Had a letter from Aust Cricket Board (David Richards) just a thank-you for my letter to them & he said that it was your own performances that won you the scholarship & he hoped you gained a great deal from your trip to England. (I also wrote to Esso – just a thank you from Daddy & me for your trip).

A letter came for you from Nth Melb last week with a restricted Members Badge.

Gary has taken to collecting ARMYS as he calls them. Packets of soldiers, guns, boats, helicopters & such from "Mervy's Shop" – he's had five $2 packets in the last three weeks (you *know* who buys most of them, don't you – Daddy).

Gary & I had a few days in Euroa. Left Thursday & Peta picked us up on Sunday (Chris went too). Gramps seems O.K. and was pleased to hear your news.

Trish has made the Aust side to go to Brazil. There is also a P. Cockrem in the Aust team (from Q'land) to play in N.Z. next month – I wondered if it might be Trish's sister. Hope to ring her & find out (and also pass on congrats. from all of us).

Beasley, Jess, Clayton were all reported last Sat. but were all cleared at the tribunal last nite. Talking of Tribunals, Peta's coach got 6 weeks – so he can't play or coach in that time.

We have our new gate – Daddy took two days to paint it but it looks really O.K. Goes from near your window to side fence.

Hope to send you some cuttings on footy – Footscray def Fitzroy but still are 7th on the ladder – out on their dreadful percentage. C'wood had a good match against the Swans in Sydney too, but they were beaten.

Kate & Debby came to lunch last Fri week but haven't seen Gav for a while.

Must go & get Gary ready for kinder – New teacher today – Kathy Walker from Mt Eliza straight from college. I'm on milk & fruit too. Bye for now,

> Love from all of us
> Freda

25 May 1983

Hi Mervy,
This is an historical letter, the first and probably the last I'll write to you.

Business first:

The young chap who bought the car came round with $1200 (we've spent it already) he said he had to pay $40 to finish the roadworthy. Do we pay him yes or no?

Werribee Panels sent you a bill they overlooked for $186.20 for work on your timing gear on 15–4–83. Do we pay yes or no? . . .

Now on to the daddy/sonny stuff.

Keep telling us about the cricket as many of your friends are very interested in how you are going. I am out as President and off the Committee of the C.C. as I feel I've had enough. It looks as though Lindsay J. is going to coach. Rumour has it that Ray Bright may become C/C of Footscray to give him a chance at the State job.

Werribee's going well in the footy. They are in 4th place behind Port, Preston and Geelong West. They play Port this week so bye bye Bees.

Back to the cricket. At the annual meeting they made me a Life Member of the Club so I was pretty thrilled with that.

I'm looking at a Commodore that's done 44 000 km at Ballan's. I'll probably buy it this weekend although it's a bit pricey.

The Basketball Tribunal scrubbed Peta's coach a MR FRANCIS CARY, for 6 matches on Monday night so I'm in the sticky stuff with Peta and all her friends.

School rolls along as always because of the brilliant principal so there's nothing new there.

Keepon (that's two words) writing as we like to hear from you.
          Love Daddy

P.S. The bar and billiard table are beaut.

MERV: Dad's always been efficient with his words. And he's a great judge – it'll be interesting to see how Werribee goes against Port. I didn't ask what Peta's coach did to get six weeks, but with the hangman Ian Hughes on the tribunal, Francis was probably lucky.

 Tuesday 31 May

Hi Merv,
Just a few lines mainly to enclose some paper cuttings so you can see how the footy teams are going and who is playing where.

Gav wasn't working yesterday and he came around for a while in the afternoon. He'll come again one night when Daddy is at home.

We watch the David Frost show on Saturday nights – live from England. We were on the lookout for you but it's arvo there and you'd be at cricket.

VCA didn't contact me re your cricket boots and Graham Yallop so you won't be getting your boots off him. Perhaps I got their message muddled. Ian said (or Pop, Daddy or Father) that you wouldn't want to be breaking in new boots anyway.

This morning we heard that Sussex were bundled out for 40 odd against Essex. You only play with the seconds don't you? Still we'll wait with interest to see who got the wickets. Is Robert a batsman or bowler?

Daddy gets a new Bluebird next Tuesday he tells me. His trade in was almost $4000 after being offered only $1500 at one place. It is pale blue with brown trim and has a cassette player among other things. I haven't seen it as yet.

He goes to Cowes this weekend (from Thurs night) with the State Council – he is also out tonight & Wed. Until now he hasn't been out for ages – almost right off beer & he can't understand why he isn't losing more weight.

Must go & get your clippings together. Gary is most upset that he hasn't written to you too but will write later,

lots of love
Freda

(R) Wednesday 1 June 1983

Hillman,

How are ya, ya pommy prick. I've just had my hair cut, I hope you like it. Nothing much has been happening around here, you know typical Werribee. Geelong was on the T.V. last night, playing against North Melb. Both the Kols played and Damien Chrisso played his first game, he did very well.

Katie is moving into a flat in Beasley Ave on Saturday . . . I worked with the Chamberlains today and yesterday. I'll probably go down to the rooms and have a few with Burnsy tonight. Time for tea, back in a sec.

Went to visit Freda & Gary on Monday, they are well. I heard a roomer that Ronny Nipples from Yarraville is going to coach Werribee. Jan still hasn't had a little Crossa yet. I saw your car around a few times. It looks different because it's clean. I've still got my shitheap and it isn't painted yet, I don't know what to do with it. I hear Pop is buying a new car, he's sick of the other one.

Lara rooms open officially on Saturday, beats the old tin shed. We are about eighth on the ladder and going shithouse. Werribee is just out of the 4. Port beat them by seven goals last Sunday. The seconds won. That's four in a row for them. A few people are trying to talk me into coming back but I say Don't worry about it. Panels are second on the ladder and going O.K. Hope you're not too homesick. Hows the cricket going and are you *scoring*. I am occasionally but not enough . . . My ex-girlfriend RANA was going out with Bugsy but she woke up to herself.

Better go now down to the rooms. I'll have a *cold* beer for you with the boys. We are all missing you. Keep enjoying yourself,

> All the best
> SNAPPA

P.S. Remember no horrors.

P.S.S. There's a cruise on for 13 nights – March 21 – April 3, 1984. How does that sound – let us know.

MERV: I told you Dad was a good judge – Werribee done by seven goals! And as for Rana being Snappa's girlfriend – in his dreams!

 7 June 1983

Dear Merv,
How are you going. We are both fine. I have got a cold (nothing new). Andrew has left Sunshine and is playing for Hoppers X-ing now (paddock football). I would rather him play for Werribee but he is happy.

We have been house hunting, but not much around. Haven't been doing that much. Andrew went away for a week Pig Shooting, but didn't even see one, the trailer fell off, back window broke, the fridge didn't work and after all of that it rained all week and they only shot (2) rabbits.

We are going up to Barwon Heads this weekend with Andrew's friend from work. (Can't go anywhere else as we are broke). I had to get my brakes fixed on my car, the Laser had a tune up and then we found out we didn't need to, because the petrol was full of water, so the petrol tank had to be taken off, sent away and cleaned. It all cost $230. So we are broke.

Well I hope you are enjoying yourself over there and going good in cricket.
> Look after yourself
> Love Gillian & Andrew

 Monday 6 June 1983

Hi Mervy,
How are things and how's your cricket? Just a few lines with clippings of footy from Banner, Sun, & Western Times. Saves me telling you and if you are not interested, throw them away.

Pop enjoyed his weekend at Cowes – arrived there Thurs. night
& home here again Sunday arvo & the only money he spent was
$1.60 (twice across the Westgate!)

Peta took Gary & I to watch Lara on Sat. They had a good
win, Gavvy played well (he doesn't kick the ball much) but
marked well and hand passed & tackled. He kept out of an all in
fight which broke out when the opposition trainer tackled Jeff
Hughes. (His first game back after a neck injury & he was captain
for the day). Their club rooms were officially open for club
members on Sat. – they look good. I sat in the car with the
wireless on & knitted away & Peta kept Gary entertained. I really
enjoyed myself & so did they.

Kristen Wiggins asked for your address so you may receive a
letter from her one day. If you have any postcards to spare, could
you send one to Nanna Noonan & another to Gramps – I know
they'd be thrilled to hear from you.

All of your friends that I have spoken to, are really pleased that
they have heard from you.

Just tried to ring Crossas – no answer – so checked the birth
notices. Guess what? They have a new baby daughter – Kate
Suzanne, 8.10½. So now I'll get your letter to them. Have been
waiting for that arrival to work out what to knit.

Best leave this unsealed as Gary was crook on things last week
because he didn't 'write' to you.

Apparently Paul Smith & Rod Harrington were models at a
mannequin parade last week – Gavvy told me.

Barry (is he the window dresser?), Joey Alifraco & Gary Jessup,
were asking about your cricket last shopping day. All hope that
you do well over there & even when you get back home. Barry
thinks you're far better off playing cricket than working in a shop.

Damian Christenson, Mary's brother, played in the night match
with Geelong last Tues & then played his first Sat match at the
weekend & did quite well. Chironee was named seond best for St
Kilda against the Magpies so Daddy said . . .

Love from all of us
Mummy

5 June 1983

9.45 pm
"It's a girl"

Dear Merv,
Thanks for your postcard. We wanted you to know there is now a little Crossa. I had a girl, on 4 June 1983 . . .

She is really lovely even if I have to say so myself. She was 8lbs 10½oz born. Steve is just so happy and proud of her. I think all this celebrating is getting to him and it's only been a day and a half. Bad luck you're not here to help, so have a drink over there to wet her head.

You sound like you're settling in quite well over there which is great. Getting plenty of wickets now hey? Or making your mark as a batsman (I know you're an allrounder) you devil! Well I had better go, just a short note to tell you the news. I will try to write again soon as I get organised.

Love Steve, Jan & Kate XXX

 Monday 13 June 1983

Hi Mervy,
Thanks for your letter – Pleased to hear you are getting a few wickets. How's your batting? [**You told me the other day my batting was going well, Mum.**]

I'm writing this late at night watching the Aussies batting against India – Chappell has just made a century – and now has gone out. Pop waited up to see his century & then went to bed about 11. He did well – now it will be interesting to see if we can last out the 60 overs. Do you go to any of these games? We'll look for you at Chelmsford in the crowd next Mon. night.

Last week I rang Trish – read in the paper where St Kilda were beaten badly after leading by 9 at ½ time in the final. She said they had a close semi but on the night the others were just too good (forgotten who). (Sorry about that) She made both Australian teams to play in Brazil & New Zealand but was down as T Cockran for Brazil & P for N.Z. She was really pleased to receive your b'day card & letter & has been too busy to write now but hopes to write from Brazil.

Daddy's news to you – (1) There are still 3 great captains still playing cricket, Lloyd (48), Illingworth (51) & Hughes (48). (2) Bruce Comben received the OAM in the Queens Honors List this weekend. It's the highest award one can receive in a Labour governed state. (3) He's (Pop that is) driving around in his Datsun Bluebird & 'cries' or carries on whenever mud or birds dirty his nice new car . . .

Haven't heard from Robyn for a few weeks, Katy either, but have talked to Gavvy on the phone. Have almost finished knitting a little pink jumper for Kate Crossley & we hope to go & see them when the jumper is finished.

Footscray defeated Geelong today & C'wood def Melb – both were pretty close games throughout. Werribee were thrashed by Coburg and have gone to 6th position. Peta & Chris went to watch Footscray but Pete isn't home yet. Brendan Ryan (M'ford) played well for North Melb 2nds on Sunday – Peta watched it on tele & thinks he's good enough for 1sts. Chironee was in the best players again & Damian Christenson did well for Geelong today.

Peta & Helen are talking about flying to Q'land during Peta's holidays in July – they hope to have about a fortnight there – leave after Gary's birthday & be back for their grand final on 25th July.

Best go, as I'm now actually going to write a letter to Jill (8 overs gone & Australia still there).

Love from all of us,
Freda

MERV: Mum's watching the World Cup in England, and still hoping to see me on the tele! The Crossas have had young Kate and life in Werribee is smooth. I think.

CHAPTER THREE

Life in Werribee

PART II

Sometimes a mate should be around when things are getting tough.

 15 June 1983

Hilly

Hows things ya pommy bastard? There's not much happening around here. The hole has been dug for the pool and all the pipes are in, they are pouring the concrete this week. So we could be twisting by the pool soon.

It sounds like the good life over there – you're laughing . . . I suppose your mum told you about the invite to Mandy's 21st, it's a pity you won't be home but I'll be going for sure. We had a big Long Weekend. On Thursday night we went to Crossa's to celebrate. We all got blind, Crossa & Robo undressed me and put me to bed at about five. I woke up at about 11 so I didn't go to work.

[I can't tell you what Snappa wrote here, but he's heard that Katie might be seeing some new bloke. Snappa described him, which is why we can't let you read it.]

On Saturday we played against Thompson at Thompson and got rolled by two goals again. It was a fairly good game, but we should have won. They are on top and we are about eighth. Went to Cats on Saturday night and got pissed again, hung shit on everyone, you know, the usual. Sunday went to the footy, Werribee got shit on by Coburg. Danny is still in the firsts, so is Chrisso at Geelong. Sunday night Ronnie Combo, Hynesy and I went to Richmond, got legless again and came home at about 7 in the morning.

On Monday we went to the Racecourse Pub for a while then to Geelong-Footscray which Geelong lost by about three goals. And just for a change I got legless there too. I saw Prissa & Whitey at Cats on Saturday night, they were their usual selves as usual.

We are going to the snow in 2½ weeks so we are all looking forward to that. It could be the break I need, to get into a few snow bunnies. **[Censored.]** As you can probably see, my writing has improved heaps. I know you'll be able to understand the shit that I'm writing . . . Bad news on the footy scene too, Mark

Jackson got the arse from St Kilda today. They had a pleasant
Sunday morning and Jacko was sneaking around putting lit
smokes in the supporters' pockets and I don't think they liked it.

I don't know if Jan told you in her letter that she called the
baby Kate Suzanne, she's a little bewdy, they are really rapt.

I better piss off now. See ya later

     SNAPPA

P.S. Look after yourself. Hillman Hunter Back 2 Fronter

MERV: In case you haven't been paying attention, Snappa Whiting has
been my best mate since school days, and his long-time girlfriend, Katie
Hughes (no relation) is also a good friend.

---

 16 June 1983

Dear Mervyn,

Hi ya!! How are you today?

I'm fighting fit, like everyone else in this town.

As you can see, I've finally got my own flat in Werribee, boy am
I pleased with it. I can't wait until you're back so you can come
over for tea and visit whenever you like. It took me two full
months to get it. It's from McNaughtons Real Estate. $45 a week,
two bedroom, oil heater, back yard, large glass windows, built in
robes, double storey. It's ace!! All I need now is a flat mate. At the
moment Nicola Ford (Robert Smith's girlfriend) is thinking about
it but until I find someone I'll pay my own way for everything.
I've applied for the phone. I got a little 160lt fridge for $110 in
Werribee, it's a cutey.

How's Crossa's BABY (not kid) it's fantastic isn't it. Kate
Suzanne. I was so happy for the both of them, Steve was as high
as a kite *when he saw her born*, she is absolutely beautiful. Jan's
been talking herself to sleep, she's so happy but also very tired.

How's your love life?? You mug!! You tell Gav but you don't tell
me, I'll bop you one, you know I like to hear it too. You see, I care!!

[I can't let you read what's in this bit, but Katie has been seeing a new fella occasionally. He sounds like he's not a bad bloke and Katie's happy. He doesn't seem to fit Snappa's description.]

Gav visits every now and then. I'm trying to keep busy with myself so he won't worry about me and come over all the time. He got his name, address & phone no. on the truck yesterday so he should pick up a few sheila's soon I'd reckon. (It looks tough, and not bad either) . . .

The footy scene's still the same.

Mrs Whiting sold me her two wall units for $150 and is giving me her lounge when they can afford a new one. They're paying off the pool first. I'll let Gav tell you all about that.

Your dad looks funny in his little *Bluebird*. I had no idea he was getting a new car. Well time to visit your mum & Gary again to catch up with them.

Cold weather! How's your's (the weather I mean)?

Cricket's good I hope! for your sake. You'd better check your letters before you send them Heapa, because some of your words were a bit indecisive and they had double meanings (bit rude) . . .

Well, I'll love you and leave you for another week or so. 'GOOD LUCK'. love ya!

> All the best
> Kato!!

MERV: What can a man do?

---

 18 June 1983

Dear Mervie

How's it going? It's really great to hear that you are writing to so many people. Mrs Day said Stephen was really rapt to get a card and letter for his 21st. She said the party went really well & the highlight was hearing from you! Naza wants to know why you haven't written to him. I see him to talk to at basketball on Wednesday nights.

They all think I like Steve Pinzone! It's really funny – he's really nice to talk to & so funny & I always get excited 'cos he's about the only person that's ever nice to me (but that's 'cos he is so nice to everyone!). The girls send their love too – Muzza (your cheer squad), Coralie & Julie. Muzz got a card from Simon Davies who is in England & he said he was trying to get in touch with you. Kathy O'Callogan was in the bank the other day & she said she was disappointed not to see you. Libby & Wiggy were rapt to hear from you. Debra May Barker was spewing 'cos she's only had one card from you. I said you were busy writing to everyone else!

Do you get out much? What's your new family like, as nice as us? (Woudn't be hard hey?) Don't forget Gazza's birthday will you – 5th July – he wouldn't let mum remind you 'cos he said Mervie will know when it is!

Chris took his waisted jacket back too. You can borrow it again when you come home. He's a real little fattie & needs it badly. Do you know when you're coming home yet? Have you seen many Aussies or met up with the Australian side?

Guess what – I threw 26 pts at W'bee the other night – rapt. We won 62–9 against Wyndham but I was rapt. Threw heaps last night too with W'bee Devils. Danny Maher said hello, so did Brett Wright!!!

Also Mrs Tardrew was asking about you, also about ½ of W'bee who bank with us. Did I tell you, any Pommies that come in with travellers chqs, I ask them where they're from & if they're going home they say they'll look in the paper for your name! One girl thought *Kim* Hughes was my brother (I was talking to her just after the Australian side was announced). I didn't like to tell her otherwise. Wasn't that great about Trevor Chappell's 110. Garry & Jeff reckon that they should pick you as Captain – that was after the Australian's two losses. Did mum tell you we went & saw Lara play. Jeff was captain. Jeff & Gav both played really well. I think Phil Snozzer is better at cricket than footy! Bobbie fired in patches too.

Chris & I went out with his teachers for tea one night. It was good but all they talked about was school! Was it like that when you went out with Tricia & her mob? Dad's new car is nice. Mines going ok. Alan Burke asked me last week when you were leaving for England – he'd seen your car around & wondered why you hadn't been playing footy. Helen & I look like going to Qld for a couple of weeks. Will miss out on a bit of basketball – spewing, but I suppose the break will be good. Jeff & Garry have been stirring me like anything lately – so you can punch their lights out when you come home ok – so keep in good condition. Dad would but he works in Laverton. Anyway, must go. Keep enjoying yourself. How many address books have you filled?

       Love Peta XXXX

Monday 20 June 1983

Hi Mervy,

Don't think much of the English teli – no cricket tonight because of their strike & after I'd geared everyone thru the week to watch teli tonight!!

Mrs Lancaster said 'Hello', & also to let you know you are badly missed in the Werribee footy team.

Your frind Choccy Choc has announced his engagement in last Sat. Sun (hope to cut it out & send) . . .

Tonight Gavvy called around before tea – he'd received your letter today but couldn't or wouldn't tell us much about it!

There were two *girls* reported in Peta's game tonight – Teresa Wright (Francis thinks she's a goner already as Pop is still Tribunal Chairman) and Nicola Barker. Peta won't tell us a thing about the report as it concerns her team-mate, and she might be called as a witness & she gets too upset with everyone when she does talk about reported players.

How are things with you anyway? Gavvy said you would probably be at the cricket today. (Even if we *did* have teli tonight, it wasn't going to be the Australians anyway).

Tomorrow there is a puppet show at kinder which Gary & Melanie are looking forward to.

Joan Sadler is picking me up tomorrow night and we are going to see E.T. at the RAAF base.

Lara got thrashed on Sat, so Gav said. Robby Barker hurt his leg & Gav didn't know if he'd play basketall tonite or not. Debby rang around people to make sure she got them all to basketball on time – BUT – she had them all there a game too early!

Katy Hughes has a flat in Beasley Av now, Gav helped her shift in but isn't seeing her these days so couldn't tell us any news of her.

(There probably won't be any newsy letter from Gary this week as he is in bed asleep now & he probably won't have time to write one in the morning.) He now knows the long blue letters are from you & he sits at the table with letter & letter opener until I sit down and read it to him.

Tonight the new Vic. coach is supposed to be announced – I'll put in a cutting if there's anything in tomorrow's paper. (You will probably hear before this letter anyway). Graf is going to WA next season – so there's one less bowler in the team.

One of Grandpa's friends at Euroa got all excited about watching Kim Hughes on Sat night until he was told – No Kim wasn't Phil's grandson, Mervyn is!

Must go, love from all of us, hope everything is going well for you.

> Lots of love
> Fre

Tuesday 21 June 1983

What on earth happened to the Aussies?? I stayed up until 4am just not believing what was happening. (Then had to get up at 7. Now I have to go and look after Melanie's little sister while Ingrid goes to school to hear reading. Gary & Melanie will be there too – hope they don't give me a hard time!)

Gary wants to know IF you could get him 3 of the Walt Disney Match box cars please (CS13 – Popeyes Spinach Wagon, CS14 Pluto's Road Roller & CS15 Olive Oyl's Sports Car. (Don't think you can get them in Australia yet) – Regards to the Leipers.

> Love, Me

22 June 1986

G'day, G'day, (Thought you'd like a bit, *of Aussie slang* that is, not a 'bit'). How's life in 'Limey Land'? Thanks heaps for the postcard; by the sound of it you're eating, drinking & sleeping cricket – lucky you! We're actually siting here watching India & England playing – can't see your face in the crowd!! By the way, why didn't you go & give the Aussies a pep talk – silly buggers!

Good news for Gill & Andrew. They bought a house last week. A four-year-old brick veneer in Ballan Rd. They're both rapt. Don't know if you've heard from Gill yet, if not, here's some more news. Andrew has left Sunshine Football Club & has signed up with Hopper's Crossing. Do you believe it? Gill is sure that he'll get the 'pisser' punched out of him.

By the way, apologies for not writing sooner but you know how slack we are. You missed out on a neat house-warming party last month – OURS! (Where's our present!!!) Got rid of the last few people at 6.00am. Christ were we tired (and whacked). Good party though.

Don't want a Volkswagen do you? My bloody car blew up on me last week – I'm throwing a party next week so everyone can watch me drive it into the Yarra! It blew that much smoke that I created my own fog! My car pegged it in the middle of the city in peak hour traffic – Jesus, was I embarrassed There was a heap of council guys working on the road . . . who were terrific. They pushed my car into a parking space, gave me a fag, a cup of coffee, listened to me swear my head off, then shoved 20 cents into my hand so I could call the RACV (which I had to join on the spot for $50.00 – shit!) Needless to say there are a few dents in the VW (like a few footprints!)

Brian is still the same – doesn't change – hey – how about me sending Brian & I'll keep the Volkswagen? NO? OK! Well, you look after yourself & write again and if you happen to visit France while you're o/s, bring me back a Frenchman and I'll give you Brian (for nothing!). See you soon. Lots of Love

Deb XXX, BRIAN

28 June 1983

Dear Merv

Hi, how are you? You sound like you're having a ball. How's the cricket going. I am so interested in your cricket, that's why you're there isn't it? I wish you all the best, you lucky thing. Furthest I've ever been is Queensland!

Well there's not much Werribee gossip I can fill you in on. Rosemary from JC's is very pregnant, she's only got till Sept. to go. I've been doing a lot of modelling. It's great fun. Big news, I made the Werribee Banner 4 weeks in a row! Wow! It's hard work though, but good money.

I broke up with Craig three months ago and went out with Paul Bugg for a couple of weeks. But that fizzled out & I was foot loose & fancy free for a while. I got back with Craig two weeks ago. That's about the most exciting news I've got. Not very exciting.

What's the weather like over there this time of year? It's bloody freezing here at the moment. I'm on holidays this week & it's too cold to do anything. Our max. today was 10°, and min. was 2°. That's warm I s'pose to over there though.

You'll have to write to me again & let me know when you'll be home. Good luck with your cricket & don't get too drunk & come home looking like an Aussie Norm! All the best & have a lovely time. Thanks for your postcard.

Take care,
Lotsa love
Rana XXX

MERV: There's no way Rana could ever have been Snappa's girlfriend.

Tuesday 28 June 1983

Hilly,

How's things ya pommy prick? Sorry I haven't written for a while
but you know me, a bit of a lazy illiterate ****. The only exciting
think that's happened around here lately was . . . [**Censored.**] . . . S
bend. No one else is home and I'm just about to watch the night footy.

Just finished training, its giving me the shits, having to listen to
Super Coach. You feel like telling him how to play the f***ing
**** of a game. I'd rather be playing in the big league – ya know
down at Winch, just turn left at Knuckey's and ya there. [**That'd
be at Winchelsea, a bush footy club.**] We can't make the finals,
Bobby, Pat and I are starting to play pretty well together. Terrific
Terry Green is playing for Bell Park in the G.F.L. on match
permits. He's going pretty well there but Lara won't clear him.

We are going to the snow this Sunday for the week so it should
be good, can't wait, a man might even pick up a ****. If he
remembers how to do it. I haven't had a f*** for about two
months. I might even root you when you get home, I hope you
haven't got aids. I haven't even seen Katie for two weeks, I think
she's still going out with the other lucky **** . . . Me oldies sold
her the wall units and couch the other day because they bought all
new stuff. Her flat looks pretty good now, but she still hasn't got
no-one else to share it with.

The old man just rolled up home after a Lions meeting, he is
president now. Ian Fairley is playing full forward for North
against Carlton and hasn't had a sniff of the ball yet.

Our pool is nearly finished . . . The weather down here is pretty
ordinary – f***ing cold in two words (its catching). It's shit. I was
in at Doves today and Ivo said to say Geday. Hoppers are second
on the ladder to Centrals. Bails is playing for Hoppers, I don't
know if I told you that last letter. He must be getting a bit of cash,
or he wouldn't be there. They just bought a house in Ballan Road
near the basketball courts.

I flaked it last night so now it is Wednesday afternoon. It is
pissing down rain, it has been for most of the day. I worked in
Melton and got soaked because I had to cover this f***ing
extension. I just read the paper and Kink is playing for Essendon

now . . . Jacko got the arse from St Kilda and he isn't playing anywhere. I still haven't got my Torana fixed completely. As soon as I do I will try to sell it. I've seen your car around a bit, it's unusual to see it so clean. We are still second on the ladder in Basketball, Burnsie is starting to play well. Steve did his ankle in town a couple of weeks ago so he hasn't been playing. The other night I was taking big grabs, you know, the usual stuff, sitting on heads, and riding them into the ground. Bluey just got home, she said to say hello.

When are you coming home? Did you get my picture of Jacko, did you like it? I thought it might make you feel at home. Are you homesick at all? You shouldn't be because there is f*** all happening back here. It really is giving me the shits lately. I better f*** off now because I've run out of things to say. All the best, see you soon.

> From
> SNAPPA

PS How's my bat going?

MERV: I am given bats by a sponsor, and every so often one slips into Snappa's bag at training. I had to borrow it back because we spent the equipment money on beer.

---

 1 July 1983

Dear Merv,

This is the 10th letter I've written to you but the first that I'm going to post. I'm saving the others up for when you come home. Karen said to say Hi and that she misses your Tarzan calls. (A housewife, working girl and mistress to her husband doesn't get much time to write letters.) She hopes you're having a good time and she's waiting to see you in the English side playing the Aussies.

Thanks for the birthday card and the postcard, its taken me ages to write this letter because I never know what to write, but I'll give it a good go. Nothing much has changed here except that Gavin has taken number one place in shit stirring and he's not doing a bad job of it. I've been going to the football each week sitting in the cold and watching the guys lose. We went to a Mash ball the other night and all got dressed up in army clothes, it was a good night, drank a bit as usual. (I'll send photos in my next letter.) Mum has just said to tell you that she hopes to have changed the dirty white Belmont by the time you get back and she misses your cheery face around the street.

On Sunday we took Pat & Terry to a breakfast for the Footy Club, they had a comedian, it started at eight o'clock in the morning and that's what time we started drinking. I'll never do that again. (Only joking give me that chance and I'd do it every Sunday morning.) By the way I played in a netball grand final on Tuesday night, we lost by about 10 goals. Debbie Cullen and I both got warnings for playing too rough – I can't see why though!! Mind you the week before in the semi final [**name deleted at the request of the defamation lawyers**] tried to kick a player, needless to say we were not very popular.

Well Merv it's about time I was going to bed (do you want to come too, it's a shame I'm a Catholic isn't it!). Until I write to you next time its goodbye and I hope you're having a great time, miss you a lot.

Lots of Love Michelle XXXXX

P.S. Please put a cute guy in your suitcase for me.

MERV: The following was included in the same envelope.

Dear Merv,
How's everything going in England. I bet they really love having you there because they're probably not used to having such a tall, dark, handsome spunk around. I s'pose you must be beating the women off with sticks. Hope the cricket's going good.

All of us girls at the Chemist really miss you. We say every day,

'Boy we sure miss MERV!' (Did that brighten up your day?)
Anyway – must go, 'cos I'm running out of paper.
See you.
Jo (The friendly pharmacist)

I'm going to tell everyone that I correspond with a famous cricketer! Will you be telling everyone that you got a note from a famous pharmacist?

 July 1983

Merv Mouth,
Hi! Things sound really good over there apart from your ankle. Debbie's due on the 12th of Sept and she's been great 'no problems' YET! Basketball's not bad we lost to Curly's mob on Monday by about 15 points. We only had four players because Gavin and Burnsy have gone to the snow. YER! Danny has been playing for about 6 weeks now. We went to 'Duran Duran' Darren Goodwin's 21st it was great they had a band, but we didn't do the WORM!
   Lara Football's not going too good we're about 8th on the ladder. We have some easy games coming up. Greeny's trying for a clearance to Bell Park, 'GFL' but they will only give him Match Permits. Marie Squires left for Bali on Sunday for 3 weeks. Werribee football got beaten on Sunday by Geelong West. Geelong West scored ten goals before W/Bee got their first, 'they got beat by six in the end'.
   Rajah says Baooooo!
   Just in case you haven't heard. Redpath's coach of the Vics next session. Richmond and Carlton will play off in the night final in

two weeks. Make sure you let us know when you're coming home so we can try and get to the airport! That's about it! Look after yourself HEAPA!!

Robbie B.S. & Debbie

P.S. Take a 'Heapa' more wickets.
P.S.S. I heard about your bellywarmer!

---

 1 July 1983

Hi ya Merv!
How's me old mate? Hope you're well! I'm fine and so is all the family. Work's going O.K. The computer has been playing up lately though, but we can't help that. I'm still on my own in the flat. I've kept myself busy so I won't get scared. I've half finished cleaning the place and I'm into making some curtains at the moment, should be all done soon. Boy time flies, how long have you been away? I can't remember! It seems like years since I've seen you. I think I could be missing you too . . .

Robyn's birthday's on July 15th. She's putting on a counter tea at the pub on the river in Maribyrnong. Our works got a do on that night so I don't know what to do. She's fallen for a guy in Sale (sorry mate). So I think you better forget her.

Our daggy team made it into the GRAND-FINAL for softball in Melb. We play off on Sunday. I'm so wrapped, because we were the underdogs and we got up and beat the top side Yippee!!

Jan's all relaxed with her baby now. She did seem very nervous the first week home with her brand new baby. I reckon it would be scary too, looking after something as precious as that all on your own. But she's fine now.

. . . How's your love life?

Mr. Whiting had his photo in the banner last week. President of Lions.

Oh well, I guess I better get back to work. You look after yourself won't you? I'll give Robyn a kiss for you o.k. I can't wait till you get back, so much to tell you.

Stay well Mervie, won't you . . .

> Lots of luck & love
> Katie XX

P.S. I'm still happy, deep down it hurts though! (losing Gav's *friend*ship).

 Sunday 3 July 1983

Dear Merv,

How's things. Are you still in England. It seems to be a long time since we heard from you . . .

Ron Nicholls from Yarraville is the new coach here at Werribee in the Cricket Club. It appears Mick Drinkall will be back too.

The Football team fell apart in the last two weeks to drop out of the four and out of contention. Frankston and Geelong West both beat them easily.

Freda just told me to tell you that Brendan Ryan from Myrtleford played full forward for North Melbourne yesterday. He just went but he has a future in front of him.

I suppose you've heard the news that Redpath is State Coach with the assistance of Stackpole. No big names recruited to the state.

The Werribee Club, getting back to the big time again, have lost Terry Moloney – he's coaching Seddon and Ken Norris is being shifted in his work to Canberra so you win some and lose some.

Would you please let us know what you are going to do at the end of July, are you coming home or staying on?

The new car is going well it costs about half as much to run as the Holden and is easier to handle. No you can't borrow it. That's it for now,

> Love from all at home,
> Ian

MERV: Don't you love a sarcastic father. 'No big names recruited to the state.' Ian Redpath played 66 Test matches and made nearly five thousand runs, and Keith Stackpole played 43 Tests.

 Monday 14 July 1983

P.S. Like your 'very own' letterheads.

Hi Mervy,
Thanks a million (from Gary) for his birthday present, and for the *two* letters and the cutting and Essex cricket book. (Please thank your captain for his note too.)

Daddy wrote last night mainly because it's 3½ weeks since we heard from you. How's your leg? You seem to be doing well bowling half pace – do you get to bat much these days?

Peta started holidays today – she & Helen hope to go to Queensland next week . . .

Did father tell you he's lost 1½ stone? . . . [**What is this thing everybody has about weight?**]

Ross MacLure left for England yesterday with his girlfriend – he wanted your address as he hopes to see you. A lady from Anthony's was in the bank when he was talking to Peta & she was pleased to find out Peta is your sister as now she'll be able to catch up on news of you. She said they all miss you at the hair salon.

There was a letter from VCA to tell you of a meeting next Wed (6th July) to meet Redpath. They realize you're overseas but thought they'd let you know what's going on.

By the way, the jumper fits Gary & is nice & long for next year too. I love that color blue – have you got one too?

Pleased to hear you are staying on until the end of Sept – (poor Jill with your washing & ironing though!). Hope you get across to France as people say that's a great day trip. Are you taking any photos? You also have to let someone, don't know who, know when you're coming home don't you? (in regard to your ticket).

Brendan Ryan was full forward for North on Sat – but Daddy told you that too I think. Damian was dropped last match but Chironee is still in the team . . .

Looking thru the Essex book, I gather Rob Leiper is a batsman & also bowls a bit . . .

Tuesday 5 July

Will just finish this before taking Gary to kinder – he's not dressed yet as he's watching Sesame Street.

The two girls that were reported a fortnight ago – Nicola Barker got 4 weeks and Teresa Wright got off. A fellow from Albert Park, Ashe or Nash, was Chairman mainly to show the Werribee fellas how to go about things – Also sitting on the Tribunal were Ron Taylor & Roger Mansey. Your father had ½ doz [**that's six for those of you born after the 1960s**] independents lined up as he thought it unfair for umpires & coaches to sit on the Tribunal.

The badge you sent with Gary's jumper, well Daddy thinks he'll wear that – I told him we'd have to get Gary's approval. Father was also very impressed with your letterheads & wants to know where you got them from. Pity we didn't know your phone number last week as the telephonists were on strike & there were free calls interstate & overseas.

Gary is just about to write a letter to you too – we *will* be late for kinder this morning.

Will go now, Peta will write in a week or so.

Love from all of us, Keep on getting wickets
　　　　　Love Fre

P.S. Hope your leg is o.k.

P.P.S. Regards to the Leipers.
Nanna Noonan just rang. Was really pleased to receive a card from you yesterday.

MERV: See, Mum, I do what I'm told, usually.

Sunday 10 July 1983

Hi Mervy,
It was good to talk to you on Fri. Hope your leg is OK & that you're back playing again.

Good, too, to find the cricket fixtures for this season in the back of the Essex book. Is your team doing well? People have asked if your team is near the top so please tell me next time you write.

Daddy went to the footy today. Werribee defeated Williamstown by 10 goals. Rod Harrington & Robert Smith played well on the back line & Scanlon played really well along with other small players.

Gavvy was at the footy – back home from his week at the snow. He didn't put anti freeze in his engine & the head cracked (I think) & now he has to go back up tomorrow to bring his car home on a trailer.

Peter was at the NBL finals last night & was talking to Trish there – she's been out suspended for two weeks by some umpire that hates her, but she (Trish) is going to write you all about it.

Gary's bike isn't a BMX, just a two wheeler with training wheels – at present it's in your room along with all his Leggos (which are set up on a little table.) Rather pleased you're coming home at the end of our winter, cos now we can keep *your* doona on *our* bed until then, & your blankets & a travel rug are on Gary's bed! I also wear your red & navy waterproof coats that you train or run in.

This weekend was a split round in the League – St Kilda & Geelong didn't play. Brendon Ryan was dropped from Nth Melb team – they beat Essendon, Carlton, who have been playing badly defeated Fitzroy, & Richmond defeated Footscray.

Your father is having trouble with Gary's Leggos – he takes hours making them up & Chris & Gary take them apart to make other things! Daddy thinks once they're made up they should stay that way but the others don't agree – Must go, love from us all.

(Peta & Helen off to Q'land Wed 13th until Fri 22nd)
      Freda

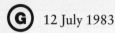 12 July 1983

Hi Merv,

I thought I should send you a postcard, not just to stop the boredom from receiving normal, ordinary, plain, dull letters but because you are an Australian & would not normally receive an *Australian* postcard.

Yes, everyone is missing you, & your mum keeps calling Peta Mervyn. Even Sniffy has been sniffing a bit harder lately. Gary enjoyed his birthday party, I enjoyed the chocolate crackles, & everyone had a good time.

Christopher Pedigrew played with Gary's Lego's for at least 3 hours. Peta & I are going to Queensland, Wednesday for 10 days. I'm just hoping she doesn't squeal on the plane. She said that she will get drunk before she goes, on the plane, so she won't feel it!!!

I believe everyone in Werribee has read your letters Merv – your language is disgusting & we are all proud of you.

> Lots of Love
> Helen XX

MERV: Isn't it great to be able to impress your friends with your command of the Australian vesicular!

 Tuesday 13 July 1983

Hilly,

Hows things ya pommy prick? Sorry I haven't written for a while, but I've had a few other things on my mind. I suppose Freda told you what happened to me shitheap car. I went to Buller yesterday morning and picked it up. It needs a new motor, real handy especially when I'm trying to sell it. Crossa and Robbo had the day off and came up to keep me company. Robbo got pissed and Cross had a few too. I've got a lend of George's Statesman for two weeks because he lost his license. Unreal, he only lost it for fourteen days.

We went to the Tarmac after basketball to watch him fight for the Victorian Light Heavyweight title but the other bloke piked it – don't blame him. So if George doesn't have a challenger in three months he automatically wins the title.

We won the last game of basketball against Mossfiel last night. I put some big smart arse prick into the wall head first, when he was doing a layup. It was great.

When we went up to the snow last week it was shit hot. We skied about six hours every day then discoed till about 3 or 4 every night. Got legless every night, none of us got a **** but what's new. Burnsy got on with a tart that worked at the chalet. We got her pissed and she was dancing on the tables and farting around. She got the sack the next day. Burnsy said that will teach her to give him a knock back. It was a barrel of laughs up there. Jacko was up there skiing so was Steven Reynoldson. I was pissed and I kept telling him 'ya got no jam tart Reno ya big sheila'. Lucky he didn't belt me. Pity that me car f***ed up because it spoiled a great week.

Should have seen us trying to play footy on Saturday after it. We were all f***ed ya know – ran out of legs. I went for a mark, one out with me opponent who was in front of me (unusual). I jumped up and stood on his head, took a chest mark, and went right over top of him and ended up in front of him. The crowd went crazy it was a fairly good grab.

Couso got his jaw broken in two places when he copped an elbow behind play. I pity the bloke if he catches up with him. You know what he's like. Damage gave a bloke a big straight arm coat hanger and knocked him out. Patty Curtain got knocked out. Bobby punched on with a bloke who tried to push him through the fence. All in all it was a pretty ordinary game. We won by about ten goals. We played Anakie.

Robyn told me about two months ago to leave the day of her birthday free. Since then she's asked everyone out for Tea or something and she didn't even invite me. They're the breaks, if you're not wanted, you're not wanted. Every other **** is going except me and Burnsy . . .

The pool is close to being finished, I'll know who my mates are when every **** comes dagging around for a swim and a spa –

I'll tell them all to f*** off. F*** em. Work is going all right at the moment, I've got a fair bit on.

I went to your house last night to give Gary a present and see Freda and Pop. They're O.K. Pete wasn't home but what's new. Better piss off now, have to get me haircut before training, less wind resistance or something like that. All the best, keep enjoying yourself.

From SNAPPA

. . . P.S.S.S. Greeny got cleared to Bell Park and he kicked thirteen. Broke the Club's record. He was rapt. Good on him. He shut all the knockers up.

MERV: Snappa's doing it tough. No chicks, his car's rooted and no-one loves him – but he's going to be my best mate when he gets the pool finished!

CHAPTER FOUR

Life in Werribee

PART III

(G) Flight 816
From: Melbourne
To: Los Angeles
Pan Am

15 July 1986

Dear Merv,

As you can see I'm on my way to Brazil for the World Championship. I believe your mother has written to inform you that I made both the World Championship team and the New Zealand team. So I'll be away from July 11th to August 29th. Then I get on a plane to Tasmania for the U14 Club Championship. Dianne (Maria) is looking after the girls while I'm away and will go to Tasmania as well.

I've been so busy organising the U14 girls my basketball schedule plus run a Grade Two classroom that I just haven't had time to write. I'm very sorry about the fact. I loved getting a card from you on my birthday. It was a surprise, a nice surprise.

I hope you're having a great time. If you have time, write and tell me of some of your adventures. I know what it's like not to have time so I won't hold my breath. Write to me in Brazil but make it plain I'm in the Australian team. (Write in big letters) . . .

The address is of the Brazil Basketball Federation. Hope you do write.

Your mum rings me to (twice) tell me of your happenings. I'm glad she does. I miss not knowing what my superstar is doing. Di and Ian had a baby girl (Suzie Jane Watts). She is fine and healthy. They send their best. Mum and Dad said to say hello and hope you are having a great time.

I hope you're not eating too many English pastries. Well I'm running out of space. Still got a lot to say so I'll write again. Lucky you. Hope this finds you in England. I am missing you. No-one else to argue with.

          Love Tricia XXX

MERV: Well if you want an argument, keep telling me to watch what I eat! Trish is playing at the World Championships, representing Australia, and she's calling me her superstar. That's typical of the modesty of most Aussie sportspeople. I said most.

 30 July 1983

To Dear Mervyn,
Hi Ya, mate! How is ya? I'm still kicking on. I feel lousy though. (Problems in the tum tum).

Thanks for your quick response to my recent letter. I really needed your opinion and am grateful for your truthfulness. I'm not as happy as what I was a few weeks ago you know. I think my high just deflated and I'm on a very LOW LOW. **[The bloke she had been seeing is no longer around.]** . . .

Gavin's car broke down at the snow, Crossa told me, as he was the lucky one who had to go with Gav to pick it up at Buller last Monday. I saw the happy Crossley family last nite after volleyball. Baby's well!! Steven's building more cupboards & Jan's having a clothes & jewellry party next week, so its back to normal in that household! . . .

Deb's fine. Fatty bumba!! I've got to put T on for Robbie now so I'll get back to you after our 2nd semi tonight, with all the results . . .

Well! Guess what? We won and so did Panels. I was so happy for them (us too). We won by 8 pts. Robyn played so well it was a shock to her system . . .

Gav didn't speak to me again last night. He must think I don't even like him as a friend which is totally wrong.

So now Panels play Colts and we've got Lakers again.

Well what else is new Mervie! Gavin's hair is really short now . . .

Marie returns on Saturday, so hopefully I'll have a flat mate . . .

O.K. Now it's your turn again Heapa!! Hope all is well with
you. I must say you've done well to keep up with the letter
writing. I didn't think you would last . . .

> See ya Merv (stay happy)
> Love Katie XX

MERV: Why the surprise at my ability to write letters? I don't know
what people think I am – illiterate, overweight and lazy?

Tuesday 26 July 1983

Dear Mervy,
How are you? Hope your injuries are O.K. and that you're
playing cricket again.

Last night the B'Ball grandfinals were played. Peta's team won
easily – they expected a closer match as Finches only lost to them
by 10 the game before the finals. Peta played really well. Panels
put up a great effort with five regular players plus Burnsie against
Commercial who had 8 players – it was a great game but they
were beaten by 10 or so. Nazza came off with five fouls with 2½
minutes to go. The Wrights carried on a bit and there were fouls
and tech fouls early & it looked as though Panels might win if
they kept their cool. They ran out of 'puff' though & I heard a
few comments like 'if they only had Merv or Brewster for the
rebounds' . . .

Saw several of your friends last nite; Gus (asking after your
cricket), Paul Smith (Angies team beaten by Jeanie Peace's team)
he's out of footy with strained groin & stomach muscles. He
thinks may be he'll take six months off sport to try and right
himself. Robyn (told me you'd rung & also told of her parties &
present – we gave her crystal glasses), Katy (her rent lowered to
$45 – Panels & Finches were kicking on at her place last night –
she's invited me to a leather bag party next Thurs week at her

place), Debby Barker (who says she's popping out *everywhere*, has only 7 weeks to go now & has the baby's room almost ready). They just have to get a wardrobe now. Gavvy (kicked five goals Saturday from the forward flank) Joanne who leaves in four weeks with Craig and her parents for Bali. Gary said to tell you he enjoyed the b'ball – a bit 'boring' cos *you* weren't playing. He slid up & down the floor! . . .

Saw where Essex lost the Benson & Hedges game by four runs. Did you watch it?

Sad news about Jack Newton wasn't it – he suffered some terrible injuries – now they're worried about saving the sight in his right eye. Will go now & *probably* send you footy news & cuttings next letter.

> Love from all of us
> Freda

 Tuesday 2 August 1983

Received your letter at lunch time. Thanks.
Gary disappointed you didn't include Sniffy – just Mum, Dad, Peta & Gary!

Hi Mervy,
How's things? Hope the heatwave (worst for 300 years so we hear on the radio) hasn't affected you. Is the heat very different to ours? . . . **[Yes, Mum, it is. When they say it's 85 degrees in England, it feels like it's only about 28 or 29 degrees. I can't work it out.]**

How's your cricket? There was a 'Meet the Coach' social night at Werribee last night – there were a couple of new players. Father Bear didn't hear the speeches as he had another meeting beforehand. Heard where John Lever got 12/95 in a match against Sussex (or Surrey) & that Essex won & went to 2nd place. Have you seen anything of the Australian young cricketers? They seem to be doing well. (Tony Dodemaide is with them, isn't he?) . . .

Four more prisoners have escaped from Pentridge – they have police all over Bonnie Doon & they have now shifted to Euroa, Benalla, Seymour & Mansfield areas. The last escapee was caught at Euroa . . .

Werribee were beaten by Dandenong by 8 points – so they've really had it now. Brewster fractured his leg & *should* miss the rest of the season but he's trying to make the team again before the season ends! His mother thinks he's crazy & again said how much they miss you, especially at C.H.B. [**For those of you who don't know much about Aussie Rules, that's Centre Half Back, the engine room of defence and the springboard for most attacks, therefore the most important position on the ground. For the rest of you, don't tell the others I'm lying.**] She sends her regards.

Gary would like to know if you have seen any of those Disneyland matchbox cars? If you do see any, bring them home with you please. [**I'll assume you want me to buy them.**] . . .

Hawks defeated Nth Melb in the game of the day & went to top position. Kink played his first game with Essendon and they were beaten by Richmond but are still in the five. Carlton beat Sth Melb – perhaps they are coming good at the right end of the season & are now back in the five. [**That's the Final Five, which came after the Final Four.**]

Am about to finish off your letter now – Gavvy has just come in and is now reading your letter. Lara were thrashed Sat & he didn't get a goal. (He did get five the week before but you have been told that.)

Gav has left now for footy training. Although he has several jobs to do, he can't work because of the wet weather. He wants to know when you'll be home, apparently Footscray are to play Werribee in a practice game & he doesn't particularly want you to play. He has 74 games up & if he gets his 100 in the next 2 seasons he'll be the youngest W'Bee player to do so. Previous youngest to get 100 was Ivo at 25. He's friends sort of with Katy again! (off-on-off-on-off-on . . .) Won't start another page,

            Love from all of us

            Freda

MERV: Did you notice how seamlessly Mum has switched from the footy season to the cricket season? Without you noticing, she has been writing about Footscray Cricket Club (my District team) playing the Werribee Cricket Club (where Snappa plays in the firsts and Dad is Captain of the thirds) in a pre-season match.

---

 17 August 1983

Dear Mervie,

Hi mate, how are you? (that's from me, the writer). Hi, how are ya! You pommy poofta!! (that's from Gavin, the *dictator*).

Freda has only just phoned to tell me the good news. Hopes you go all right. So do I Merv. I've finally recovered from my operation. It's still a bit swollen though. It's no way near as bad as yours because I hit a much weaker, slender bloke than you did. Rocket's was broken in two places, they cut his face right back near his ear. He's still off work. I went back today. Rod looked shockin in the rooms after the game. I felt for him. (only because he couldn't find it). (only joking)

Me and Harry played 18 rounds (golf obviously) on Monday, I won by one stroke 137–138. Blitzed 'em mate!

Great news, Conni's (Gary Conn) playing for Panels. He did well. Egmond will be in the team too after he gets over his corky. We beat Chevrons by 25 pts great score.

Merv, I played in Albert Park with Pete & Helen last week, I'm trying to keep a bit fitter (so lazy living alone). I also did well in the Melbourne softball comp. I got best and fairest. I was rapt!!

... Gav and I are good friends again (not together) though. I feel it's better this way so we can still go our own ways. Gav's laying back watching Benny Hill, oh now it's Dad's Army.

Footy at Werribee this week, we'll go watch their last game against Port. Joey Alifraco won the volleyball final. His team I mean. We lost our final, bloody useless.

Gav just read this, he says his are much better, especially the spelling and writing.

The old's are packing this week. The pools not finished yet, spewing, no skinny dipping while they're O.S. Bodie and Doyle is on (pommy mugs always get their man) . . .

I won the goal kicking between Joffa, Bobbie & myself. Me 11, Bobby bullshit four, Joffa four.

Robbie's ankle swelled heaps. Yukky, it bled under the skin profusely (big word eh!).

Well Merv, how's New Zealand, you should have beaten them by now. Helen's here now, Bodie and Doyle just made contact, nearly another win to them. We went out raging last week after basketball. 11pm we got there, Darby's disco in Caulfield, Chapdjian, Clive (the pom) Marie/Darren and Buck. We had a ripper of a time, got home at 2am. Then Friday I went out with the girls to Vegetarian restaurant, good change. It was called Lord Lentils. Nice food.

Meanwhile, Gav's bored stiff with me ranting & raving, he's got a cold. I've got a gut ache. Helen just left and I have to finish off the letter on my own. I hope you're not bored. I hope you've done all the touring you've wanted to do.

I wish you well in your games over the next few weeks. I think this will be the last letter till Deb has her baby early September. I'll write and tell you what she has. I'm helping her the first week she has at home. Oh well, I'd say that's about it for now.

> All my best
> Kato
> Gavin XX

MERV: How's that for a bit of 'stream of semi-consciousness'! It was written in Katie's handwriting, from Katie's flat. Snappa's had an operation on a fractured cheekbone (I think that was the swelling he was referring to). I had a similar injury when he and I banged heads during a basketball match a few years ago.

The New Zealand news is my selection for the Essex First XI in a First Class game against the touring New Zealand team.

The rest of it you can work out for yourselves.

19 August 1983

P.S. Everyone from work sends their regards. [**What is it with the Hughes family, putting the PS at the start of the letter?**]

Dear Mervyn,

We only got your letter yesterday so sent chq off as soon as we could. I had to send it in English pounds or the cheque would have taken six weeks to clear ok? I hope I've done the right thing. Your friend Suzanne will be able to cash it for you straight away this way. Everyone here is well. I have to bolt I'm doing this in my arvo tea. Everyone rapt about your game against the Kiwis. Jeff helped me do the draft.

You'll have to come to the flat for tea when you come home. Looking forward to seeing you. Mr Findlay (from school) sends his regards. Mum must have told $\frac{1}{2}$ of Werribee about the game against N.Z. Now she'll tell all of Euroa. She & Gazz have gone there for a few days.

I'll write a longer letter next time. Hope your money lasts if not ring us.

Peta XXX

MERV: When you're 21, away from home, and running out of money, it's very handy to have a sister who works in a bank.

 Tuesday 23 August 1983

Hope you rec'd your money O.K. We were lucky to get your letter – found on lawn across the road. [**See what I mean about the PSs?**]

Hi Mervy,

Thanks for ringing to tell us about your match against N.Z. Saw in the Border Morning Mail where you got two wickets with successive balls and that Sneddon did well for N.Z. Trish Cockrem may pick up more news of the match in N.Z. Hope you enjoyed the game – Have you heard any more about a contract for next year? How's Kathy – please tell us more about her (tall? short? fair? dark? – that sort of thing – a photo would be better!)

The league five is finalised – North, Fitzroy, Hawks, Essendon & Carlton; only the order could change. Peter Bosustow is out for four weeks after striking John Law from Nth. He was also reported for striking Gary Dempsey but he cried & got off with a reprimand. Bortolotto is also out for two matches . . .

Daddy is going to have a word to you over the page . . .

Here's Daddy now. Bye.

Merv,

The season here starts on the first Saturday in October which is the 1st of Oct. this year. I don't want to tell you what to do but it may be a good idea for you to be here a week or two before this to make sure you start off the season in Footscray 1sts and give yourself a chance at making the first Shield side. Give it some serious thought. This season will make or break you.

Daddy

Gary is in bed so not around to ask about Disneyland Toys! Skippy Breen (219) won the W'Bee Player of the Year Award – trip to Gold Coast! Parkes 2nd (213).

MERV: There's no doubt about Mum, hard but fair. Dad, too.

 Monday late August 1983
(too lazy to find the date)

Hilly.

How the goodness are ya? And how's *our* missus going, you know one in all in (only having a lend of ya – or her). Sorry I haven't written for a while, but you know how it is being a Bachelor. Actually I've hardly been home since the olds left last Sunday. I just wrote them a letter so me hand is a bit f***ed already. We had a bit of a porno night last Thursday around here sorry I didn't invite ya but it was on the spur of the moment. The guest list was – Crossa, Danny (his missus was away), Egg, Barnsy, Dick, Robert Smith, Hynsey, Goody, Boonga and Hot Cock & Harry & George. They were treated to an Electric Blue movie, with this sheila, Marilyn Chambers, Jack O'Tooles daughter or what. She had the biggest [censored]. Next day I had to clean up, there were 66 stubbies, four Crownies and two tins. The boys hate a beer.

We play basketball at eight thirty tonight and we've got a pretty good side. Egg, Conny, Barnsy, Terry, Steve, Naz, Bobby (still injured) and me. On Wednesday we are going to look at this brown H.J. premier 4.2. If its all right I'll buy it but I'll get Panels to check it out. The bloke, a mate of George's wants about $3500 for it. About the same as Bobby wants for his but if this one is better I might indulge. How's the cricket going? Has your old man wrote to tell you to come home about a week earlier so you can get a training run or two in before the first game. It's not a bad idea you know. Pop told me you're getting married over there. I think it's just a nasty rumour. We started training last week and I am sick of it already. I hope you're back when we play Footscray in a practise match so I can find a bit of form and get a few runs under my belt and a bit of shit in me undies. [**I was always good for Snappa's form. Often I would go to state training twice a week, and when I couldn't get up to Footscray, I'd train at Werribee. I'd always try to knock the blocks off as many batsmen as I could, but pitch it up outside off-stump for Snappa. Selectors would say, 'Snappa's handling a state player better than anyone, we should give him a run in the firsts'. Dad was the only one who worked out what I was doing, and he kept it to himself.**]

At the moment I'm doing a bit of head banging to Midnight Oil. Danny, George and I are going to North on Thursday just for Recreation sake to [censored]. Speaking of Lara which I wasn't but Coop's won the B&F by 50 votes to Duggo second and Matto third. I got four f***ing votes (spewing) which was four more than T.M. (dominator) Craig Courtney and Quicky. They all made ducks. Then again I'm not much better. I should have got more than that though.

Me face is back to its good looking normal self again. I was in a little bit of pain for a week or so but it wasn't too bad. A couple of good, little, cute, ********, spunky, single, very eligible, wouldn't kick 'em out of bed if they farted, young nurses in the hospital. The day I left, the couple I had me eye (in) on were on a different shift so I dipped out.

When I was coming out of the anaesthetic it was great. I felt pissed and I was singing and shouting out to all the nurses. This bloke beside me in the recovery room was moaning and groaning so I told him he was a weak **** and to shut up or I'd belt him again. In the end they had to kick me out of the recovery room and back to the ward so I carried on in there as well, it was great. They were all glad to get rid of me, you know what I'm like when I'm pissed.

Debbie hasn't dropped her bundle yet but she's only about a week or two away. Bobby hopes she drops it while my olds are away so he can stay and drink piss with me but I told him that I don't usually drink. I'm probably getting the rust taken out of my car tomorrow or Wednesday, rub it down, get it painted and sell it. I hope.

I had better piss off now and go out to basketball. Catch ya later big feller.

From SNAPPER

We won basketball 60–25.

P.S. Let us know exactly when the f*** you're coming home.

P.S.S. Say geday to your missus for me.

30 August 1983

Dear Mervie,

How goes it. Looking forward to you coming home. I suppose
you're split in two with all the new friends you've made & coming
home to your old faithfuls. I suppose Ma & Pop told you that you
got picked in Vic & the Colts squad. Congrats . . .

Debbie has only two weeks to go she's looking really big & fat
& healthy. She looks really happy. Swan from Port Melb won the
Liston trophy & Port are in the finals – preliminary. They then
play Preston or Geelong West . . .

As usual millions of people have been asking about you –
everyone was rapt that you got a game against New Zealand! . . .

How's the mighty Bulldogs – finished up with 10 wins & 7th
place!! Centrals snuck in at their semi final – by 96 pts. Don't you
pity who they meet in the grandfinal. Mum's birthday is the 18th
Sept. Miss you heaps. Lots of Love & safe trip.

Love Peta XXX

 Sunday 4 September 1983

Regards to the Leipers

Hi Mervy,

How are things with you? Ray Bright has been appointed Capt of
the Vic team for the coming season – I hope to write soon &
congratulate him. Carlton were thrashed on Sat by Essendon &
they are finished for the season. Hawks just won in a close last
quarter against Fitzroy & Werribee Centrals won a premiership
today by 10 goals or so.

We went into VCA last Wed & met Andrea, Elaine & Frank
Tyson. He asked when you were coming back home & said
because cricket finished $1/2$ way thru Sept there that you would
probably want a break before starting the season here!

In a Sunday paper today, Ray Steele had an article in & he thought the Vics were in for a good season with Yallop, McCurdy & yourself a chance of making the Aust. team this season! How about that. [**Settle, Mum, I'm a long way from that I would think. But keep dreaming.**]

Katy was around yesterday – she was going to Gav's for tea. He was preparing something in the seafood line. He told Pop he'd come here through the week for tea. Debby has left work – her baby is due 12th Sept.

On Saturday mornings there is a sports summary on the ABC radio station so we've been listening in to hear of Essex. They seem to think that Middlesex will finish on top as they've got a couple of games to go. But, if it rains Essex will be OK won't they??

How's Kathy? Is your money holding out? Tony Dodemaide has done well on his trip – did you see them at all? [**She keeps asking me, but I can't tell her. If I do, she'll ask me what we did and I'll have to tell her we drank for eight hours.**]

Today Gary & I went into Albert Park & we had a lovely morning at the parks & lake while Peta trained & then she took us over to Heidelberg to see Nanna, Grandpa & Aunty Kate.

Peta is to play in a grand final next Wed nite – their Thursday team has two games to go & they *could* make the four but will only have five players if they do make it.

Best go now, love from all of us. School starts again tomorrow & kinder on Tues. Gary is in bed so no messages from him.

> Freda

 Monday 12 September 1983

Hi Mervy,

Thanks a lot for your letter that arrived today – Gav received one too. We were getting a bit worried as NOBODY had heard of you for 3½ weeks. There is usually *someone* around who knows something of you!

Have just read today's paper & saw some sad notices – the death notices of Katy Hughes' grandma & Donald Laird's father. Mr Laird had a stroke quite a while back. I didn't even know Katy's Grandma was sick. Katy, Helen & Pete were here to lunch on Friday. Deb's baby is due today so I hope the news isn't too upsetting for her.

Frank Tyson is down at the Werribee rooms tonight – I cut two jumbo loaves for the night for which they pay me $10 to cover costs. ALSO, I received a box of chocolates – How about that? Told Robbo when he picked them up I'd do them anytime but there was no need to give me chocs. Just think how fat I'll get!

Essendon & North Melb are to play in the Prelim Final next Sat. North were thrashed by Hawthorn & Essendon won an exciting game against Fitzroy. Brendan Ryan may get a chance to play with North – he did well with the seconds on Sat. They were beaten also & are finished for the year.

How did you go with Mike Denness? Hope you got the contract you wanted. Heard on Sat morning that Essex were still 14 in front of Middlesex as they were unexpectedly defeated in their last game & they each had one game to go. *How* many points can a team score in a game?

How are Woodford Wells going – Must of just about played your last game by now – Hope you & your team did well. **[Woodford Wells was the club team I played for on weekends after playing Wednesday to Friday for Essex seconds. You'll meet my team-mates later . . .]**

Daddy has just arrived home after a couple of school meetings of some sort & didn't get to the cricket night. He thinks your spelling & writing have improved to billio this year – doesn't seem particularly upset that you're not coming home earlier. We didn't realize that Woodford Wells still had matches to play.

Gary is quite happy to think that your are looking for those Matchy Toys. Peta is finding it a bit of a struggle (finance wise) at the flat. She was upset not to have her name included in our letter today. She is still nearly as much home as she is away. Did you get the money she had sent over? – You didn't say in any of your letters home but we think you must have it or you would of let us know before now.

Will go now, love from all of us & Peta,
See you in 2½ weeks,

Regards to the Leipers
Mummy

So glad we heard from you today as people are always asking about you – Now we have news for them.

Tuesday 13 September 1983

Just a few more lines.
Forgot to tell you that we received a card from the Whitings yesterday; they are due home Thurs morning & Gav & George will pick them up.

If Gav can't pick you up, Daddy said he probably would. Gav will let us know. There will be someone to meet you anyway. Gary doesn't think he'll be able to meet you because of kinder.

It is pouring rain here today but the dams still need plenty as they are only just over ½ full & water restrictions are on again for this summer . . .

Am enjoying my last couple of weeks washing & ironing-free – I scratch around to get enough clothes to wash two days a week!

If you get a contract for next year, will you leave some of your cricket gear over there? Shouldn't of started this page as the big hand is nearly up the top & if Gary happens to see that we'll be off to kinder in a flash – rain and all.

Really must go, may get one more letter to you.
See you in two weeks & two days.

Lot of Love
Fre

MERV: I think Mum's missing me. I'm sure I'll be able to give her plenty to do when I get home.

Thursday 15 September 1983

Regards to the Leipers!

Hi Mervy,
Hope this isn't too much for you to get two letters in a week
(*that's* if the other one reached you – it wasn't in an airmail
envelope).

Main reason for writing, is to tell you the Barkers have a baby
son. Due 12th, he arrived on 13th – everyone is well. His name is
Lee Garth & Robbie is almost jumping over the moon.

Congratulations to your Essex firsts on winning the cricket.
Told you they'd be right if it rained! How about your team. You
won't want rain – you have to win your games don't you?
Anyway, guess it's all over as you read this.

We enjoyed our shopping day today as we were able to tell
people what you are doing. Robert said the cricket board had
rung a few times, to see what you were doing. I did tell Andrea &
Elaine you wouldn't be back until the end of Sept. so don't know
just *who* was after you.

Nancy Alifraco wants to know if you have written to her at all
as if so, your letter has been lost in the mail somewhere! I was
supposed to tell you ages ago she was waiting for a letter . . .

Daddy is getting quite tired as he's been on the go for a
fortnight now & he's looking forward to a quiet time next week.
Last night at the tribunal, they suspended three players for four
weeks each.

Helen rang a while ago & if *nobody* else is at the airport, she
will meet you. We are pretty sure that Gav will meet you – Helen
& I might still go too. Gary hasn't quite decided whether he can
miss kinder for a morning or not. See you soon – this *could* be the
last letter to you. [**I would think that is very unlikely.**]

> Lots of love from all of us
> Fre

Tuesday 20 September 1983
[**Told you.**]

(P.S. Regards to the Leipers)

Hi Mervy

Just a short quick note as it's nearly time to go to kinder (and it's pouring rain!)

How did your cricket team go – do hope you won that championship (and that it's not raining there).

Elaine from VCA rang last Thurs about five to clarify what you are doing.

M'ford were beaten in the prelim final. Preston won the VFA flag from Geelong West by 7 points. Essendon won the prelim final against North M by heaps & Ross Glendenning won the Brownlow with 24 from Rioli 23, & Simon Madden 22.

McCurdy & Yallop are going to court with a writ against VCA & Richmond & Ringwood Cricket Clubs as they want to play for South Melb . . .

Will go now, lots of love from all of us & we are looking forward to seeing you on the 29th.

Gary has just gone to kinder with Ingrid – his ONLY message – Have you been able to get his toys yet??

Bye for now
Mummy

MERV: When I returned from Essex, I was required to give a written report on my time there. I think Dad might have helped me with the commas and the full stops.

 10 October 1983

Mr. G.W. Halbish
Administration Manager
Australian Cricket Board

Dear Sir,
I wish to thank the A.C.B. and Esso for giving me the invaluable experience I received playing cricket in England on the Esso Scholarship. Not only was the cricket a great experience, but it was my first trip overseas which I thoroughly enjoyed.

The following is my report to the A.C.B. covering aspects of the Scholarship season.

1. General Arrangements

Travelling arrangements went smoothly and the board provided at the home of former Essex player Jack Leiper and his wife Jill was excellent. Their son Robert, also played with Essex seconds during the season.

I stayed for five months to see out the full season.

2. Playing

My 'local' club was Woodford Wells who competed on a Saturday in the Richard Veneer's League. We finished second and I took 55 wickets at around an average of 13.

Woodford Wells also played 'friendly' games of a Sunday in which I participated. These were purely social matches.

The County side I played with was Essex Seconds. We played on Wednesday, Thursday and Friday in three day matches in the County Championship.

On Mondays in June and July I played in the Essex Under 25 side in a 40 over competition and on Tuesday in a 55 over competition with the Under 25 side.

My performances for Essex seconds were as follows:

Bowling	Overs	Mdns.	Runs	Wickets	Av.
Essex 2nds	594	87	1119	60	18.65
Essex U25 (40)	29	4	97	7	13.85
Essex U25 (55)	36	6	76	8	9.50

Batting	Runs	Completed Inn.	Av.
Essex 2nds	119	5	23.8
Essex U25 (40)	13	1	13
Essex U25 (55)	1	1	1

I also represented Essex Firsts against the touring New Zealand team. In the first innings I took 2/91 in the N.Z. score of 4 Dec/321 and in the second innings I took 4/71 in their innings of 220.

Essex Firsts had a similar schedule to the Seconds, playing 3 day County matches on Friday, Saturday and Monday, a 40 over competition on Sundays and Benson and Hedges competition on a Tuesday. Essex won the County Championship in the Firsts.

Essex had a number of internationals who assisted me with coaching. These including G. Gooch, P. Lever, D. Pringle, N. Foster, K. Fletcher and the Essex 2nds Captain M. Denness, who is a former English captain.

3. General Impressions of the Season

The standard of the County firsts is above district level but below State level.

The standard I played at in the seconds is below that of district cricket. Most of the players have to be professionals on contract to the County as playing cricket is a full time job in the season.

There is little atmosphere in the games and players don't get 'fired up' as they do in District Cricket. The games are played in an easy-going manner and lack the desperation of District Cricket.

The constant playing makes it hard to be flat out all the time and a high level of fitness is needed to try to maintain top form particularly for quick bowlers.

Once again I would like to thank the A.C.B. and Esso for giving me such a wonderful opportunity.

Yours sincerely,

M.G. Hughes

MERV: Or perhaps I told Dad what happened, gave him my scrapbook and went to the pub.

CHAPTER FIVE

A Mother's Letters to Home

I returned from Essex in September 1983 and only managed four Sheffield Shield games for Victoria. I had hamstring troubles at the start of the season and then I was diagnosed as suffering from stress fractures of my back. That was the end of cricket for me for the summer.

At the beginning of 1984, Mum left home. Dad was transferred to West Bairnsdale Primary School, in East Gippsland. Mum, Gary and he left Peta to look after me in the family home at Werribee. Sniffy went with Mum and Dad.

(M) Tuesday 13 March 1984

P.S. How did you get on with your back?

Hi Mervy,
How's things? And what is all your news. Did you enjoy that concert you went to at the showgrounds the Sunday we came home from W'Bee?

What did you think of all the cricket at the weekend? Tony did well, so too, did that Mark Hooper, Simon O'Donnell & McLaine seems to be doing better with Nth Melb.

. . . Pete said you were working last week – guess the money was OK. How was the work? How is Gavvy and any of your other friends? Did you enjoy Moomba? I owe Kate a letter & will write one of these days.

Yesterday we went to Lakes Entrance. – The Surf beach there is fantastic – the beautiful sand is beautifully clean and there is just so much of it.

Looks like, W.A. will win today, and also Botham & his teammates could be in a bit of strife if all the paper talk is true. Must go, write soon & tell me your news.

Love from all of us
Fre

Tuesday 20 March 1984

Hi Merv,

How's things? Did you enjoy your game of footy at the weekend?
How was your back afterwards?

Sorry to see two of Footscray's teams are finished for the
season. Also saw where Tony didn't bowl & that Raynor Reber
did bowl – who wicket kept?

Katy sent me some of her photos to look at. Saw a nice one of
you & also some of Smithy's wedding.

Tomorrow I'm going to Lakes Entrance again – third time in
two weeks. This time on a bus with C.W.A. Should be good fun.

Had any luck with a job yet? . . .

The procession here at the weekend was really good. *May* be
able to show you some photos next time we're home.

Will go now, write one day & tell me what you are doing with
yourself.

> Love from us
> Fre

MERV: Mum really likes to know what I'm up to, God bless her.

 Monday 26 March 1984

Hi Merv,

Thanks for your postcard – hope you enjoyed your stay in S.A.
(last cricket season, or the season before?)

Did you enjoy your day's work with Pris? What did you do?
Did you play footy over the weekend? Brian Wilson had some bad
luck – bet he won't enjoy being out of footy for 12 weeks.

My Aunty Greta & her daughter Gwen were here today – it
was great to see them and have a talk and laugh over old times.
Gwen asked if you would be here over Easter. (Told her it
probably depended on your footy.)

Footscray Presentation Night is on the same night as Werribee's, isn't it? Saw in the Sun where F'sray's was on April 6th. Are you going to it? Do you know how Tony Dodemaide's back is – see he didn't bowl in the semi-final & Rainer Reber did (Think I said that last letter too).

Gary is home from school now – Pop had to go out to the school camp – 17 km out & the sixth graders rode out there. Hope they had a tail wind – we just walked Sniffy and almost got blown away.

Gary's messages: Except for Robbie and Kate (who are on holidays in Bright just now) he doesn't like anyone else in the street very much.

All the kids hate Mrs Davis because she won't give their balls back to them if they're hit there during the cricket games. (She does have a lovely garden though & probably doesn't like little people breaking down her plants.)

He's off to play with Lincoln tomorrow night – he's the doctor's son and lives about a mile the other side of school from here. That's all of his news for now.

How is Gav's ankle – hope it didn't keep him out of his footy. Say hello to him from all of us. Have you heard anything about the cricket pitch or who dug it up? Pete said she hadn't heard anything.

Must go now & see about tea.

Love from all of us

Freda

 9 April 1984

Hi Merv,

How did your footy go yesterday and did you play in the ruck? How did Steve go & where did he play? Next week hopefully we'll be able to see your results in the Sun – no results of practice matches that we could see today. Tell Gav I'm sorry we missed him Sat. morning – hope his ankle is OK.

The Australians aren't going the best again – they need some good fast bowlers, so get in there next season, Mervy . . .

Did you ever send your friend in N.Z. that shirt (or whatever) that he wanted? Is he going back to England this year?

When you know what you're doing at Easter will you let us know please. Peta and some of her team mates may stay here, but except for Pete they'll probably go home Monday.

I think Katy Hughes may be staying with Robyn – she wasn't sure when she wrote a fortnight ago but Peta said she thought Katy was staying at Yarram.

I don't think Gary & I will be up next weekend – we'll let you know if we change our minds. (Gary & I might get to watch your footy *if* we do go.)

Looks like being another nice day here today – sometimes it takes a while before the sun comes out. There is a lot of burning off in the forests (similar to what was done when we were at Myrtleford) and because there is no wind, the smoke is around for ages.

Have you heard anything of Choc at all? Is Ady Black going back to Ireland?

Can't think of anything more now, hope to see you at Easter (I'm pretty sure Gary and I won't be up next weekend) hope you enjoy your footy season.

Bye for now,

Love from all of us

Freda

Monday 16 April 1984

Hi Mervy,

Thanks for your letter – Gary thought the card terrific (I did too – I love those guards) and he took it along for morning talk today.

Did you see where Trish made the Aust. B'Ball side? – under P. Cockerem in Sat. Sun? Hope she does really well and has a great time. Have you heard from her at all?

Sorry to hear about your ankle – looks as tho' they missed you a lot or aren't they very good this year? Hope it comes good soon & that you will be able to get a bit of money playing.

Last week there were several big fire trucks in the yard next door and the kids in the street had a great time climbing all over them and playing their own games.

Have you worked out what you're doing over Easter yet or does it depend on your footy? You will probably be last out at home so don't forget to lock up securely will you now.

Pleased that you did a bit of visiting – Jan was saying at the cricket presentation she hadn't seen you for a while. Hope the Blairs are well – I'm still waiting to hear from them . . .

This week I hope to get the trophies cleaned – looks as tho they need to be cleaned every two months. They will then look goodo for the Easter visitors.

How did the disco go? Did you do much dancing? If so, hope your ankle is O.K. today. [**Mum, blokes don't go to discos to dance.**] . . .

Competition tennis starts of a Thursday after the May hols – I put my name down as an emergency but may see if I can get in a team.

Did you get your blind fixed?

Will go now – hope to see you over Easter . . .

Father enjoyed the cricket weekend although he was pretty tired and he feels his blood pressure could be up a bit; from now on, he is really going to crack down on his food. [**If it was a cricket trip, I don't think it is food that is the problem.**]

>Bye for now, love from all of us
>Freda

P.S. Say Hi to Gavvy.

Tuesday 12 June 1984

Hi Mervy,

Thank you for your card you sent here with Peta – good to hear from you.

Enjoy your game Sunday? See where you were in the best players again – good on you. Have asked Katy to send me the Banner footy news each week (did ask you to last week but you didn't. Katy sent it though & I thought if I asked her nicely she might send it each week.)

How do you like your cricket training? Is that at Graham Yallop's in South Melb? What is the set up like (*there* is something you can tell me about in your next letter). Where did you go last night with Katy & Steve? Hope you enjoyed yourselves. Footscray & C'wood didn't go too well Monday, did they?

Now that Petey is working in town try and help her a bit will you please? She will probably have trouble getting the washing done.

Best of luck in your b'ball finals, that is another thing you can write & tell me about.

Love from all of us
Fre

Regards to any of your friends that are my friends too

 Monday 23 July 1984

Hi Mervy,

How's things?

Congratulations on your win yesterday – how did you enjoy the game?

The parent-teacher interviews were on at school last Wed., & Gary's teacher is pleased with his progress. She said he was shy at first, and that all the noisy boys were gradually quietening down now. [He's the son of the principal – why wouldn't she be pleased with his progress?]

I finished a big thick jumper for my brother John at the weekend – it was 14 ply wool & only took 2½ weeks to knit. Now I *might* do some knitting for the Bairnsdale Show – first week in Nov.

Gary had a big weekend – he slept at Robbie's Sat night & had most of his meals there & then on Sunday morning they rode to the B.M.X. track & then after lunch he went to Scott's 6th birthday. He wore your Essex jumper again (or the one you gave him) & it looked great. It really fits him well this year & that is his bestest jumper for going out.

Daddy is still off bread, spuds and ice-cream (although he does lash out a bit over the weekends.)

Do you think Wessells has any intention of coming to Victoria for the cricket season? Saw him on teli say that he'd have to be captain. Brighty has already been appointed so the paper said earlier, so what is going on?

Will go now, still waiting for your letter to tell me all you are doing.

Lots of love from all of us
Fre

 Monday 30 July 1984

Hi Mervy,
How's things?

Bad weekend for Werribee, Lara & F'scray footballers – did you enjoy your game? There wasn't a great lot of difference in your final scores – haven't read the paper yet to see what the ¼ by ¼ scores were. Your father did say that Parkes (I think) had been reported again and that there were only a few hundred at your match.

Today I'm going to make enquiries at Coles about the Herograms they suggest sending across to the Olympic Games. *If* they are not out of this world, cost-wise, I'm going to send one to Trish . . .

Gary is off to another party on Wed (two last week!). He wasn't sure about going as David told him he had a pet SNAKE. So I said that on the reply & his Mum went into see Daddy & told him they haven't a pet snake at all & that David had his photo taken with one at some park or other – so now Gary is quite happy about going to his party.

Lots of floods here over the weekend but the water is all going down now. We are high and dry here.

... I was able to play tennis last week – 1st time for a few weeks. Played with the top team – had a great time. Won two of my three sets & my team won 40–28. Was quite exhausted afterwards as I tried like billio in the 2nd set & we were beaten 8–3.

Don't think there is any more news just now – Daddy still just under 17 stone – will, if I have time, cut out a few clippings from M'ford Times that Boris sent to me.

Lots of love from all of us. Still waiting to hear from you. (letter or phone)

Fre

Monday 6 August 1984

Hi Mervy,

Great to see your name in the best players *and* first in line too. Your father was beginning to think they had their print set and nothing would change it.

(Bit hard to write to you without a letter from you to answer – I can only tell you what we are doing here & ask you more questions which you never get around to answering!!)

Did you help Katy celebrate her birthday? Gary told me that now she is 23 and she is older than you & Gavvy cos you are both 22. She is old as Pete now, & he has the first birthday in our family each year. [**Gary clearly got the brains.**] ...

Have you any cricket gear that needs mending? If so, better get it out for me. Holidays are only a fortnight off & I'm hoping

Gramps O.K. to travel as I want to see you people & HEAR all your news because you don't write letters. [**That gives me two weeks to clean the house, mow the lawn and fix the blind.**]

What do you think of Dean Jones being vice captain? And Ian Callen is still around – I thought he was out of Shield cricket – Is McCurdy going to Tassy? Wiggy was at some coaching clinic at South Melb Sat & Yallop & Jones were there. He enjoyed it greatly as there was a baseball coach there with suggestions to liken cricket fielding to baseball fielding with hand signals.

The cricket psychologist was there too & showed how he did his work – on Dean Jones. [**That would have been interesting to watch.**]

I watch teli all day when I can just to get a glimpse of Trish. They were just on (11.45 am) but Trish wasn't on the court. The first half was only less than half way through, Aussies were one point down AND THEY CROSSED TO HOCKEY! How dare they, when Trish is the only person I know there, so the basketball is much more important! Sent her two herograms – second she won't get as I forgot to put her number (from the book) in place provided. Do hope you sent one – if not, send her one now. By all accounts they are thrilled to get these herograms as everyone that is interviewed all say so . . .

Looking forward to the Holidays (only if I can get to W'bee though). Will go now, congrats on your good footy game yesterday.

Love from all of us. Regards to those of your friends who are my friends too.

> Hope to see you soon
> Fre

12.05 B'ball back on – Trish still not there – Aus are down 29–24.

P.S. Just saw Aust def Yugoslav by three. Trish got on for last minute or so. NOW I can get my work done – that is the finish of our B'ball.

Monday 20 August 1984

Hi Merv,

How's things? Hope your knee is O.K. [**I'm glad I'm using the winter to recover from my injuries.**]

Peta was just talking to me (from work) & said you didn't play yesterday. Did you go to the game? Your father said Lara were beaten on Saturday – that must just about finish them as far as the finals are concerned. Did you enjoy the party Sat night?

Gary *was* thinking about writing letters to you & Peta, but decided to go & play with Aaron instead. He said to tell you that he's got 20 something Star Wars men now and that he played with Aaron yesterday. Robbie is on holidays.

Heard anything of Trish yet?...

The school spellathon has just been completed – I think about $1400 was raised. Gary raised the most in his grade, INCLUDING $1 from you, $1 from Chris & $2 from Peta. (I will collect from you when next I see you!) (I knew you would *want* to sponsor him so I put down 10c a word – or sound actually – from you & Chris & 20c from Peta (on her say so). [**If I'd known Peta was going to give 20c, I would've given 30c.**]

Will go now (you can now write to me just in case I don't get to Werribee).

Love from all of us
Fre

 Monday 3 September 1984

Hi Mervy,

How are you? And how did your practice go at Footscray? Hope you do well at Mildura – good not having to drive up, isn't it? Just go easy & don't try to bowl too fast, too soon. (I'm sure your coaches would tell you that, wouldn't they?) [**If they don't, I can give them this note from my Mum.**]

Thanks for taking Katy's card around – was she all ready to go

when you saw her? Pete said Hynesy was around Fri night &
didn't know what to do with himself. (Did you get the washing in
for Peta the day we left? If so, thank you.) . . .

How is work? Stacky's cricket practise starts today, Monday
3rd, doesn't it? Hope that goes well. You must nearly be one of
the oldest there now aren't you?

Can't think of any more now, help Peta as much as you can
please as she is pretty flat out with her work and sport too.

   Love from all of us
   Fre

P.S. It was really great to get home & see you even if you do carry
on with fights & things. [**What fights? She started it.**]

 Monday 17 September 1984

Hi Mervy,
Nice to hear your voice on Sunday – forgot to ask if you were still
working – are you?

This has to be pretty short today as I have several letters to
send off today – to Gavvy, Nardine Cody & Robyn Souter
(engagement cards), Gramps, Sympathy card to a friend in Euroa
who lost her father, and you & Peta & that all has to be done
before the box is cleared at 1.30 – it's almost 11 now!

Dav Whatmore was in Violet Town a while back – John was
talking to him – he thought you should do well with your cricket.
John wondered if he might be moving up that way as Brian Hayes
& other V.T. cricketing people were talking to him for ages.

Done anything about a car yet? Are you still going to get
Whitings teli? We thought that perhaps you wouldn't be home
enough to watch that & perhaps the money from that could go
towards a car.

Looking forward to your weekend in Mildura? Have fun –
work hard. [**You just told me not to bowl too fast.**] Ian Callen was
on the 3LO Sports Show Sat morning & he thinks that with

McCurdy gone he might be No.1 Strike bowler & *he isn't even going to Mildura* – he thought the training might be *too hard* for him. So how can he be considered for the team!!! [**He's probably got a better note from his Mum.**] (That is only my opinion)

My new shoes & socks were terrific both for tennis & aerobics last week & it was good to finally get to use them . . .

Will go now Mervy, please let us know how you go in Mildura.

Love from all of us

Fre

 Monday 24 September 1984

Hi Merv,

How did your weekend go? We listened for news of your game on the radio last night but there was nothing. And this morning the paper was late, just when we really wanted to see how you went. Your father was pacing up & down & carrying on about the paper boy. It finally came a few minutes before he left. Did you enjoy your game? We were pleased to see you got a couple of wickets. Who do I have to put a 'mos' on this season? Who is the Mohr fellow? Your father thinks he's an older player who has been around for a while.

Have you heard who won the trophies for W'bee? How did their presentation night go? Hope Gavvy got away OK.

My brother John was at the airport to pick up friends from Queensland around lunch time Thurs. and was looking around for you cricketers for quite a while. Told him Friday that your plane left at six. How was the trip? Was it very wet in Mildura?

Had a card from Katie last week – is she home yet? She was having a great time.

Look after Pete this week as she is playing in two grand finals and a prelim final on Tues, Wed & Thurs nights at Albert Park. She is looking forward to the holiday Thursday.

Will go now Mervie, nearly your turn to write isn't it???

Love from all of us

Fre

CHAPTER SIX

Life in Essex

I made many friends in Essex, both at the county club, and also at Woodford Wells, the local league team with which I played on weekends. I also received a few letters from fans while I was over there. After I got back to Australia a few of my team-mates kept in touch.

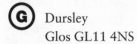 Dursley
Glos GL11 4NS

20 June 1983

Dear Merv,
I am a keen cricket fan and autograph collector. My collection includes many of the games greats past and present. I would be very pleased if you could sign for me.
   Could you also ask Neil Burns, Michael Field-Buss, Andrew Golding & Kevin Maye to sign for me as well. Thank you Merv.
   I enclose a stamp addressed envelope and look forward to hearing from you.
   Best wishes for the future.
                Yours sincerely,
                [signature illegible]

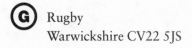 Rugby
Warwickshire CV22 5JS

2 July 1983

Dear Sir,
I am a very keen cricket follower, and I am trying to make a collection of players' autographs. I should very much appreciate it if you would please be so kind as to send to me your autograph, to add to my collection please.

If you will do this for me, will you please write it on a piece of paper, and forward to me in the enclosed envelope?

I note that you played for Victoria in five games during the 1981–82 season, and in four games last season. I find that in 1981–82 you took four wickets for 69 runs and 2 for 73 against Queensland and 4 for 71 and 1 for 19 v N.S.W. and finished the season with 18 wickets for 567 runs.

Congratulations on your fine achievements in the Sheffield Shield.

Every good wish for continued success, and very many thanks, if you can oblige me.

> Yours faithfully,
> D. G. C.

MERV: Buttering me up is one way to get an autograph!

 Lancing
W. Sussex

18 July 1983

Dear Sir,

I am an enthusiastic collector of Cricket autographs. I wonder if you would be kind enough to sign the enclosed card.

I enclose a S.A.E. Thanking you in anticipation,

> Yours faithfully,
> Tim B.

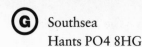 Southsea
Hants PO4 8HG

9 August 1983

Dear Mr Hughes,
I hope you are enjoying your season with Essex. I see you have
been taking wickets for the Second team. I am a keen follower of
Sheffield Shield cricket which is not too well covered in this
country.

I'd be grateful if you could supply me with some details about
Victorian cricketers.

As you can see from the list enclosed, I don't know which way
round any of the listed players bat or who they play grade cricket
for. I am missing some christian names and methods of bowling.

If you could fill in any of these gaps it would be a great help to
me.

Thank you in anticipation.
John T.

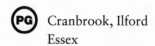 Cranbrook, Ilford
Essex

7 October 1983

Good Day Merv
Hope you had a good flight back. Did you manage to chat up any
of the waitresses or hostesses. I doubt it, anyway if you did it
might take you back to Milton Keynes. I'm still not certain what
happened there. Did your so-called loony mates meet you at the
airport alright or did you have to walk it back home? I suppose
once you got home, you later went out for a couple of pints and a
curry.

How did your first training session go that week seeing that
you went back pregnant. I bet you get a bollocking for that. Seen

the missus yet – I cannot remember her name – hope you have and are making up for lost time. Dirty git. I also bet you have been showing everyone all six of your jumpers and no doubt been telling them of your First XI game.

The place somehow doesn't quite seem the same without you, it's a lot quieter now and I don't seem to be getting pissed so much . . .

I heard that someone from the Well's has offered you some money to come back and play for them again next season. That's good news in a way, but it would be a shame if you couldn't make it to play for Ilford (with the lads, without the Male Model). Well I trust that everything has gone well since your returned home, including trying to find a new job if your other one had gone. You will have to keep me informed of your progress during the season . . .

By the way don't forget to ask your club (Footscray) whether or not they would mind if I came over and played for them next season, that's of course if I have the cash to do that. Also, don't forget to send me those Foster's Lager T-shirts you said you'd send me.

Have you heard from Kathy at all since you've been back? Don't suppose you have, in which case you probably won't have heard the latest on her, or might not want to hear. Well, she's getting engaged to what's his name. Never mind when you come over again we will have to go down to the west country. You must remember that trip. That's where you told Pritch to take that woman out of his mouth.

I saw Paddy and Scanlon just after you left and they wanted me to pass on their regards and they hope to see you next season. By the time this letter reaches you, you would have already heard the news about G. Boycott being given the boot. Such a shame, it couldn't have happened to a nicer bloke. I think also by now, Alan (Dad) would have written and told you about the latest on his career whatever might have happened. I hope you have been out somewhere special so that you can wear your Ilford tie (don't swear). I think you made a few friends over here, and they will

certainly miss your nutty capers. Did you give Gaffer's and
Suzanne your address so that they can keep in touch. Still you can
see them all next season if you make the effort to come back over.

Well, I hope to hear from you soon.

all the best Merv

Mouse

P.S. Mum and Dad mouse send their best wishes.
Keep Smiling (give it the mouse grin).

MERV: Mouse played cricket with me at Essex seconds. He is keen to
get to Australia, thinking it might change him from the timid little bloke
that he is.

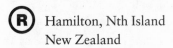

(R) Hamilton, Nth Island
New Zealand

26 November 1983

Dear Merv (I don't really mean Dear),
How the f*** is it? I thought I'd better write about now to find
out what you're up to next year and all. I've got a job as a
storeman driving a fork lift all day which ain't too bad. I get
about $170 a week. My club here have said they'll pay my airfares
next year to England – it might be all bullshit (you know these
kiwis!) so I can't definitely say whether I'm going back next year
or the year after. I'll let you know though.

I suppose it would have been a few weeks after we left England
that I saw Werribee on T.V. flooded out – couldn't believe it. I
wonder if your place got sunk.

You'll be happy to know that Graham 'SKIPPER' May wasn't
too pissed off about the jumper. I think he knew you had it all
along!

I've been following the Pakis over your way. They took a hiding in the first Test. How come David Hookes wasn't playing – someone told me he was dropped. I can't believe that.

I've only really seen one Aussie cricket mag with a preview on each state. I read that you were 'hampered by a hamstring injury'. Well if you get that again don't worry because you've always got your keeping to fall back on!! Speaking of that sort of carry on I bowled 10 overs of dazzling off spin for Hamilton and took 3 for 6!! People laughed when they saw I was about to bowl! I don't think I was half the bowler as I was with you behind the stumps! I reckon that Rod Marsh should look out.

As far as cricket for me has gone since I've been back I've been quite pleased. I've had eight bats because it's been raining so much. Bit like April–May in Pommie Land.

Tomorrow I'm going to Dunedin (Sth Island) to play in the Under 23 tournament. I wonder if the NZ team plays you guys – hope so. Remember if we ever meet on the field the first ball has to be a bouncer.

Looking forward to hearing from you and getting my Victoria one day shirt (remember!!)

> See you in the final
> Kiwi

P.S. Didn't I do well in the Melbourne Cup!!
Ye Mighty Spurs!!

MERV: In 1983, Kiwi, trained by Snowy Lupton, arrived from New Zealand just days before the Melbourne Cup, was last into the straight, and won by several lengths.

Nick played with me at Woodford Wells, where I played on Saturdays and Sundays, having played for Essex seconds Wednesday to Friday. I seem to attract mates with strange senses of humour. Nick is a Kiwi version of Snappa.

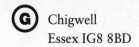 Chigwell
Essex IG8 8BD

6 January 1984

Well Merv, must thank you for your Christmas Card – we're sorry
you're having such a rough time there! It's not been too bad here –
no white Christmas – but I'm getting concerned that we might
have a white wedding (and I mean snow) otherwise it is going to
be a white wedding!

It's been relative quiet here since you and Nick departed – we
had Christmas drinking sessions up at the Club and there was a
dinner & disco on New Year's Eve. There were over 200 people
there so you can imagine the chaos.

No doubt you've heard that Val & Richard Harrison will be
parents in May? And I think Rob and Allison will be down the
aisle in 1985 – the rest of the gang are no different – still propping
up the bar, playing the fruit machines and everything else men do!
The cricket season doesn't seem far away now – perhaps we can
have another bash at the League title – will you be gracing us with
your bowling & antics in 1984? You know the form – if you are –
come over early and come and see Webs sign his life away!! (April
14 1984). How's your 'home' cricket season going – I trust that
after the fine training you had here that you are doing well!
Anyway boring I'm afraid this is but at least you know the Wells
is still alive and kicking!!

Take Care

Love Liz and Mark Webber

MERV: Mark played at Woodford Wells. For some reason they think
they want me back. I'm nowhere near as shy on my second visit to
somewhere.

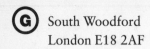

South Woodford
London E18 2AF

10 February 1984

Dear Merv,
How are you, you old growler, it's your world famous (nearly)
SKIPPER here, G'day.

Thanks for your card at Christmas and I can understand that
you are busy playing a lot of cricket. Actually I heard via Nick
Lloyd that you had had injury problems again and were in and
out of the state side. That's bad luck but I hope you're fit now and
knocking the bastards over.

What about the bloody Kiwi's then, Christ we must have batted
badly. I was very embarrassed, And all the poor Englishmen have
to look forward to now are three tests in Pakistan!

Well now what news from POM. I'm still enjoying myself and
working pretty hard in the family business. Actually it's going very
well and I will be getting a new company car pretty soon which
can't be bad.

One very sad bit of news is that Richard and Val Harrison lost
their first child last Tuesday. It was a tragic story, for some
anatomical reason the baby was born, alive, after only 25 weeks
(about 3 months premature). It gave one hell of a fight for a boy
of only 1lb 10oz but unfortunately died after living for just over
two days. Everybody is a bit choked but I'm sure they'll bounce
back and they have been given the go ahead to start trying again
pretty soon.

I hear from Nick that you won't be over here next year. Is this
for a special reason or is it just the financial side? If it is the latter I
can confirm that Mike Darbyshire will support you through the
summer if you really want to get over here. I'm not pushing you at
all but do let me know either way.

Our hockey season is going pretty well. We are, yes, you
guessed it, second in our league and we are playing the league
leaders tomorrow. We've got our work cut out but I think we can
do it. If we do win or even remain as runners up it will have been
a pretty good year.

Mark Webber gets married to Liz on April 14th. He's asked me to be an usher for some reason, actually it should be a bloody good day out.

Everyone at the club sends their regards and still talks about you and it would be great to see you over here again. Nick is probably coming over in 1985.

News from a few quarters: Mike Darbyshire is still not married but having a ball, Graham Ayres is playing Rugby and talking a lot, Mike Rogers is still farting around, Rob Leiper is getting closer to marriage, Don Leiper is still making excuses, Barney Miller is still as black as the ace of spades and Wally is still a Wally! Also to your disappointment Leigh-on-Sea cricket club have not disappeared from the face of the earth.

Well I'll sign off now. All the best Merv, keep taking the tablets and keep in touch.

    Graham

P.S. I have not forgotten the photos.

MERV: Graham May, Woodford Wells captain when I was there. One of the good guys.

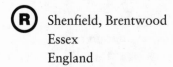

Ⓡ Shenfield, Brentwood
Essex
England

20 February 1984

Hello Hughsy,
Thanks for your letter which I got this morning (Saturday), everything's going pretty well here, I'm managing to keep pretty fit by playing soccer on Saturday afternoons & Sunday mornings, although I can't play at all this weekend because I cracked a rib bone playing last Sunday, I ran full pelt straight into the f***in'

goalkeeper he had 3 broken ribs & a broken arm, I got a cracked rib & a goal!

You mentioned Paula in your letter – well Hughsy I'm afraid that ended just after you went home, I must admit I miss those tits! Thanks for the photographs you left with Lil, perhaps you should have kept the f***in' things – only joking.

I'm sorry to hear about your back, I hope things get better soon for you, but I'm glad you're enjoying life on the beach with all that crumpet (lucky Bastard) give em one or two for me will you!

I hope you're back on the beer by now, you'll make me feel guilty if you're not. Kingy & me have had a few beers over the last few months as you can imagine, although he's got tied up now, about three weeks ago this bird moved in to live with him . . . so I haven't seen much of him lately.

I've been having a few beers with Pony (Ian) he's just as mad as ever, he sends his regards.

Not much activity going on around the English beaches at the moment – f*** knows why! It's been pretty cold here lately about -5 at night and 2° at day.

I ain't been doing much work here over the winter just a bit of coaching her & there in the cricket school.

Burnsy passed his driving test and has got a brand new sponsored car (Alfa Romeo) he's only crashed it twice! (poor bastard). He still takes a lot of stick especially Tuesday nights when we all have to go to indoor nets, he's had his hair cut shorter and his ears have got bigger! What a laugh eh!

I've seen quite a lot of Lil, he's doing weight training 3 times a week to make himself stronger (Lil stronger f***in' hell!) he'll be able to hit the ball eight miles instead of five!

Everyone's dreading pre-season training to start except Leips because he's been running five miles a day for four months so he's pretty fit!

Anyway my Mum & Dad are fine thanks, my Mum says you're always welcome to dinner, Dad say's as long as you don't eat the whole f***in' lot! Only joking . . .

Well Hughsy I'm gonna go now because the winter Olympics are on telly, what do you think of the Aussie skiers? About as good as ours eh!

Anyway, take care of yourself, keep in touch soon.

Best wishes

Prich

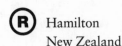

Hamilton

New Zealand

Friday 7 April 1984

Merv,

Thanks for your letter and how did you know my dong was pox ridden? Did that naughty granny from Loughton tell you?!

Seriously, thanks untold for the shirt – I still haven't taken it off. F***ing magic.

Now to more serious things – what the f*** are you telling Graham May that I'd take his jumper back for – I've sold it!! I don't know if you know, but Mark Jessop gave me his – and who the f*** needs two anyway?

I followed your season (and in particular one M. Hughes) as closely as possible. No doubt that back injury of yours got worse. You'll have to get it right for next year as I am definitely planning to go back – even if it's just for a President's Day (!) Seriously though I should be going again next April (1985) – it wouldn't be bad trying to win that f***ing league for the Wells – they sure as shit won't do it this year. We'll keep in touch about that. Hopefully April 1985. We can always stay in Sqiji's office like he said! Mike Darbyshire (Happy new year) will have us too.

To answer your questions about growlers here. I've actually got my own little one at the moment – she's not too bad a looker and she's not F***ING 55 either. I think, however, that I've got the same problem as you though – the girls just don't seem to be able to appreciate my good looks and natural charm – and what's more, you know how fussy I am . . .

It's a bit strange, even for you, that you've managed to make your parents leave home and I may well take you up on your offer to race over and stay one day soon.

In your last letter, you said you had no job – have you yet? We might need to save a bit for next year – and I'll probably have to buy Graham a new jersey too.

As for my family over here – not too bad. You remember my brother and his little growler who used to come to the Wells sometimes – well they both came here about a month ago. We had a few drinkies (actually we got pissed) and reminisced about things in England. He went up to the Wells just before getting home. I think they'll probably go back at the end of the year though – somewhere else to stay, you beauty!!

By the way, in that Under 22 team, I spoke to Martin Crowe who remembered you as a 'Mad Aussie'! NZ did really well beating the Poms. I went to see the first game against Auckland, and as Neil Foster was coming in to bowl I was (drunkedly) shouting out saddle bags at the top of my voice – just like you told me to do – anyway that day I ended up in a police wagon. I spoke to him at the ND game here in Hamilton – he got six wickets for f*** all in the first innings. They thought he was a cocky Pom!

I got a wedding invitation not long ago for Mark Webb's and Liz's wedding on April 14th. I might ring the Wells when the reception is on.

Well mate that's about it so show us your ugly hairy growler and we'll see you in the final.

> Best wishes
> Kiwi

P.S. It lets you down, doesn't it?!!?!

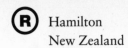

Hamilton
New Zealand

22 May 1984

Dear Merv,
How the f*** are you? Now it's my turn to find out why you
haven't f***en written. It would be great to hear from you –
you've got to let me know whether you're going back to England
next year. I've got a mate here who's a pretty handy allrounder
(but he can't keep as well as you!!) who wants to play in England.
If he comes he'll come with me, but if you're there (which you'd
better be – ****!?!) then we may have to send him down the road
to Wanstead or even Ilford.

I wonder whether you got my last letter or not – about 1½
months ago – but if you didn't I said that I was going to ring the
Wells on Mark Webber's wedding day. Well I did and Mark Jessop
answered the phone. He was a bit pissed I think as they had been
in the bar for six or seven hours. I also spoke to Graham and that
guy Tom Dawlins and also Don Leiper.

Well you'll have to let me know how your football's going. I've
played quite a bit of rugby in the last few weeks and actually
broke my nose two weeks ago. Some bloody hori thought he was
a bit of a boxer and smacked it in. I think that I'll have to get him
back in the return game. We're actually winning our league with
only one game to go in the first round.

Now onto important things. I hope the Melbourne growlers
have started to change their ideas about who to f*** and who not
to – and that you're getting a bit more now! My situation hasn't
improved too much. I'm still dorking the same old growler
without too much variation.

I hope your folks are well and that your sister's boyfriend
doesn't need a broken nose as well.

How's your old man's new job mate?

Well you'll have to let me know what you're up to soon so I'll look forward to hearing from you soon.

Regards

Kiwi

P.S. Have you heard from anyone in England? What about those photos from Graham? I saw that Graham Gooch started the season with a 200!

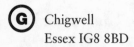

Chigwell

Essex IG8 8BD

18 July 1984

Dear Merv,

I must apologise that you never seem to receive a letter personally written by Mark but then nobody has up to now and I don't expect this will change! Thank you for your letter – nice to know you are o.k. – it does not seem possible that it is over a year since you were here mind you the 'firsts' are not doing as well in your absence – however they have not disgraced themselves either (not too many 'bad' Saturday nights due to defeat!)

Incidentally I am certainly not intending to get pregnant for some time to come – I'm letting the Val's etc of this world lead the way. She & Richard are trying again & we are all hoping things will be o.k. this time – Sue (sister) & Chris are trying although I gather she is stopping for a couple of months so she's not fat for their holiday! No doubt next time I write there will be some news on the reproduction programme at Woodford Wells!

The rest of the Wells crowd are just fine – we had a good cricket week and last week we had a Summer Ball which was fantastic. It started at 7.30pm & went on till around 5am – there was a marquee, a jazz band, brass band & disco, a full meal, plenty of booze & breakfast from around 1am onwards. A good time was had by all & plenty of sore heads the next day!

Have you started any serious saving towards a visit here next year?? I'm sure you won't be short of places to stay it's just travel & beer money really!?

Anyway one of these days we may just ring you in the middle of the night but until then take care & keep in touch.

Love from Liz xxxx

Regards from Mark

 South Woodford
London E18 2AF

3 August 1984

Dear Merv,

How's it goin! Thanks for your letter and I'm sorry it's taken me such a long time to reply but this summer it seems that there has been little time to sit down and do anything.

Good to hear that you are fit again, so fit that you can even argue with referee's now! Keep it going and all the best for next cricket season when I hope to be reading a lot about you in the Victorian side.

Nick wrote to me just about the same time as you and you both asked a similar question of me. WHERE ARE THE F***ING PHOTOS??

What can I say apart from I'm very sorry that I haven't done anything about them. Actually that's not quite true because I have asked Mr. W. Webber to look them out for me but I think he's having trouble finding them as when they moved in after their wedding, things like that just got chucked in bottom drawers.

However I will have another go at him I promise and as soon as he gives them to me I'll do the necessary and get you some copies.

The season's been going fairly well, a little up and down (rather like those two in the grass at Colchester!) but it's very wide open this year with no one side running away with it like last year. We have chances though. Of individuals, Mark is batting very well and Rob can't score a run, although I think his luck is just about to change. Barney is really bowling well and taking a lot of wickets with Yorkers, perhaps he caught this from you?

You'll be pleased to know that in a weeks time we play your favourite side, yes you guessed it LEIGH-ON-SEA!! WOW! I hope we can roll them over again. By the way, you obviously remember the idiot who started shouting at me that day, well believe it or not he came about 10th in the League 1st XI averages, incredible isn't it.

Essex are doing very well again, leading the Championship table again and also the John Player Sunday league. However I'm sure you will have read that our fabulous England side is four down with one more Test to play and probably by the time you receive this letter will be well on their way to a white wash.

I think what sums up the encounter is that the W. Indies, when they put someone in hospital, they do it good and proper (as per Andy Lloyd who has literally only just started playing County Cricket again and Paul Terry). When England do it as per Malcolm Marshall, we break his wrong hand and he chimes in with 7 wickets in an innings to beat us. I must admit though they are a bit good aren't they.

What news of me, well not a lot really, enjoying life as usual, getting it regularly now, still enjoying work and I'm an Uncle again for the third time. Oh also I'm getting a few runs believe it or not!

Cricket Week went very well again, the President missed you of course but it was a very good drunken week.

Darbyshire has been banned from driving for a year on account of driving when pissed. Actually you have to laugh. He and Gary Golden were coming back from a fancy dress type party early in the morning. Mike was dressed in full Judo gear and Guy was changing clothes as his fishing gear was soaked. Consequently when Mike jumped a red light and was stopped, Guy was virtually nude in the passenger seat and all Mike could say was 'It's a fair cop. I had it coming to me.' The funny thing was that for the first three or four weeks of his ban Mike stopped drinking. Interesting logic!

Well I'll sign off here. I promise to get those photos moving as quickly as I can and I'll drop you a line to let you know how we got on against LEIGH.

All the best Merv.

Yours

SKIPPER

P.S. Hope to see you next summer over here, we need you if we want to really win the league.

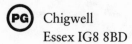

Chigwell
Essex IG8 8BD

Dear Merv,
This is the first letter I have written as Captain of Woodford Wells C.C. having been elected just days ago. As you may have heard we finished in 10th spot this year so it was time for a change. Rob Leiper is captain of vice as he has lost his contract with Essex & has decided to give up pro cricket.

How's your cricket going – over all injury problems, hope it wasn't anything serious enough to stop you knobbing any birds. How is the love life, you're not getting any younger & I can thoroughly recommend married life.

Having said that you can't get married until you have paid another visit to England & Woodford Wells. Some of the sides we played this year were determined to make us suffer for not having you around this year – sides like Leigh-on-Sea (Have you saved those studs) just batted on all afternoon, so we want you back to knock their heads off. We really have the making of a good side. Kiwi looks as though he will be coming over & bringing a friend with him (hopefully not a 'growler'). We are to have a 'Paki' over on a scholarship not dissimilar to the one you were on. We also have one of Barney Miller's mates joining (he's black too), and another quick bowler from the Lord's groundstaff. So if you can come over we will make sure you go back with a winners medal this year.

Everybody also over here is OK. Dick Harrison has just got Val pregnant again, let's just hope everything goes OK with this one. David East & Jeanette got married and have just gone to South Africa to winter over there. Other than that everybody's doing fine. By the way no sign of any little Webber's yet!!

Must go now Liz wants me to do the washing up! Anyway keep in touch & don't forget to come over next April.

See ya soon
Mark & Liz

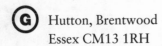

Hutton, Brentwood
Essex CM13 1RH

31 December 1984

Dear Merv,
Thank you for the Christmas Card – you're right it did take me by surprise! Anyhow things have been fairly quiet over here for Santa's homecoming although Dec 24th resulted in lots of grog with Prich, Burnsy, Brother Keith and Graham Gooch – a motley crew, not to be trusted.

Well I'm still up at Stowe School, Bucks, coaching away although the cricket bats have long since gone and have been replaced by rugger & hockey posts. We had a couple of weeks holiday here at home and I'm due back for the new term on Jan 7th. Yes, it's all go.

I had another very good season, this time in the Cherwell League in Oxfordshire, taking a record 55 wickets at 10 a-piece so I unfortunately did not get back to play for Hutton. Since August, I've lost over a stone in weight and worked really hard at my bowling and hopefully, something contract-wise, may result at Essex. I feel so much better now at 13 stone 12 lbs with another 12 lbs still to come off. You can only really get to grips with cricket in the off-season and mentally it can be a long, hard winter.

Speaking of which, it's been good to see the Aussies struggle as well, against the West Indies! See, England aren't so bad after all! How the hell anyone is meant to beat a team like that, I'll never know. There have been a couple of new Aus. names in the Test side, perhaps we may have seen a certain M. Hughes? C'mon Aussie, don't let your Essex mates down! How has it been going for you? To be honest, we get but very little coverage of your shield matches in fact just the scores and not even a scoreboard. So I've not seen how Victoria have been doing at all. Have you been in the squad? I hope so. I know you have to be very lucky to get on in cricket and you have to get all the breaks. As well, of course, as having someone to push you at the top level and sing your praises to the men who matter. Good luck for the second half of the season.

Your certainly left a favourable impression here with the ball. I wonder if you have any plans to come back?

Listen Merv, in running out of space, needless to say, Happy New Year – we'll be thinking of you tonight on New Year's Eve, have a great season and keep in touch. You can write here at home and Dad will send it on to me at Stowe. No worries.

See you soon Hughesy

Regards

Ian

 London N6

7 January 1985

Dear Merv,

I did not realize that kangaroos celebrated Christmas. Thanks for remembering me at the festive season. I do not believe in sending cards to anyone because I am such a mean bastard.

I have seen your name in the newspapers over here having

taken a few wickets on a couple of occasions. I have not been able to follow your progress but I would like to know how you have fared this season.

Are you hoping to come over to England this year for the cricket season? If you are, please write to me and let me know and I will try to help you with the air fare provided you promise me that this year you will behave yourself and concentrate on your cricket. There is a lot of time yet for you to concentrate on birds, booze and the good things in life generally after you have made it at the highest level, i.e. playing for Australia or even maybe for the struggling Poms.

Mark Webber is captaining Woodford Wells this year and old Mike Rogers has taken over the second team captaincy from Dilip. I am therefore hoping to be the first spinner in the side having done pretty well last year with the ball. I think I pushed Rogers all the way and the pressure seems to have caught up with him. What a big head! As Alan Border says, the lad is confident and cocky. The lads and I will be more than pleased to see you and therefore I await your reply.

Just as a by the way, Robert Leiper has been released from his contract with the county. He has been appointed the Vice Captain in our side and therefore will be playing regularly this coming season.

See you mate!

Yours truly

Wiji

(K.M.WIJESURIYA)

MERV: Wiji was a generous bloke. When I was in Essex and playing for Woodford Wells I was running short of money and didn't think life was too much of a challenge and he questioned me as to why I wasn't taking wickets – and I said it wasn't a challenge. He knew I was running short of money, so he offered to give me 50 quid every time I took 7 for in an innings. So for the next three weeks I took 7 for in an innings and got the 50 quid off him each time. Then I told him it wasn't a challenge anymore . . .

 Nick Lloyd
N.Z.

14 February 1985

Dear Merv,

Thanks for your letter and all the news. I think you're a big ****
for not going to England so now what I'll have to do is come to
Aussie at the end of this year and see you there. I suppose a couple
of week's holiday in Melbourne around December won't go
astray! Honestly mate it's a shame.

I'm leaving in April for another exciting year at Woody Wells.
I've been in contact with the Rt Hon Mark Webber and it looks
all set for another season in the LAND OF THE WINGEING
ONE!!! What really pisses me off is that I'll have to pay Mike
Rodgers his £10 I owe him. Do you think I should steal back my
car off Wiji?

Glad to hear your cricket has gone much better this year. I've
told the boys to watch out for this fiery **** in Aussie. Don't
forget, the first ball *has* to be a bouncer! As far as all my cricket
goes, well I made the New Zealand Colts again this year which
was great, and I played for Northern Districts 2nd XI which
doesn't say too much. Actually when I come back from Pommy I
plan to play in Otago, bottom of South Island, as I had a bit of an
offer down there.

To be totally frank, I haven't had a root for ages, in fact I think
it's just for pissing out of now. I hope you've done far better.

I'll write again before I leave, 'show us your BUSH' – I mean
growler!!
                    Regards
                    Kiwi

MERV: That's one of the joys of travelling by playing sport: it
introduces you to vastly different cultures.

Rugby,
Warwickshire

2, July, 1983.

Dear Sir,

    I am a very keen cricket follower, and I am trying to make a collection of players' autographs. I should very much appreciate it, if you would please be so kind as to send to me your autograph, to add to my collection please.

    If you will do this for me, will you please write it on a piece of paper, and forward to me in the enclosed envelope ?

    I note that you played for Victoria in 5 games during the 1981-82 season and in 4 games last season. I find that in 1981-82 you took 4 wickets for 69 runs and 2 for 73 against Queensland and 4 for 71 and 1 for 19 v N.S.W. and finished the season with 18 wickets for 567 runs.

    Congratulations on your fine achievements in the Sheffield Shield.

    Every good wish for continued success, and very many thanks, if you can oblige me.

Yours faithfully,

Douglas C

CHAPTER SEVEN

Mum's Advice Pays Off

Hi Mervy,

How's things? If we were selectors, after reading the paper, we would have had you in the team. Perhaps this year with the competition so fierce, it might be an idea to ask Redders if he has any suggestions on how you can improve your batting – and, I'm only trying to help you, you know, – it might be wise to get up ½ an hour earlier so you can have a shave. You wear nice clothes, and it always seems a shame to me, that with whiskers you don't look as terrific as you do without them. Now I'll talk about something else . . .

Played tennis Thursday for a team called 'Snowy'. In my team there was a girl called Lynne (Peta's second name) with a mother called Freda! How about that? (Forgot to tell Petie that one – so tell her please if she's around). Also played social tennis Wed, Aerobics Friday & bike riding Sat & then my knee was sore. Don't know if it went out in sympathy with Peta's knee or that I did too much last week!

Daddy doesn't think he'll miss cricket at all here & thinks perhaps we might get to W'Bee occasionally during summer if he doesn't play. There are a few teachers in the team & they'd finish up just talking school so he's not keen on that & with lack of practice he thinks he'd go downhill fast. [I think he'd be much better off playing cricket, otherwise I'll have to cut the grass every week.] . . .

Have you been doing anything much? The weather here today is fantastic & I spend the morning sunbaking while I gardened. Last week I forgot to tell Peta this too, we had peas and lettuce that Daddy grew!! The cabbages went to seed without forming a cabbage, but we've had some spring onions too. The plants (flowers) that I've planted are all growing which astounds me greatly – I didn't know I could do that.

        Love from all of us

        Fre

P.S. Hope the Vics win in Q'land but hope the fast bowlers go badly. Nasty aren't I?

Monday 15 October 1984

Dear Mervie

As usual this is getting written in a big hurry (and my pen just ran out so had to get another one) . . .

Is Gavvy back yet? – we haven't received a postcard from him yet!

Vics got beaten too, but a few of them did well. Your father hopes that they don't fall into bad ways & try & pick all rounders to bat & bowl instead of fast bowlers!

Are you working this week or has that finished now?

Will go now Mervie, hope your leg is O.K. and that you will be back at cricket soon.

Bye for now.

Love from all of us
Fre

 Wednesday 17 October 1984

Hi Mervy,

Today it is almost snowing here so far too cold for me to go to tennis. A teacher asked me to help with school tennis Friday arvos so I said yes as long as the weather is fine! No way would I go out in weather like this. Hope tomorrow is much, much, better as I *have* to play in a team.

How did you enjoy your counter tea with Katie? I tried to ring you Friday night to tell you Sean was playing with Melb 4ths. Now I know why you didn't answer.

Now for some sad news Mervyn. Last night Daddy took Sniffy to the Vets and left him there – the Vet was going to put him to sleep because he couldn't do anything for him. The new treatment he tried him on last month didn't work. Gary thought the W'Bee vets would've fixed him but nothing could be done for him. He has been very sick for the last few days. Gary just sobbed & sobbed last night but is a lot better today. He did think he might be too sad to go to school but after a few tears was OK. Daddy wanted to wait until we saw you to tell you but I thought it better to tell you now. Hope that is OK. Don't be too sad as nothing could be done to make him better.

> Love from all of us
> Fre

Monday 22 October 1984

Dear Mervyn,
Thanks a million for your letter, cricket draw & booklet – that is really great (what I would like one day, is for the cricketers to autograph their write-ups – any chance of that?)

We were sorry that you didn't make the Shield side for the weekend – it's really hard to get back in. Keep trying though and good luck next Sat. We didn't know until Sunday that your match was washed out – you didn't have any chance of impressing selectors! . . . What did you do Sat when your cricket was washed out? Sean made the Melb. 4ths again but haven't heard if he's doing any good there. Daddy *may* play cricket here after all as Lucknow 3rds only had six players last Saturday and had to forfeit their game. [**That's a relief.**]

Do you know if Robbo's & the Larkin babies have arrived yet? Had a letter from Katy last week (but now I remember telling you that last letter).

My tennis was very poor last Thursday 2–8, 3–8, & 8–6. I'm filling in for a section 3 team on Thurs & as that is the bottom grade, I hope to win a few more games . . .

Daddy had to buy [Gary] a cricket bat on Sat as his fell to pieces last week at school. He plays cricket all the time at school with the big kids or anyone who will play with him.

Look after yourself. Hope your back is OK with the brace and keep trying with your cricket and hopefully you will be back in the team soon.

> Love from all of us
> Freda

P.S. Thanks again for the cricket info book – have you got one too? Do you know if that 'Cricketer' magazine (monthly, that I used to get last year) is out yet – haven't seen any here in the shops.

 Monday 29 October 1984

Hi Mervy,

How are you? See where you got a wicket, took a catch, weren't out and that Footscray won. [**Mum's so good at finding the positives.**] Your team mate did well taking seven wickets! Pleased to see Scholesie make another century. Melb & Dandy 2nds were both beaten.

The Shield match was broadcast a fair bit on Sat., but yesterday there were only half-hourly reports from about 2pm. The wireless is on again today so hope I hear something before the day is over. How about S.A. having four injured players off the field in their match against the West Indies?

May ring you later on in the week, just in case this is your last week with Prissa. Where did he play Sat? Also Gavvy? See that the fourths won, thirds lost, don't remember what Ian told me about the firsts & seconds.

My tennis was poor (again) last Thursday BUT, we were behind all day & in the last set, the captain & I had to win 8–6 to level the match & we won 8–0. Immediately there were protests about the emergencies being too strong – my other sets were 5–8 & 3–8 so the captain was just told to watch who she got to fill in another time. Neither the other fill in or I played very well at all – it was the captain herself that won the match.

Will go now Mervy, good luck in S.A., hope you get lots of wickets and then be a chance for the next Shield game.

     Love from all of us

     Fre

Regards to Gav, Prissas and any other people you see.

P.S. Just received a phone call & am now playing tennis before
C.W.A. Thursday.

 Monday 5 November 1984

Hi Mervie,
This will probably be short as I was talking to you Fri, and intend
to ring you about 3.15 Wed.
    See where you made 13 Sat – that was good. F'scray finished up
with a good score – it sounded a bit poor at tea time. Great to see
the Vic's have a win yesterday. But didn't WA collapse in their
second innings against the Windies? By the time you receive this, I
have just realized, it will be after I talk to you on Wed, as the Cup
Day holiday is tomorrow. You will of also completed another
cricket match.
    Did you get to the beach Sunday? It was cold here so unless the
weather was better there, you probably missed out.
    Gary & I went to the circus on Friday night. It was really good.
Gary was impressed mostly with Spider man . . .
    Will go now Mervie & have some lunch. Love from all of us,
hope Gav is OK.
                    Love Fre

 Sunday 18 November 1984

Hi Mervy,
How's things? Hope you enjoyed your trip to Portland – how did
you go? We thought that you would probably all travel together
in a bus. The weather forecast isn't the best, so hope you were

able to get your match played. See where Grafy got you out; hope you can do likewise to him next Sat! Good to see the Vics get the 4 points and of course we thought you SHOULD HAVE BEEN *in* the 11. [**Are you confused yet? Mum's referred to three different games in one paragraph. We flew to Portland for an exhibition game against Tasmania, Grafy is Sean Graf who I played against in a District game (Footscray v St Kilda), and the Vics got the four points in a Sheffield Shield match for which I was twelfth man.**]

Hoggy didn't do a great lot, did he? [**Hoggy's one of the Australian fast bowlers who played a Test against Pakistan this weekend. Don't get ahead of yourself, Mum.**] Bill Lawry, in one of the Sunday papers, wasn't very impressed with a few of the Australian players. It will be interesting to see the next Test side.

Gary's cricket is now improving steadily – he can now take catches and the kids, all older than him, in the street, ask him not to hit the ball so hard. He takes his bat & ball to school every day & plays with 5th & 6th graders before school.

Pop thinks he'll give away volleyball and make a comeback at cricket, if he can gear himself up enough. [**Put the lawnmower back in the shed, Peta.**]

Last week Kevin Heinze was here & there was a night for him. We had to cut sandwiches, so it was just like the good old cricket days. Kevin Heinze was at school all Thursday morning & all the kids got to see him but some of the groups were pretty big & some kids missed out hearing him. Gary and I planted some cuttings today & each one, Gary gave three cheers cos Kevin Heinze said that helps them grow – so he heard *something* . . .

What is happening with your work now?

Perhaps I'll go now Mervy, hope your back is OK.

Love from all of us, Regards to any of our friends that you may happen to see. Have written to Gav tonite too – he tells me he's looking after you!

Bye for now

Fre

Sunday 25 November 1984

Hi Mervie,
How's things? And how did Friday go? Did you get to Statewide on time, to V.C.A. & then to Yooralla OK, (not Euroa!) [**Your hearing's not as good as it could be, Mum.**]

See where St. Kilda had a win – your father thinks you must of had good figures early as you got the two openers.

Gary played cricket today at Lake Tyers with Daddy, his teacher friend Tony & his two sons. Gary won – he was the only one who ran! . . .

What night & what time is the Ossie Ostrich show on? Some telies here get Melbourne stations & I WOULD LIKE to see it.

Have fun with the ESSO ad Wednesday.

I'll go now & watch the rest of the movie – not too bad tonite for a change.

Love from all of us. We'll see you in 3½ weeks or so.
　　　　Fre

 Monday 4 February 1985

Hi Mervy,
Thank you for your letter – it was great to hear from you. Thanks for the cigars too.

How's your back after the weekend? Good to see you get three wickets. Pop thinks it must have been really slow as they made 150 for the arvo. Did you see where Blacky made 108 with C'wood seconds? . . .

We watched Trish play her b'ball on Sat. before we went to cricket. Although we stayed up (Pete & I) until 1.15, we didn't see them win their final. Make a few phone calls, will you please, & try and find out what she's up to. I'd quite like to write to her.

Pop played with the Seconds – he got a bowl this week but for the second match in a row didn't take a wicket!! [**That won't help his blood pressure.**] Took two catches in slips though. A teammate, Michael Atkins, played his last cricket game here on Sat. He is off to play footy with Footscray. He has a job as a cadet journalist with Western Times.

No more news now, Pete is getting ready to head off,

Love from all of us

Fre

P.S. Caroline rang last week (Pete forgot to tell you).

MERV: England is playing Australia at the MCG in a One Day International today. I hope to catch up with Neil Foster, with whom I played at Essex.

 Sunday 17 February

P.S. Did you see Trish during the Australian Games?

Hi Mervy,

How are you – hope you enjoyed the cricket at the MCG today – who did you take? Have you seen Neil Foster yet? See in the paper yesterday where he has had back problems too. How is your back now? We often wonder & lots of people here ask after you but we aren't able to tell them much. Great to see in the Sun where Tony won an Esso scholarship – hopefully I'll get a card off to him.

Gary continues to play cricket all the time at school and out in the street. I ask how school goes each day and he tells me all about his cricket.

I won my three sets of tennis last Thursday – would be fantastic if I could do that each of the next six games with my new team!

Pop took 2/22 off 11 yesterday & his team had an outright win against Lakes. I'm watching the cricket *and* writing letters today. Where did you sit? Haven't seen you yet. [**In all her years of trying, I don't think she's ever seen me in the crowd at a sporting event. I bet your Mum's never seen you at one either.**]

Hope your back is OK and that you can play in the last two
Shield games.

Will go now,

        Love from all of us

        Fre

P.S. Great to see the Aussies have a win – hope you enjoyed the
game. Jonesy was great – felt sorry for Kim Hughes.

 Monday 25 February 1985

Hi Mervy,

How are you? Daddy thinks your bowling at the weekend was
tremendous as you bowled 24 overs & finished with 8/49. So,
hope, with that effort, you make the Shield Team this weekend.

Heard on the wireless before, that the W.I. played a N.E. team
on Sunday. The people there weren't impressed as they took it so
easily. But *I* think they must need a bit of a break when they play
so hard for so long. Have you seen your Pommie friend yet? Pakis,
19 yr old?? Wasim Akram had a great day yesterday. Pleased for
him, but not for the poor old Aussies.

An ex-team mate of yours from Footscray, Lindsay Davidson,
played with B'dale's country week team last week. John
Kinnburgh, from Daddy's school played too. They won their
section, defeating Albury & Border at Essendon (Section Four I
think). Kinna said Lindsay had been talking about your early days
at F'scray.

Because Pop goes and hits the ball on the clothesline before he
plays on Saturdays, Gary now gets up early enough to do likewise
before he goes off to school. Because the grass was wet this
morning, he got his sneakers all dirty, & my nice white bathroom
mat had to be washed because of his dirty shoes!! . . .

Daddy and a team mate finished up at one end of the pitch
when they were batting Sat; Peter was yelling 'go go go' & Daddy

thought he was saying 'no no no'. So Pete was run out & then Daddy went out very next ball. [**Good to see Dad stood his ground and made the other bloke pay for his bad calling.**] . . .

Will go now Mervy,

Love from all of us

Fre

 Tuesday 12 March 1985

Hi Mervy,

Pleased to see you batted well & got five wickets – how about the run outs? Did you get either of those? Pop had the two Sunday papers & The Sun & The Age, & in each of those you had 21, so he said, if he bought another paper somewhere you would have had 100!!

Sorry Footscray didn't make the finals.

Next weekend will you check and see if Peta needs car rides anywhere, please? The surgeon did say she *should* be able to drive, *but*, she may not feel like it. We can't do much from here so would you please help. [**Peta's got Hughes knees.**]

Daddy's game on Sat was a disaster too. Lindenow made 180 odd & then Lucknow didn't even reach 80! So they batted on & declared 40 past but then Lindenow only lost two wickets before stumps. Pop made around 7 & took a catch in slips & got one wicket.

Will go now Mervy. Big week ahead.

Love from us

Fre

(M) Monday 25 March 1985

Is Tony going to Essex too? Said so in a Sunday paper yesterday –
we thought he was going somewhere else.

Hi Mervy,
Thanks a million for looking after Peta for us – she was thrilled
with your flowers too & thought *I'd told you* to get them for her.
How are you – Pete said you are working at Sands & Mac.
Someone told Gary those shorts you gave him were bathers, so
they serve two purposes: going out (all dressed up) or swimming
(thinks he's trendy I'm sure).
Did Pete tell you the jury had to be locked up last week? We
hadn't reached a decision by 4.45 Wed, so all 12 of us had to
make out lists of our needs; these were rung through to each
home, then a police van went and collected 11 bags & they were
at Swan Reach, where we stayed, by 9.45. Ian wasn't home – the
police called here twice & then left a note at the *front* door, which
he didn't see because he uses the *back* door. I finally got my things
at midnight. We were back at court by 9am . . .
We couldn't believe that we were being locked up – there were
two other mums. It was all very interesting though, but *no way*
did we think it would last six days (collected $150 each & then
those who lived more than 8km away collected more for petrol or
whatever.
At Pop's final, several photos were taken & he's been given
three which are quite good . . .
Because of jury service, I missed out on two weeks of tennis so
may of forgotten how to play! Our team is second *bottom*.
Will go now. Love from all of us.
Thanks again for looking after Peta.
Fre

MERV: Then, suddenly, the letters stopped. It had nothing to do with
the decision of the jury . . . Snappa has just had a hernia operation and
was told that he needs as much as twelve months rest from his work as a
roof-tiler for it to heal properly. I've had a second season of cricket
interrupted by the stress-fractures in my back, so perhaps its time for me

to stand out of footy for a while and just get my body right. We're off to follow the coast north as far as Cairns, then across to Darwin. I am about to become a person of no fixed address.

I'm back, I'm fit and I'm hairy. Four months on the road without a shave, plenty of rest and plenty of fitness work.

Monday 19 August 1985

Dear Mervie,
How are you?(So long since I've written to you, I've forgotten how to print!)

Have you been around and seen all of your friends yet? We're not going to see your beard after all! Please get a photo taken before it comes off.

Daddy nearly busted his boiler on Sat. at the fair. He started at 7.15 & finished at 5.15 & ran the whole time in between. It was a great day though, & over $5,000 was raised.

Gary forgot his wallet! So spent our money on himself. He had 9 goes on the lucky dip & bought a show bag, a C'Wood spider (From a stone & pipe cleaners on a stick) food & drinks. We worked all day & didn't get to spend much money at all.

Do you know if the W'Bee cricket annual report is out? Daddy would like one if you could get it for him please.

We'll probably leave here at six Fri night so see you four hours later (if you're home!)

Bye for now,
Love from all of us
Fre

MERV: Mum hasn't changed in the five months I've been away: it sounds like she might be missing me though! Suppose I'd better get home by ten on Friday night.

Monday 2 September 1985

Hi Mervie,
How are you? Hope your practice with Dimma was OK & that
your B/Ball team won, without Steve & Naza.

Wonder how Border & Ritche will go tonight? It would be
great to see them hang in there for a couple of sessions. [**Bad luck.
England defeated Australia in the Sixth Test by an innings and 94
runs.**] Viv Richards, did you know, has just made his 8th century
in England this season. Wonder if he & others, who play cricket
non-stop, ever get sick of the game? . . .

Daddy went through our papers & cut out the cricket info, so
now I just have to get them into a book & do it each week instead
of getting a great stack of papers. He enjoyed Fathers Day – sat &
watched the Essendon–Swans game right through while drinking
his Darwin stubby – first time he can remember sitting out a
whole televised match. [**How's that blood pressure, Dad?**]

My new spoon rack is up with *12* spoons – we called into that
park, Gumbuya Park, near Warragul & I bought one there.

Will go now, we saw your name in the Vic Squad which pleased
Pop greatly.

> Love from all of us
> Fre

 25 September 1985

Dear Mervyn Esq,
Greetings from Zimbabwe. I'm writing from Mutare where we
have destroyed the 'B' team. Bishop made 129 n.o. out of 1/189 to
win in 29 overs. The cricket is going OK. The first game was
against the country team which we won well. Then we drew with
the national team in 3 days and lost the 1st in a 5 one day series.
We batted OK & set Zimbabwe about 236 to win & they needed
about eight per over in the last five overs & a bloke called Buthout

came in and smashed Dave Gilbert for three sixes & a four in one over, then Sniffa for two successive sixers & the game was over!

The lads are getting on pretty well, most of which are happily getting stuck into a cocktail party at the moment, but after getting pissed on cordial & ice I came home early. Sniffa is proving to be a top one day bowler (he sat out the 3 dayer) & Dodders is doing v. well with the bat in all games he played in. The Legend is in great form churning out runs in his own 'teddy bear' fashion. He is in the process of a great tour, so we may not see too much of him this season. I'm looking after Dodders so no need to worry . . .

See you soon buddy
Michael

MERV: This is from my Victorian team-mate and wicket keeper, Michael Dimattina, who is on an Australian Under 25 tour. Tony Dodemaide (Dodders), Dean Jones (Deano) and Simon Davis (Sniffa) are all Victorians.

 Monday 7 October 1985

Hi Mervie,
How are you? Katie sent me the photo of you. It's a good one too. How are you fitting all your sport & practice in? You can't get much time for socialising. My tennis friends wished they were a few years younger when they saw your photo . . .

Pop starred at cricket on Sat. Top-scored with 13 of the team's 36 & then collected three of the four wickets that fell. He said it's the first time in a long time that he's really thought about his bowling and that he's still got it!!

There is supposed to be a really big day at school today but it is raining. So there go the bark huts, damper making and tons of other things. Don't know where the mothers club will BBQ sausages . . .

Tuesday 8.50

Hi again.

Yesterday was a great day at school even though it rained most of the day ...

Daddy is now awaiting your phone call – he is home most nights after nine (depending a lot on the teli). Once before, I know, he thought it might be a good idea for you to be paying off something ...

Love from all of us. Good luck with all your sport

Fre

G VICTORIAN CRICKET ASSOCIATION

14 October 1985

Dear Merv,

Queensland v Victoria, Sheffield Shield Match – Brisbane 18–21 October 1985

You are invited to play for Victoria in the above match. The previously announced Team is –

Ray Bright (C)	Merv Hughes
Dean Jones (VC)	Simon O'Donnell
Simon Davis	Michael Quinn
Michael Dimattina	Jamie Siddons
Tony Dodemaide	Dav Whatmore
Paul Hibbert	Peter Young

Manager: Manager for the match will be Mr. Ian Redpath, M.B.E. ...
With best wishes for a successful start to the Season which everyone hopes will see Victoria re-emerge as a power in Australian Cricket ...

Monday 14 October 1985

Dear Mervie,

Thanks for your phone call last night – sorry we knew already.
Lucky that we *do* listen to the ABC station at the weekend. We
still haven't heard the team on the local station. Do your best &
we hope you clean up Queensland & that you get plenty of
wickets. You were your Father's son last night when I told him
you'd made the team! . . .

   Will go now Mervie, all the best in the Shield game – say hi to
Dodders too.

> Love from all of us
> Fre

 Mon arvo 21 October 1985

Hi Mervie,

Well bowled!! And didn't the Vics get off to a great start. Border,
Ritchie, Trimble & McDermott must of batted extremely well –
horrible people. Last report I heard at 4.00, Vic was 4/75 needing
108 to stop outright defeat.

   Today I've been to Sale shopping with a friend – you now have
fans here, too, who take clippings from the Herald & Weekly
Times along to Daddy at school. My friend's daughter (6th Grade)
kept her informed all weekend on your happenings on the cricket
ground.

   Gary is hoping to grow bigger than you & then when *you* want
to fight *him*, *he'll* say 'come back when you're big enough, sonny'!

9 PM

Cricket is now over & apart from the score, Vics 6/137, there
wasn't much else on teli, & *nothing* on the radio. So we still don't
know all Vics' bowling figures only that you had 3/116 &
Dodders 4/150.

Hope you enjoyed your game – a few did really well & others not so well. *We* think *you* were tremendous.

Marie Squires engagement is in today's Sun (Monday). Is she home from W.A. yet? Say congrats from me please (just in case I don't get a card off to her.) . . .

Will go now Mervie, hope your back stood up OK. Keep up your good bowling. We'll be in Werribee the second weekend in November, so see you then. [**Peta, do you know where I put the lawnmower?**]

> Love from all of us
> Fre

 Monday 28 October 1985

Hi Merv,

How are you? See where you got two wickets for 19 – did you bowl many overs? And how was your back afterwards? Quite liked the article in the Age on Sat. – didn't think the photo looked much like you though . . .

Did you get your hair cut? (You did hope not to play Sat. so that you could have your hair cut) [**I did not, I would never have such an unprofessional thought as that. But the haircut looks good.**] How did Terry's Buck's night go? And what did you do Sunday . . .

Will go Mervie, good luck at the weekend. Bye for now.

> Love from all of us
> Fre

P.S. Hope you do well against N.S.W. next weekend, & then the following weekend we might see you in the game against Tassy.

Monday 4 November 1985

Dear Mervy,

Well done on your first innings bowling. Sounds as though you were a bit stiff to miss out on wickets in the second innings though. It is only lunchtime now but Vics aren't doing as well as the papers thought they would.

We went out & bought the papers on Sat. Have you seen the Australian? You look like Mossy, we thought, with your bushy moustache.

I took my knees to the Doc on Wed & he's given me Arthritis tablets. Real bad to get old, isn't it?

We are going to W'Bee on Friday, now, instead of Thurs, & calling in on Junction Oval on our way through. We hope to leave here around eight or so.

May talk to you later on tonite. I've finished your jumper so you'll get an early birthday present from me on Friday.

Hope your back is O.K. after all the bowling.

See you Friday, well done again.

>   Love from all of us
>   Fre

Daddy played with the seconds on Sat. He made three & was run out. His team were beaten. He worked at school all of Sunday so was really tired Sun night.

Gary takes his bat to school & plays with the 2nd graders who also have trouble with the big bat. He was in strife this morning for running thru the house practising his fast bowling action.

Monday 11 November 1985

Hi Mervy,

Well done with your bowling – sorry we didn't see any of your four wickets. Your father thinks we should of left earlier & then you would of got your wickets more quickly. Each time you bowled, Gary would go & stand on the steps of the grandstand; I still don't know why.

Poor Aussies are going badly (3/19) & I haven't heard a Shield score. Feel sorry for Jonesy who is having a terrible run at present. Hickey didn't get wickets yesterday, so Daddy said.

Lawson is injured and out of the next Test so someone will have to replace him. Hope you get wickets in W.A. & you may be a consideration!

Will go now Mervy, good luck in W.A.

Love from all of us

Fre

MERV: Mum has always been a great encouragement and also a good judge . . .

 Monday 18 November 1985

Hi Mervy,

How are you – hope you enjoyed your trip to the west & that you saw a few people you knew. Do hope you get an outright win this match. We don't hear any cricket reports after 7pm so we won't know the results until Tues. paper. Congrats on your nine not out, your two & one wickets so far. The selectors, I should imagine, will have a horrible job picking a team today . . .

Give us a ring if you have any news from the W.A. people.

Love from all of us

Fre

Wednesday 20 November 1985

Dear Merv,
How are you – Happy Birthday on Saturday.

I've now got 10 transformers – the most in our class. Now I've only got seven cents left.

How is cricket and how is work. Unreal six you hit. (Did you hit anyone with it?)

Hope you have a great birthday and that you get some presents.

> Lots of Love
> from Gary

 Wednesday 20 November 1985

Hi Mervie,
Enclosed is a cheque from Daddy for the strides you wanted. With leftover money buy yourself something from Gary (something exciting like undies, socks, hankies or a t-shirt). If you like, wrap up the jumper I made you so you will be sure of at least *one* birthday present!

Tomorrow I've got a game of tennis, so hope *my* arthritic knee is OK. I gardened today & my knee is always sore after that.

Pete *might* come for the weekend – *if you* feel like a quiet weekend, come with her!

Have a lovely birthday.

> Love from all of us
> Fre

VICTORIAN CRICKET ASSOCIATION
2 December 1985

Dear Merv,

Victoria v India, Melbourne Cricket Ground
6–9 December 1985

You are invited to play for Victoria in the above match. The previously announced Team is –

R. Bright – Captain	M. Hughes
D. Jones – Vice Captain	G. Parker
S. Davis	M. Quinn
M. Dimattina	J. Siddons
T. Dodemaide	D. Whatmore
P. Hibbert	P. Young

. . .

The umpires for the match will be Messrs L. King and D. Holt . . .

Monday 9 December 1985

Hi Mervy,

How are you? From all accounts you must have bowled very well – *AND* your batting! Can't wait to hear, from you, about that!

Did you think to get all the Indian autographs for Mummy?? Did you ever get the paper reports from Tassy?

Surely you can't be real far away from test selection. Wish the *selectors* would listen to the wireless, the teli, and read the papers!!!

Have you any Xmas list made out? If not, think about it before we get down. *OTHERWISE* you will get some crummy thing that you don't even want!

Good luck for your next match – how many days work this time before you play again? Do you think it will ever stop raining? Will go now.

Love from all of us

Fre

MERV: I'm not too sure how much work I will be able to fit in between now and my next game, Mum. I might have something on. A season off footy, hard work on my fitness while I was on tour with Snappa, and for the first time I've played all of Victoria's matches so far this summer. I wonder . . .

CHAPTER EIGHT

My First Test

AUSTRALIAN CRICKET BOARD

GWH:PMM

9th December, 1985.

Dear Merv,

FIRST BENSON & HEDGES TEST - AUSTRALIA v. INDIA

ADELAIDE - DECEMBER 13 - 17, 1985.

I am pleased to extend on behalf of the Board a conditional invitation to
you to play in the above match. The conditions of this invitation are detailed
in the attached 1985/86 'Australian Players Handbook'.

The selected team is:

A. Border (Capt)   R. Kerr
D. Hookes (v-capt)   G. Marsh
D. Boon   G. Matthews
R. Bright   C. McDermott
D. Gilbert   W. Phillips
M. Hughes   G. Ritchie

Team Manager: Bob Merriman   Physiotherapist: Errol Alcott

Twelfth man will be announced on the morning of the match.

Accommodation in Adelaide will be at the Hilton, 233 Victoria Square, Adelaide,
Telephone (08) 217 0711.

Please read the Handbook and attached memo carefully, to familiarise yourself
with the general arrangements which have been set in place for the 1985/86
season.

Don't hesitate to contact either Ron Steiner or myself if you have any queries,
at any time.

Best wishes for a successful first Test.

Yours sincerely,

GRAHAM W. HALBISH
GENERAL MANAGER
AUSTRALIAN CRICKET BOARD

cc: R. Merriman, E. Alcott, D. Richards, I. McDonald,
    B. Taber, Board Representatives, States.

70 JOLIMONT STREET, JOLIMONT, VIC. 3002. TELEPHONE: (03) 654 3977. TELEX: ACBMEL AA39163

(G) AUSTRALIAN CRICKET BOARD
9 December 1985

Dear Merv,

First Benson & Hedges Test – Australia v. India
Adelaide – 13–17 December 1985

I am pleased to extend on behalf of the Board a conditional invitation to you to play in the above match. The conditions of this invitation are detailed in the attached 1985/86 'Australian Players Handbook'. The selected team is:

A. Border (Capt)	R. Kerr
D. Hookes (v-capt)	G. Marsh
D. Boon	G. Matthews
R. Bright	C. McDermott
D. Gilbert	W. Phillips
M. Hughes	G. Ritchie

Team Manager: Bob Merriman, Physiotherapist: Errol Alcott
Twelfth man will be announced on the morning of the match.

Accommodation in Adelaide will be at the Hilton, 233 Victoria Square, Adelaide.

Please read the Handbook and attached memo carefully, to familiarise yourself with the general arrangements which have been set in place for the 1985/86 season.

Don't hesitate to contact either Ron Steiner or myself if you have any queries at any time.

Best wishes for a successful first Test.

Yours sincerely,
Graham W. Halbish
General Manager

MERV: Better men than me have tried to describe their reaction to selection for their country, and failed. So I won't.

G MYRTLEFORD PO VIC

MERVYN HUGHES
. . . WERRIBEE

CONGRATULATIONS GREAT NEWS
MUZZA LEAHY

G AYR QLD

MERVYN HUGHES
. . . WERRIBEE

CONGRATS GIVE IT YOUR BEST
TRICIA AND THE COCKREMS

G BAIRNSDALE

MERVYN HUGHES
AUSTRALIAN TEST TEAM ADELAIDE OVAL

CONGRATULATIONS GIVE IT ALL YOU'VE GOT
POP FRE PETE GAZZA

(G) MELBOURNE

MERVYN HUGHES
... WERRIBEE

CONGRATULATIONS ON YOUR AUSTRALIAN
SELECTION. A WELL DESERVED HONOUR. A TRIBUTE TO
YOUR DEDICATION AND SACRIFICES TO CRICKET.
JOHN FORBES WARREN WHITESIDE AND ALL AT PUMA

(G) LONDON

MERVYN HUGHES
... WERRIBEE

CONGRATULATIONS ON YOUR SELECTION. KNOCK EM
FOR SIX.
LOVE AND BEST WISHES FROM THE GIRLS AND BOYS AT
WOODFORD WELLS

(G) HIGHPOINT WEST

MERVYN HUGHES
... WERRIBEE

CONGRATULATIONS MERVE. WE KNEW YOU WOULD
MAKE IT. GOOD LUCK.
THE DODEMAIDE FAMILY

(G) FOOTSCRAY

MERVYN HUGHES
... WERRIBEE

CONGRATULATIONS MERV, A FANTASTIC EFFORT. HOPE
YOU KILL EM.
WERRIBEE CRICKET CLUB

(G) MERVYN HUGHES
... WERRIBEE

CONGRATULATIONS ON ATTAINING THE ULTIMATE IN
YOUR CHOSEN SPORTING FIELD
WERRIBEE FOOTBALL CLUB

(G) MERVYN HUGHES
AUSTRALIAN TEST CRICKET TEAM
HILTON HOTEL
ADELAIDE

CONGRATULATIONS ON YOUR SELECTION IN THE
AUSTRALIAN TEST CRICKET TEAM. WISHING YOU
EVERY SUCCESS FOR THIS TEST AND THE FUTURE.
EUROA SHIRE COUNCIL AND RESIDENTS

(G) MERVYN HUGHES
... WERRIBEE

MERV, CONGRATULATIONS ON YOUR SELECTION. IT
WAS YOUR BATTING WHICH FINALLY GOT YOU THERE.
GOOD LUCK AND BEST WISHES
GEOFF COLLINSON

MERV: And many, many more ...

First Test v India at Adelaide Oval
(13, 14, 15, 16, 17 December 1985)
Australia 381 and 0 for 17 drew with India 520.
M Hughes 38 overs, 6 maidens, 1 for 123, one catch,
fifth ball duck.

Bruce Reid came into the twelve in place of Dave Gilbert, and in fact made his Test debut that match, as did Geoff Marsh. Robbie Kerr was twelfth man.

It was the only Test match David Hookes and Wayne Phillips were to play with me, mainly because I was dropped and didn't make it back into the team for twelve months.

Bruce Reid took 113 wickets in 27 Tests over the next seven years before he was forced by injury to give up the game. Geoff Marsh became a stalwart of the team as an opening batsman, making 2854 runs in 50 Tests, before being dropped for the Fifth Test of India's tour to Australia in 1991–92. He was replaced in that Test by my Victorian team-mate, the other Wayne Phillips, who also only played one Test with me.

The Australian Test Team was changing, and I thought I might have ruined my chances of being part of the evolution, by my performance in my First Test.

Sunday 15 December 1985

Hi Merv,

How are you? You were fantastic today. Did you hear *me* cheering when you got your First Test Wicket?

Pop said he did better than you yesterday. He made 45 – top score – & got two wickets. His team (B Grade) won a one-dayer.

The Vics are going well. Great to see two centuries and a 90.

One A.B.C. announcer wanted to know if your moustache is insured & John (my brother) wants some pups – if it ever has pups!! (silly fellow)

What did you think of your banner & the girls with *their* moustaches. Will go. Great to see you on teli!!

           Love Fre

. . . Good luck with the Vics at the weekend! If you get a chance, please ring Pop one night – he'd love to hear from you. We hope to go out Thursday & I will see you Friday probably.

MERV: At last, Mum's seen me on the television! Peta, and a couple of her friends travelled over from Melbourne to be at the match, and wore false mos.

 AUSTRALIAN CRICKET BOARD
17 December 1985

Dear Merv,

Please find enclosed the Board's cheque representing your match payment for the First Test in Adelaide – Australia v. India.

Gross	2,500.00
Less Tax	750.00
Net	$1,750.00

           Yours sincerely,
           Graham W. Halbish

(G) WERRIBEE PARK GOLF CLUB
19 December 1985

Dear Merv,
Your elevation to the Australian Test Team is applauded by all
members of the Werribee Park Golf Club who wish you the very
best of luck for your debut in Adelaide.

Your dedication to achieving the high standard of fitness
required to become a test bowler, reflects great credit on you and
no doubt the difficult decision you were required to make in
giving up your football is now, obviously, worth the sacrifice and
we only hope that you become a permanent fixture in the squad.

Once again, congratulations.
              Yours faithfully,
              G. O'Brien
              (Club Manager)

And a well done from all at College Rd.

(G) CITY OF FOOTSCRAY
24 December 1985

Dear Mr. Hughes,
At the last meeting of Council it was unanimously resolved that
a letter of congratulations be forwarded to you following your
selection in the Australian Test Cricket Team.

Accordingly, on behalf of Council, I extend to you hearty
congratulations on this achievement and best wishes for
continued success in your cricketing career.
              Yours sincerely,
              R. J. McQuillen
              (Director, Administration)

South Launceston TAS 7249

19 December 1985

Dear Mr. Hughes,
Congratulations on making your Test debut against India in
Adelaide.
    I have a large autograph collection including signed photos of
every living Australian Test player, and I would be most grateful if
you could kindly sign the enclosed prints. Three are for fellow
collectors I exchange with in England, Zimbabwe and India.
Could you also please send me three signatures on plain paper?
    Thanking you very much for your trouble, and wishing you
success in your future career.
                    Yours sincerely,
                    Don W.

MERV: My first written request as a Test cricketer. I wonder if Don
knows?

 Prime Minister
Canberra

24 December 1985

Dear Merv

**Prime Minister's XI v New Zealand
Canberra – 22 January 1986**

I am pleased to extend an invitation to you to play in this match.
The conditions of this invitation are detailed in your 1985/86
Australian Players Handbook.
    The team chosen for this match is as follows:

Allan Border (Capt)	Greg Mathews
Glenn Bishop	Bruce Reid
Keith Bradshaw	Glenn Trimble
Michael Dimattina	Michael Veletta
Anthony Dodemaide	Stephen Waugh
Merv Hughes	James Pyke (12th man)

The match will be played under the auspices of the Australian Cricket Board with the ACT Cricket Association being responsible for match management.

I look forward to your participation in what promises to be another outstanding match, and to welcoming you at the Lodge on the previous evening.

Should you be unable to accept this invitation, or should you not wish to accept the conditions of selection as attached, please advise the ACB office immediately. Attendance for the match will be taken as acceptance of the conditions of selection.

Yours sincerely

R.J.L. Hawke

Attachment to Australian Players handbook
Prime Minister's XI v. New Zealand
Canberra – 22 January, 1986.

Accommodation: Canberra Parkroyal, 102 Northbourne Avenue, Braddon . . .

Hours of Play: (To be confirmed)

1st Session	11.00 a.m. – 1.00 p.m.
2nd Session	1.40 p.m. – 3.10 p.m.
3rd Session	3.20 p.m. – 4.50 p.m.
4th Session	5.10 p.m. – 7.10 p.m.

Official Functions: Official Australian team uniform or similar appropriate uniform is to be worn to the Prime Minister's reception at The Lodge 6.30 pm – 8.00 pm on 21 January 1986 by those who will be in Canberra.

Playing Conditions: Benson and Hedges World Series Cup playing conditions will apply for this match, except that one red ball per

innings will be used. White cricket clothing is to be worn.
Remuneration: A match allowance of $250, inclusive of meal and
laundry expenses, will be paid.
Reserve Date: If no play is possible on 22nd January, the match
may take place on 31st January. Players required for B&HWSC
and Sheffield Shield matches on that day will be replaced.
Travel: The A.C.B. office will arrange Ansett air travel for players
to arrive in Canberra either on Tuesday 21st January or on the
morning of the match. Departure will be Thursday 23rd January.
The Department of the Prime Minister and Cabinet will be
responsible for transport in Canberra.

MERV: It was almost the perfect match: five overs bowled, we batted,
game washed out!

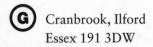

G Cranbrook, Ilford
Essex 191 3DW

7 January 1986

Hi Merv,
Sorry this letter has taken so long in coming, kept putting it
off. In the end it was worth it, because I can now say
CONGRATULATIONS on becoming a Test star.

Just before you played, I had received a letter from Steve
Waugh from New South Wales telling me you were having a very
good season up until now, and that you must be quite close to
getting a call up for the side. Then when we saw the side that they
picked on the TV, us here thought of you and how pleased you
must be feeling at that moment.

The coverage of the Tests have not been too good, so we are
getting most of the information from the newspapers, of which I
have cut out and enclosed them, so that you may read them.
When the test was played we were pleased to read D. Vengsarkar,
c. Phillips, b. Hughes, unfortunately you did not get many more
which we thought you might, but we thought at least he is playing

and hoped for the second innings (what went wrong?)

At the end of the game the papers were saying something about Kapil. He was making a fuss about you and a disagreement that you had on the pitch. (Write and let me know all the gossip about it.) Still we thought that what you had done in the first Test would keep you in for the rest, but not to be, you were standing by for someone in case they failed a fitness test. Tough luck. Hope that the cricket is still going OK even though you are not in the side.

Shortly after that Test Steve Waugh who was here with us last season, and who I got close to, also made the Test side, so there was more celebrations here, when that team was announced. Would you please give him our regards if you see him before I do. Tar very much.

Anyway mate what are you going to do with yourself after the season down under, will you be coming over to visit us, or going on another trip like last winter. By the way, I have started to save the pennies so hopefully I might make it over to you. If you *still* have the room still made up that is. That also depends on whether or not Essex give me a new contract, because that is up at the end of the summer (time to sweat).

Apart from the cricket how's life treating you, have you found a lady if so what's her name, send a photo. What has happened to your writing hand, has it been broken, because I have not heard from you for ages. Write to me you lazy git, no messing about. Everyone in Essex is OK, or they were the last time that I saw them. A few of them including Paul Pritchard is in Aussie, or he will be in the new year, so if you bump into him give regards. Don't suppose that you have heard that Kevin Moye has been released by the Club, and he is at present looking for another county. Also at Essex we have signed a novice player called Allan Border, you may have heard of him he comes from your country. Rubbish so we gather. Right that's that, also everyone at Ilford is ok, and by the way Cap's get married . . .

So take care and don't forget to write. Give regards to family.

Regards

Mouse

(G) AUSTRALIAN CRICKET BOARD

MEMO TO   Merv
                   Australian Team Players
SUBJECT   Fitness Test Results
DATE   9 January 1986

Attached is a copy of your results on the Tests conducted by ACB Physical Fitness Consultant, Dr. Frank Pyke on December 31, 1985.

As pointed out by Dr. Pyke, the tests were designed to assess some of the specific fitness demands of One-Day Cricket and to assist in your preparation in the future.

You will note that your report includes the following scores:

(i)   Group average
(ii)   Your personal score
(iii)   The rank order in the group of your score (weight and body fat ranking are from highest to lowest; other test results are from best to worst).

Dr. Pyke has made a personal comment on your performance. If you have any enquiries, don't hesitate to contact me or Dr. Pyke.

> P.R. Spence
> Development Manager

A.C.B. – CRICKET FITNESS TESTS

MELBOURNE: 31/12/1985
NAME: Merv HUGHES

TEST	GROUP AVERAGE	SCORE	RANK IN GROUP
WEIGHT (kg)	82.8	99.0	1/16
BODY FAT			
Arm (mm)	8.4	9.1	
Back (mm)	10.5	10.7	
Hip (mm)	12.9	21.7	
Abdomen (mm)	15.3	26.8	
TOTAL (mm)	47.1	68.3	3/16
FLEXIBILITY			
Sit + Reach (cm)	+9.0	+15.0	4/15
SPEED			
Run 3 (sec)	10.04	10.14	10/13
Turing speed (sec)	2.26	2.30	10/13
INTERVAL SPRINTS			
Sprints 1, 2 (A)			
Average (sec)	5.17	5.13	5/13
Sprints 3–6 (B)			
Average (sec)	5.43	5.22	
Index (A x B) (sec)	28.1	26.8	4/13

1/1/86

COMMENTS: Body fat levels are excessive, particularly for a fast bowler. This is affecting running speed especially the ability to turn quickly. Despite this handicap interval sprint performance is quite reasonable. It is recommended that efforts be made to restrict dietary intake and to engage in a regular program of supplemental endurance and sprint running. At this stage of the season short interval sprints (less than 10 sec efforts every 20–30 sec) are recommended.

MERV: I think they're being a little bit harsh. I've got above average speed in the interval sprints, my flexibility is way ahead of most of the batsmen, and did you note that they don't mention my height: of course I'll be heavier than everyone else, I'm the tallest! I'm criticised for my turning speed, well it stands to reason – taller, heavier, quicker – of course I'll take longer to turn around. As for a slower than average time to run three, well I only ever score ones, fours and sixes so I'll never need to run three.

(G) VICTORIAN CRICKET ASSOCIATION
13 January 1986

Dear Merv,

**Victoria v. Western Australia, Sheffield Shield Match
18–21 January 1986**

You are invited to play for Victoria in the above match. The previously announced Team is –

R. Bright – Captain	G. Parker
D. Jones	M. Dimattina
D. Whatmore	A. Dodemaide
M. Quinn	M. Hughes
J. Siddons	P. Hibbert
P. Young	S. Davis

. . .

The umpires for the match will be Messrs. L. King and B. Guy ...

MERV: Back to state cricket: will I ever get another chance at the highest level? The One Day series is beginning and I don't think I'll be considered for them.

 FOOTSCRAY CRICKET CLUB
16 January 1986

Dear Merv,
It is the wish of the committee to congratulate you upon your Test selection, and selection in the Prime Minister's eleven side.

We hope these milestones help further your cricket.

With best wishes.

> Yours sincerely
> Gary M Crane
> Secretary

 Tuesday 21 January 1986

Hi Mervie
Hope you enjoy your match with the Prime Ministers XI & that you do well. I did want to ring you this morning, but it was 8.09 when I woke, so it was too late to do so.

The big time cricket is on now and it is very hard to get a score from the shield game – last I heard it was 4/185.

The cricket just got the better of Gary – there was a lot of cheering (on the wireless) with Marsh on his 99, so Gary has switched off his game & has the TV on now.

He's got his century now – how tremendous for him.

Today I sent an engagement card to Lindsay Jennings from all of us.

Best go & get tea,

> Love from all of us
> Fre

P.S. Good luck in your next shield game – hope your knee is OK. Enjoy your trip to Tassy. Give us a ring sometime.

MERV: Geoff Marsh, who made his Test debut with me, makes a century in a One Day International, while I am playing in a Shield match. Good on him.

 Tuesday 28 January 1986

Hi Mervy,

How are you – hope you enjoyed your trip to Tassy. It is only midday here and, at present, it *looks* as though your Shield match will be a draw. Drew Morphett thinks you may have had another warning from the other umpy. [**For running on the wicket!**] So do hope you get through the rest of the day OK.

Last week I sent an engagement card to Lindsay Jennings from all of us. Do you know if Brighty got our card? I sent it to the V.C.A.

The boys have their Maxie Walker shirts on today and are really pleased with them. I took their photos before they started their cricket match.

What did you think of Jonesy getting back in the Aussie team? (I'm wondering how they'll go when there is no second innings!)

Best go now & get our lunch. Thanks for my Souvenir Booklet & the boys t'shirts.

> Love from all of us
> Fre

P.S. We really liked the Sun photo of you today. Very serious tho!

29 JAN 1986

Mr M. Hughes
152 Tarneit Road
WERRIBEE   VIC   3030

Dear Merv

I should like to thank you for agreeing to play in the
Prime Minister's XI against New Zealand.

It was most disappointing for all concerned that the
match which promised to be such an exciting one,
especially after the good start by the team, was washed
out by rain.

My best wishes for the future.

Yours sincerely

R.J.L. Hawke

Monday 3 February 1986

Hi Mervy,

How's things? This will be short & sweet as Gary & I are off to catch the bus this morning & then, perhaps, riding to the pool this arvo.

Sorry to see you had bowling problems *or* umpire problems again – hope things were better for you Sunday.

Sorry, too, that your team was beaten.

Did Brighty get our card? (Keep forgetting to ask you on the phone.)

Will go now Mervie,

Love from all of us
Fre

MERV: It's not me having umpire problems, it's the umpires having Merv Hughes problems.

 AUSTRALIAN CRICKET BOARD

MEMO TO 1986/87 National Training Squad
                 cc: State Executives, R.B. Simpson, E. Alcott
SUBJECT   Pre-Season Preparation
DATE   16 June 1986

Merv,

Congratulations on being nominated by the Selectors for inclusion in the 1986/87 National Training Squad.

The Board's recently appointed Cricket Manager, Bob Simpson will shortly be visiting each State to meet and talk with you personally.

In co-operation with your home State administration, Bob, assisted by Australian team physiotherapist and fitness advisor Errol Alcott will devise a program aimed at ensuring that you are properly prepared to represent Australia, in the future.

According to where you are located, you will need to be available for a meeting at your State Association on:

(tba)	New South Wales	at
30/6	Queensland	at 1.30p.m.
2/7	South Australia	at 5.30p.m.
4/7	Victoria	at 1.30p.m.
3/7	Tasmania	at 1.30p.m.
1/7	Western Australia	at 1.30p.m.

Your State Executive will advise you further, where necessary.

Any queries in relation to your inclusion and participation in the squad can be directed to either Bob Simpson or myself . . .

MERV: Still under consideration at least. And I so look forward to those fitness programs.

Lancashire
England

10 July 1986

G'day, Mervyn!
How's the lazy Melbourne winter treating you? I suppose the 'Crownies' are still slipping down beautifully!

I'm well settled in here in Lancashire.

After spending the first few weeks in a thoroughly boring lodging house with about eight other blokes, to save going insane I found Grant Jordan and Darren Foley had a spare bed in the house they are renting. So now the three of us are sharing the bills along with Jordo's girlfriend Danielle who has also come across for a while.

Life here is really very slow. We usually struggle up & out of bed around 10.30 – 11.00 or so and have a leisurely breakfast, read the paper and take things from there. Most days would include a trip just down the road to the local sports centre (bet you thought I was going to say pub!) where we are now members. A gym workout, sauna or game of squash is usually on the cards.

The cricket has been a little difficult to get used to. The wickets early on were terrible due to the poor weather (wet & bloody cold), but the weather has picked up remarkably recently, and the wickets have likewise improved. Unfortunately my club has probably the worst track in the league which is a little disappointing. I'm still trying every match but I think the trick is not to take things too seriously. As they say in the classics – who gives a f***!!

I must tell you one part of my game that has improved TREMENDOUSLY is – my keeping! Yes, mate, I kept during a friendly the other day and finished with no byes, one run out, one catch and – wait for it – two stumpings! Watch out 'The Nomad' Reber!

I bought myself a car as soon as I got here which is essential to preserve sanity. So I've been able to do a few trips as well. I spend a week back down at Sussex not long ago which was great. Caught up with a few old friends and basically was drunk for a week. Magic! We've also had numerous trips to Old Trafford (Manchester) for various matches. In fact Essex was there last Sunday for a John Player against Lancashire. Lancs won in a thriller and I managed to run into 'A.B.' and 'Prich' in the bar afterwards. Prich is making a heap of runs including an unbeaten hundred in that JP game. He's playing in Sydney this summer so we'll probably catch him there.

Emmo came down from Scotland for a couple of days recently so we decided to go down to Birmingham for the last day of the test and managed to track down the 'Big Fella' himself, who is playing in the leagues there. We had a few laughs there and got horribly pissed as well. Paul Quinn has also been up for a few days in his borrowed Saab Turbo. He's 'doing Europe' for a while. C. Miller is over too, of course. Causing havoc at the nightspots, of course! Aussies left, right & centre.

That's about it for now from this end. Basically enjoying life around here and taking it easy.

How were all the end-of-season trips? I'm sure there are a few stories there. Regards to everyone there. Take care of yourself. Bye for now.

Cheers!

Dodders

P.S. Jordo says to make sure you can find someone who will read this letter out to you nice and slowly so you'll understand it all.

 There are a few legends mentioned in this letter. The writer, Tony Dodemaide, started his district cricket career with Footscray, then played with me for Victoria and made his Test debut against New Zealand in December 1987 (after I pulled out with a hamstring injury). AB is the great Allan Border. Pritch was a team-mate of mine at Essex when I was there in 1983 and went on to play over 300 First Class games. Emmo was David Emerson, a left-arm unorthodox bowling Victorian team-mate and C Miller is, of course, the spin bowling find of the late nineties. Colin Miller, who played with Dodders and me in Victoria, then went to South Australia and Tasmania as a medium-pace bowler before making his Test debut in October 1998.

(G) Prospect TAS 7250

18 August 1986

Dear Mr Hughes,

Some time ago you were kind to sign some photographs for my collection for which I thank you. The photo's were of a very young Merv Hughes and I promised to take some of the Merv Hughes, 1986 vintage.

Enclosed are some photo's I took of you at Devonport last season. There are three copies of each picture and I would be honoured if you would keep one of each for your scrapbook.

I would be most grateful if you could sign the others and return them to me in the envelope provided.

Thank you very much for your time and trouble.

Yours sincerely

Rick S.

P.S. If I get any other good photos this season I'll send you a copy.

 Monday 8 September 1986

Hi Mervy,

How are you? This will have to be short so as I can catch the Post Office by ¼ to 3. I've been to see our CWA President who has been out of action with a very sore leg for a couple of weeks, and I finished up having lunch with her. Now I've missed the mail (1.30) around the corner and the two o'clock bus so have to ride into B'dale for you people to get this Tues.

Daddy is off to a Grey Nicholls sale of cricket gear in a hotel at Sale tonight. Kim Hughes is to be guest speaker.

He is gearing up for a big cricket season – he's on the Executive & selection panel & also captain of the thirds, so looks like late tea Tues, Thurs, & Sats for the next few months after having 6 o'clock teas for 21 months!

On Thurs I bought the wool for your jumper – hope you like it. The other two colors for the top are dark brown & off white. The kids in the street had their first cricket match of the season yesterday. The best four play the weakest four, but give them 50 start. Gary was in the 'best' team.

Daddy bought himself a shirt & scales with your Fathers Day money. He also bought himself hand weights. He brought home a medicine ball & we throw that to each other 25 times a day, sitting & lying on the floor, if you know what I mean. I then drop the ball ten times on his stomach. [**I think they may have both gone mad!**]

We had a lovely day yesterday at a park near Lakes Entrance (which his school are visiting on Nov 11th).

Kristin wishes you well with your cricket this season, she sent me some of her Deb photos.

Will go now, hope your sport is OK.

Love from all of us

Fre

P.S. Please thank Katy for the photos she sent me. I like you *without* your beard, better.

 AUSTRALIAN CRICKET BOARD

MEMO TO Selected Players and Officials
SUBJECT   Team Clothing
DATE   3 November 1986

The Board will supply the following items of clothing to you for the season. Distribution will take place, preferably prior to your departure for Brisbane, otherwise in Brisbane at the Park Royal.

1. **On-Field**

Trousers – 2 pair	(via Puma)
'Batting' pants – 2 pair	(via Puma)
Shirts – 4	(via Puma)
Jumper – needs basis only	(via A.W.C.)
Sox	(via A.W.C.)

2. **Training**

Tracksuit – one	(via Puma)
Shirts (lemon) – two	(via Puma)

3. **Casual/Travel**

Trousers (and belt) – one	(via A.W.C.)
Shirts (lemon, green) – two	(via Puma)
Sleeveless jumper – one	(via A.W.C.)
Longsleeved jumper – one	(via A.W.C.)

The travel clothing will this year feature the Australian cricket coat of arms making it an outfit exclusive to members of the Australian team.

> Yours sincerely,
> R.E. Steiner
> Office Manager

NOTE: WITH THE EXCEPTION OF PLAYING JUMPERS (AND SOX), ALL OF THE ABOVE ITEMS ARE NEWLY DESIGNED AND MUST BE WORN THIS SEASON INSTEAD OF PREVIOUSLY ISSUED ITEMS.

CHAPTER NINE

Another Test Match

(G) AUSTRALIAN CRICKET BOARD
5 November 1986

Dear Merv,

First Benson & Hedges Test – Australia v. England
Brisbane – 14–19 November 1986

I am pleased to extend on behalf of the Board a conditional invitation to you to play in the above match. The conditions of this invitation are detailed in your* Player Contract and in the attached 1986/87 'Australian Players Handbook'. The selected team is:

Allan Border (Captain)	Chris Matthews
David Boon (Vice-Capt)	Greg Matthews
Merv Hughes	Bruce Reid
Dean Jones	Greg Ritchie
Geoff Lawson	Stephen Waugh
Geoff Marsh	Tim Zoehrer

Cricket Manager: Bob Simpson
Media/Team admin. Manager Ian McDonald
Physiotherapist: Errol Alcott

Twelfth man will be announced on the morning of the match.

*Not applicable . . .

MERV: Not applicable because I don't have a contract. I suppose they must have some doubts about how long I will be in the game. Still it means when they point at the fitness program and tell me I have to do it because it's in my contract, I can tell them what to do with their program. Or not.]

(G) 6 NOVEMBER 1986

MERV CONGRATULATIONS ON REGAINING A BERTH IN
THE AUSTRALIAN TEAM HOPE YOU GET PLENTY OF
POMMY SCALPS ALL THE BEST TO YOU AND YOUR
TEAM MATES
LARA SPORTING CLUB

(G) 6 NOVEMBER 1986

ALL THE BEST FOR THE TEST STAY THERE
SHIRLEY DARREN TRUDY GOODWIN

(G) 14 NOVEMBER 1986

ALL THE BEST MERV
FROM POP FRE GAZZA

(G) Guest: HUGHES   Room No: 223

Message: Peter & John want to go to the cricket tomorrow.
Ring your sister.
Time: 9:34pm   *Date:* 14/11   *Taken by:* The Brisbane ParkRoyal

MERV: Peta's been skiting she can get tickets to the cricket because her
brother's in the team! Good on her.

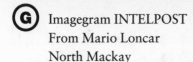 Imagegram INTELPOST
From Mario Loncar
North Mackay

Merv Hughes
Australian Dressing Rooms
The Gabba
Brisbane QLD

Scheduled for delivery by 4.10pm

Dear Merv
Gidday Mate. Hot day out there was it? Congratulations on
making the Test team. A little luck and a lot of G&D and you'll
eventually succeed. I wish I could make it down to Brisbane to see
you play but unfortunately that's not possible. Remember Aust
cricket needs people with heart like you've got so dig it in and give
the Poms a hiding they wont forget.

>Best wishes for the coming Test
>Mario (what no hugs & kisses!)

Love that Mo Mate.
PS Say hello to Terry, Ross, Naz, Gav, Bobby and the rest of the
crew back home. Carn the slabs. How's Peta's knee coming on?

First Test v England at the Gabba
(14, 15, 16, 18, 19 November 1986)
Australia 248 and 282 defeated by
England 456 and 3 for 77.
M. Hughes 3/134 and 2/28, first inns bowled Botham (0),
second inns bowled DeFreitas (0).

MERV: How well am I going? Three Test innings, three ducks. A journalist asked me the other day what ambitions I had in cricket. 'To play in consecutive Test matches and score a Test run,' was my reply. I read somewhere that if a bowler averages more than four wickets a Test through his career, then he is considered a top class Test bowler. I must be looking good for the next Test in Perth on 28 November.

 VICTORIAN CRICKET ASSOCIATION
18 November 1986

Dear Merv,

Victoria v. Queensland, Sheffield Shield Match
Wangaratta Showgrounds, 21–24 November 1986

You are invited to play for Victoria in the above match. The previously announced team is as follows –

R. Bright (Capt.)	M. Hughes
S. Davis	D. Jones
M. Dimattina	G. Jordan
A. Dodemaide	S. O'Donnell
I. Frazer	J. Siddons
P. Hibbert	D. Whatmore

... Please note that departure from Wangaratta will be on Monday, 24th November at the conclusion of play by bus.
　　With best wishes,
　　　　Yours sincerely,
　　　　K.W. Jacobs
　　　　Executive Director

MERV: From the dizzy heights of Test cricket to the Wangaratta Showgrounds. By bus.

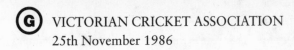

(G) VICTORIAN CRICKET ASSOCIATION
25th November 1986

Dear Merv,

South Australia v. Victoria
Adelaide Oval – Adelaide, 28 November – 1 December 1986

You are invited to play for Victoria in the above match. The
previously announced Team is –

R. Bright – Captain	M. Hughes
S. Davis	P. Jackson
M. Dimattina	G. Jordan
A. . Dodemaide	S. O'Donnell
I. Frazer	J. Siddons
P. Hibbert	D. Whatmore

. . .

MERV: You guessed it, I won't be in Perth for the next Test. Before we
leave Wangaratta, I must do some promotion of the game in North
Eastern Victoria.

(G) Indoor Cricket Arenas
(Australia) Pty. Ltd.
Wangaratta 3677

26 November 1986

Dear Merv,
Just a quick note to once again express our thanks for your co-
operation with us at 3NE whilst obviously bitterly disappointed
during Monday's interview with us. We were all impressed with
the tremendous character you showed us all as you knew when
talking to me that you would not be going to Perth.

You delighted everyone with your willingness to mingle with the crowd and sign autographs for the kids etc . . . which was far more than what some of your colleagues did. The people of North East Victoria eagerly wait for the next time you wear the baggy green cap as we have no doubt you will.

Many Thanks

John Dunne 3NE

P.S. Make sure you drop in when you're up here next winter and there will be a cold one waiting.

MERV: People everywhere are encouraging and hospitable. It's a pity they haven't read my fitness program. 'Get in the Aussie Team and come and drink beer with us.' It would be unfriendly not to.

 Monday 1 December 1986

Hi Mervy,

Hope you enjoyed your trip to S.A. At least at this stage, you have first innings points – hope you can manage full points for an outright win. We were barracking for the Poms this Test – they're doing well aren't they?

Hope to catch you at work *this* week, IF you make it there. We were wondering what to get you for Xmas & wondered about car seat covers.

Peta was here for the weekend & yesterday we went to Lake Tyers Beach. It was really cold though but we played cricket & then had fish & chips at Lakes Entrance on the way home.

Best go now, hope to talk to you in a couple of days – if not have fun against the Poms next weekend.

Love from all of us

Fre

P.S. Did you like your shirt & joke book?

(G) VICTORIAN CRICKET ASSOCIATION
5 December 1986

Dear Merv,

Victoria v. England, Sir Robert Menzies Memorial Match
M.C.G. – 6–9 December 1986

You are invited to play for Victoria in the above match. The previously announced Squad is as follows –

R. Bright	P. Jackson
S. Davis	D. Jones
M. Dimattina	G. Jordan
A. Dodemaide	S. O'Donnell
I. Frazer	J. Siddons
P. Hibbert	D. Whatmore
M. Hughes	

The Umpires for the Match will be R. Bailhache and D. Holt.

Ground Admittance and Parking Tickets are enclosed.

The contents of the Players Handbook and Code of Behaviour, as previously circulated will apply to this match. Hours of play are from 10.30 – 6.00 p.m. on days 1–3 and day 4 will commence at 10.30 a.m. and conclude at 3.40 p.m.

A special Man of the Match Award of $400 will be made available and all players will receive an engraved medallion for participating in this match.

Compulsory attendance will be required at the Official Sir Robert Menzies Memorial Dinner to be held in the V.C.A.'s Official Area, Olympic Rooms, Northern Stand directly at the conclusion of the match. Those players that are married may be accompanied by their wives. Dress for the Dinner is Team Uniform.

Should you be unable or unwilling to accept this invitation, please contact me as soon as possible.

Yours sincerely,
K.W. Jacobs
Executive Director

MERV: I wonder if those players who are not married can get two servings?

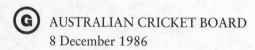

 AUSTRALIAN CRICKET BOARD
8 December 1986

Dear Merv,

Third Benson & Hedges Test – Australia v. England
Adelaide – 12–16 December 1986

I am pleased to extend on behalf of the Board a conditional invitation to you to play in the above match. The conditions of this invitation are detailed in your Player Contract and in the attached 1986/87 'Australian Players Handbook'. The selected team is:

Allan Border	Greg Matthews
David Boon	Bruce Reid
Ray Bright	Greg Ritchie
Dean Jones	Peter Sleep
Merv Hughes	Stephen Waugh
Geoff Marsh	Tim Zoehrer

. . .

M Monday 8 December 1986

Hi Mervy,
How are you? Great news you being back in the Aussie team – hope you do really well.

Kev Schneeberger & his mates are going to S.A. next weekend – they met girls there on a recent footy trip with Avenel and have been across a couple of times since then.

We went to a Sunday School picnic yesterday & had a great time. Gary played cricket & I chatted. Will go, all the best for the Test.

>Love from all of us.
>
>Fre

MERV: I hope Mum's not getting blasé about my achievements – I haven't scored a run yet. Perhaps she doesn't want to put me under any pressure.

> Third Test v England at Adelaide Oval
> (12, 13, 14, 15, 16 December 1986)
> Australia 5 dec. 514 and 3 dec. 201, drew with
> England 455 and 2 for 39.
> M. Hughes 1/82 and 1/16. Did not bat.

MERV: It didn't work, I still haven't made a run. But we only had two fast bowlers and I was one of them. That has to mean something.

> Fourth Test v England at MCG
> (26, 27, 28 December 1986)
> Australia 141 and 194 lost to
> England 349 by an innings and 14 runs.
> M Hughes 1/94. First inns 2 runs, second inns 8 runs.

MERV: Two ambitions fulfilled in the same Test! I stayed in the team for the Fourth Test at the MCG, and I made runs. Unfortunately, after four Tests, I have made more runs than I have taken wickets. And I've only made ten runs.

Fifth Test v England at SCG
(10, 11, 12, 14, 15 January 1987)
Australia 343 and 251 defeated
England 275 and 264 by 55 runs.
M. Hughes 2/58 and 0/52.
First inns 16 runs, second inns 2 runs.

MERV: Now it is back to the Sheffield Shield competition.

(G) VICTORIAN CRICKET ASSOCIATION
13 March 1987

Dear Merv,

W.A. v. Victoria, Sheffield Shield Final – Perth
20–24 March 1987

You are invited to play for Victoria in the above match. The previously announced team is –

R. Bright (Capt.)	P. Jackson
S. Davis	S. O'Donnell
M. Dimattina	M. Quinn
T. Dodemaide	J. Siddons
P. Hibbert	D. Whatmore
M. Hughes	P. Young

. . .

It has been a long and hard cricket season for everyone involved in the cricket world, more so for the players, and to bring home the Shield will top off what has been an exciting step forward for the Vics!

Good luck . . .

Sheffield Shield Final at WACA
(20, 21, 22, 23, 24 March 1987)
Victoria 8 dec. 404 and 6 for 215 drew with
Western Australia 654.
M. Hughes 2/113 from 42 overs.
Western Australia won the Sheffield Shield due
to its higher position on the table.

 (G) 19 June 1987

Dear Merv,
No doubt you have mixed feelings about the party announced for the World Cup. On one hand you will be disappointed that you didn't make the team and on the other pleased to see your name in the reserves.

If I was in your shoes I would take great heart in the fact you have been included in one of the groups, for it indicates to me that the selectors feel you have a future in Australian cricket. I concur on this and feel you haven't yourself given your potential the chance that it needs. You have done well to reach Australian standards with the application you have shown.

However, as we have discussed, you have to do more to secure a position as a strike bowler for Australia. You have the talent and love for cricket to succeed, all it needs is a little more dedication.

I will look forward to seeing you in Brisbane.

> Regards for now,
> Bob Simpson

MERV: I haven't played any One Dayers yet, so I wasn't really expecting to be picked for the World Cup campaign in India. For Bob Simpson to take the time to write to me is typical of the man and very encouraging for me. Now that I'm going to the training camp before the team departs, I'll be able to bowl at the fast bowlers in the nets and with a bit of luck, one of them won't survive, and I'll need to replace them. Not that emergencies ever wish injuries on team-mates. Bullshit.

(G) LARA SPORTING CLUB
September 1987

NAME: Merv Hughes
NO. OF GAMES: 6 : 6

POSITION(S)	COMMENTS
Ruck	Worked very well in all positions – using
Centre Half Back	strength, mobility and abilities.
Full Back	Attacking in all positions

(Scale: Poor / Fair / Good / V.Good / Excellent)

FITNESS	V/Good
COMMENT	A sound basis, however all aspects – stamina and interval work over short distances could be improved upon.

SKILL LEVEL

Handball	Excellent
COMMENT	Both hands work very well – fast and accurate

Kicking	Excellent
COMMENT	Covers great distance and is accurate – wrong foot is functional.

Marking	Excellent
COMMENT	Strong both at overhead and chest level.

ATTITUDES

Training	Excellent
COMMENT	Despite spasmodic attendance, when training – hard working, enthusiastic, supportive and with purpose

Match	Excellent
COMMENT	Apart from one moment of loss of concentration an excellent attitude – supportive of team members, good concentration and always positive.

OFF-SEASON ACTIVITIES
All the very best for this year's cricket season.

MERV: I had planned to spend another year acting as Coach's Runner for the firsts at Lara. Snappa was playing in the seconds and it gave me a chance to keep fit by training with him. One week, the first's full-forward was injured and the team was one tall short. (Are you with me?) The coach asked if I could fill in for a week. I told him I was not going to play in the second half of the season as I needed to be right for the beginning of summer, but if he could cope with that, then I was happy to play. With injuries and suspensions, I ended up playing six matches all over the ground.

At least the coach didn't mention my weight.

ACB PLAYER CONTRACT

> **THIS AGREEMENT** is made the 1st day of October 1987
> **BETWEEN**
>> **THE PLAYER** named in Part 1 of the Schedule
>> ('the Player') of the one part
>> and
>> **AUSTRALIAN CRICKET BOARD** a company incorpo-
>> rated in Victoria of 70 Jolimont Street, Jolimont, Victoria
>> ('ACB') of the other part
>
> **WHEREAS:** The Selectors have recommended to ACB that it is necessary for ACB to have players of the quality and experience of the Player available for selection and, if selected, to play in cricket matches organised by ACB and on that basis have recommended to ACB that ACB enter this Agreement with the Player.
>
> **NOW IT IS HEREBY AGREED AS FOLLOWS:**
> . . .
> 7.2. **Availability and Fitness**
> . . .
> 7.2.3 The Player shall undertake the fitness programme prepared for him by the fitness advisor appointed by the ACB and shall when requested by the fitness advisor, the Selectors or ACB undertake such tests as are reasonable to satisfy ACB that the

Player has reached or maintained the required level of fitness.
[Can't see anything in here about weight!]
. . .

Page 19
SCHEDULE

Part 1:   The Player: Mervyn Hughes
               of . . .

Part 2:   The Selectors: L. M. Sawle (Chairman),
               G. S. Chappell, J. D. Higgs, R. B. Simpson

Part 3:   Term: Two Years
               Commencement Date: 1st October, 1987
               End Date: 30th September, 1989

Part 4:   Retainer Fee: $3,000
               The Retainer Fee shall be paid monthly by twelve
               equal instalments each equal to one twelfth of the
               Retainer Fee.

Part 5:   Guarantee: $8,000

Part 6:   Match Fee
               Test Matches: $2,750
               One Day International: $900

Part 7:   Tour Fee:

[The ACB's not that confident, they don't want to commit to a
Tour Fee yet. Perhaps they're still trying to work out how much
it's going to cost to feed me.]

Part 8:   Number of Days of Cricket Promotional Activities:
            20 days

Part 9:   Coaching Activities:
            not more than 10 days and not more than
            an aggregate of 40 hours.

Part 10:   Tours:
            Sri Lanka   April–May 1988
            Pakistan   September–October 1988
            England   May–September 1989

Part 11:   Retirement Benefits Payments Scheme Credits
            Test Match: One
            One Day International: One third

MERV: My first Australian Cricket Board contract. For the first time I will be paid a regular income for playing cricket: $250 a month. I suppose this means the selectors are still looking at me.

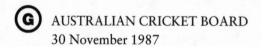

G AUSTRALIAN CRICKET BOARD
30 November 1987

Dear Merv,

Benson & Hedges Test, Australia v. New Zealand
Brisbane – 4–8 December 1987

Congratulations on your selection for the above match. As you are aware the conditions of your selection are set out in your Player Contract and in your 1987/88 Australian Players Handbook and shall apply for all matches for which you are selected during the 1987/88 season.
    The selected team is:

Allan Border (Capt)   Tim May
Geoff Marsh (V-Capt)   Craig McDermott
David Boon   Bruce Reid
Greg Dyer   Peter Sleep
Merv Hughes   Mike Veletta
Dean Jones   Stephen Waugh

. . .

First Test v New Zealand at the Gabba
(4, 5, 6, 7 December 1987)
Australia 305 and 1 for 97 defeated
New Zealand 186 and 212 by nine wickets.
M. Hughes 3/40 and 2/57.
First inns 5 runs, second inns dnb.

MERV: I took a few wickets, but the selectors took two spinners into the Adelaide Test, and before the Melbourne Test I had to pull out because of a hamstring question mark. My good mate from Footscray, Tony Dodemaide, made his Test debut in my place, and starred with a 50 in the first innings, and six for 58 in the second.

(G) LARA SPORTING CLUB, FOOTBALL SECTION
27 November 1987

Dear Merv,
I would like to take this opportunity to congratulate you on behalf of everyone associated with the Lara Sporting Club on your selection in the Squad chosen to represent Australia in the First Test against New Zealand.

Your determination and fighting spirit is a credit to you and I can assure you that these qualities are noticed and appreciated by all of us at Lara.

Good luck for not only the First Test but for the entire cricket season and may you establish yourself as an automatic selection in the team for the future.

Looking forward to seeing you in the not too distant future.

Yours sincerely,
Peter Kelly
Chairman

MERV: No such thing as an automatic selection for me at this stage. The Bicentennial Test in Sydney required two spinners, but I was picked for the single Test against Sri Lanka.

Test v Sri Lanka at WACA, WA
(12, 13, 14, 15 February 1988)
Australia 455 defeated
Sri Lanka 194 and 153 by an innings and 108 runs.
M. Hughes 0/61 and 5/67.
First inns 8 runs, second inns dnb.

MERV: My first five wickets in an innings at Test level. Allan Border didn't like the attitude of a few of us, and gave Steve Waugh, Dean Jones and me a blast. He reckons I'm overweight.

I was then selected as an emergency for the tour to Pakistan.

(G) AUSTRALIAN CRICKET BOARD
23 May 1988

Dear Merv,
Please find enclosed a copy of all the Pakistan tour information forwarded to players recently.

You should follow through with all the requirements of the letter so that, should you be required to join the tour party, all necessary preliminary arrangements have been covered.

You will also need to maintain a suitable level of preparation, as a lead up to the pre-tour training camp in Brisbane which you will be required to attend.

If you have any queries, please don't hesitate to contact either Ron Steiner or myself.

Yours sincerely,
Graham W. Halbish
General Manager

1988 PAKISTAN TOUR

I am pleased to confirm your conditional selection for this tour. Please read the information provided below; a further team letter will follow closer to the tour.

TOUR PARTY

Allan Border (Captain)	Bruce Reid
Geoff Marsh (VC)	Jamie Siddons
David Boon	Peter Sleep
Tony Dodemaide	Peter Taylor
Ian Healy	Michael Veletta
Dean Jones	Stephen Waugh
Craig McDermott	Graeme Wood

. . .

Of prime concern to you is obviously your performance and future in the Australian side. Don't let injury or lack of fitness inhibit your performance or chances of selection.

At the pre-season camp in Brisbane you will be required to demonstrate your total fitness level. Your aerobic, anaerobic and flexibility limits will be tested.

The assessment procedure will include:

BODY FAT CONTENT

Key Area Flexibility Back x 2
Hip
Hamstring
Shoulder

Run of 3 With pads, bat and spikes

Sprint x 6

Aerobic Capacity Now termed 5–25–250

5 Activities 5 minutes duration

25 minutes finished with 5 sets 50 reps abdominal work

Cycling   Stationary
Distance covered
number of revolutions

Arm ergometer number of revolutions

Skipping

Jumping Jacks number performed

Skills   running crouched
underarm short distance
number of reps.
accuracy

Abdominals 5 types of 50 reps.

1. Regular situps knee bend
2. Abdominal crouches
3. Abdominal cycling
4. Leg lifts
5. Bilateral leg & pelvis
   rotation with leg extended

Please don't hesitate to give me a call or to talk with your State fitness advisor, if you have any queries concerning any of the above.

Best regards,
Errol Alcott

MERV: Errol's starting to get serious with organising each player's approach to the game. Good to see that they are testing for body fat before the team leaves. You don't want to go over there underweight, and then lose more because of the unfamiliarity of the local cuisine. I reckon if some of the blokes don't bulk up, I'll be joining the party.

CHAPTER TEN

The Hat-Trick

(G) AUSTRALIAN CRICKET BOARD
28 November 1988

Dear Merv,

**RE: Benson and Hedges Test, Australia v. West Indies
Perth, 2–6 December 1988**

Congratulations on your selection for the above match. As you
are aware, the conditions of your selection are set out in your
Player Contract (where applicable) and in your 1988/89
Australian Players' Handbook and shall apply for all matches for
which you are selected during the 1988/89 season.
The selected team is:

Allan Border (Capt)	Geoff Lawson
Geoff March (V.Capt)	Tim May
David Boon	Craig McDermott
Tony Dodemaide	Mike Veletta
Ian Healy	Stephen Waugh
Merv Hughes	Graeme Wood

Manager:	Ian McDonald
Coach:	Bob Simpson
Physiotherapist:	Errol Alcott

Twelfth man will be announced on the morning of the match . . .

MERV: I didn't make it for the First Test against the Windies in
Brisbane, but I'm pretty happy to get this.

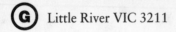 Little River VIC 3211

28 November 1988

Merv Hughes
IF NIA – LEAVE UNDER DOOR

. . . Congrats Skater,
Knew you had it in you.
Give em hell.
                    Trudy, Bluey & Louie

MERV: Trudy is Bluey's sister. Bluey is Darren Goodwin alias Duran Duran. Louie is Bluey's girlfriend.

 Kenmore 4069

29 November 1988

Dear Mr Hughes
My name is Rupert B. I'm writing to congratulate you on your re-call to the Australian Test Team. I play cricket at school. I bat at number 7 and bowl off spinners.

My father has been a fan of yours for many years. He likes your consistency and your attitude to the game. Dad and I will be watching the coming test in Perth with great interest. Good luck to all the team.
                    Yours faithfully,
                    Rupert B.

PS: Your photo appeared in today's Courier-Mail. Will you be kind enough to autograph it for me. Thank-you.

Second Test v West Indies at WACA
(2, 3, 4, 5, 6 December 1988)
Australia 8 dec. 395 and 234 lost to
West Indies 449 and 9 dec. 349 by 169 runs.
M. Hughes 5/130 and 8/87.
First inns saved by a declaration after Geoff Lawson
had his jaw broken, second inns 0.

MERV: I think life may be about to change.

(G) AUSTRALIAN CRICKET BOARD

TO   Merv Hughes
COMPANY   Australian Cricket Team
FROM   G. Halbish
SUBJECT   'Hat Trick'
DATE   5 December 1988

MESSAGE/COMMENTS
It was great to see you steam in & make history yesterday. My
kids went wild. Well done.
   Let's hope it's the start of a good run for you & the team.
        Best Regards
        Graham

(G) VICTORIAN CRICKET ASSOCIATION

TO   Merv Hughes
            c/- W.A.C.A.
FROM   V.C.A.
DATE   Monday 5 December 1988

MESSAGE
Merv,
Congratulations on your 6 wickets to date, including
your HAT TRICK.

You've done us proud and we look forward to the rest of today's play.

> From the ever-loving girls – and male members
> of the V.C.A. STAFF

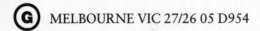 MELBOURNE VIC 27/26 05 D954

MERV HUGHES
AUSTRALIAN CRICKET TEAM DRESSING ROOM
WACA OVAL
PERTHWA

CONGRATULATIONS 'HEAPA'. CLEAN UP THE REST IN
THE NEXT OVER AND A HALF.
ROSS AND JOSIE

G MELBOURNE VIC 39/37 04 2057

MERV HUGHES AUSTRALIAN TEST SIDE
WESTERN AUSTRALIA CRICKET ASSOCIATION
W.A.C.A. GROUND
PERTHWA

TO MERV, CONGRATULATIONS ON YOUR HAT-TRICK.
KEEP THE BOWLING UP. WE'RE RIGHT BEHIND YOU
BACK AT WERRIBEE.
PAUL AND JANET PORTOGALLO AND BRIAN LENNON

(G) FROM   Woody, Darwin, NT

TO   Merv Hughes, C/- WACA Ground,
         Nelson Crescent, East Perth

Merv, Congratulations on your second Hat Trick and 5 for in the
first dig. Knock a few heads off.
         Cheers, Woody, Darwin

(G) FROM   M & EJ Cockrem
         . . . AYR 4807

TO   Merv Hughes
         C/- Australian Cricket Team
         C/- WACKA Cricket Ground
         Perth 6000

'CONGRATULATIONS'
KEEP UP THE GREAT BOWLING.
WILL HAVE A PRAWN AND BEER FOR YOU.
HAVE A MERRY CHRISTMAS AND A HAPPY NEW YEAR.
AYR COCKREMS
EVA. BOB MYLES

(G) DEAR MERV, OUR HEARTIEST CONGRATULATIONS. SO
PROUD OF YOU.
DAVID AND CAROL LYONS, STEWART, SCOTT AND
ALANA

(G) AUSTRALIAN CRICKET BOARD

TO   Merv Hughes
COMPANY C/- WACA
FROM   Ron Steiner
DATE   5 December 1988

MESSAGE/COMMENTS
MERV,
WELL BOWLED! KEEP CHASING THOSE RECORDS!
RON STEINER
(Above message was phoned through by Ron currently holidaying on South Mole Island.)

(G) 5 December 1988

W.A.C.A.
East Perth

Please forward onto Mr. Mervyn G. Hughes, c/o Australian Cricket Team.

CONGRATULATIONS!!!!
    Good on ya Merv, all the best for the rest of the match, so happy to see you get a hat trick . . .
    Lots of congratulations from
    the Hughes' of Werribee,
    the Barkers of Lara,
    the Tooheys of Hoppers Crossing.
          See Ya when you get home.
          Love KT

(G) Werribee Sports Club
PO Box 222
Werribee VIC 3030

05/12 10:45 COURIER 05 December 1988

Mr Merv Hughes
C/- Perth Cricket Ground
Perth WA 6000

Congratulations on your bowling efforts over the week-end.
Your have done Werribee proud.
  From the Werribee Football Club & The Werribee Sports Club

(G) MELBOURNE VIC 27/26 06 0929

MERV HUGHES
C/O WACA GROUND
PERTHWA

MERV CONGRATULATIONS ON A GREAT EFFORT. BEST
WISHES FROM PRESIDENT TINO AND MEMBERS OF THE
WERRIBEE ROTARY CLUB
TINO BALLAN

(G) LONDON/LM 43/41 05 0952 DEVIE

MERV HUGHES
C/O WESTERN AUSTRALIAN CRICKET
ASSOCIATION (WACA)
PERTH CRICKET CLUB
PERTH

MERV
FROM EVERYONE AT WOODFORD WELLS CRICKET CLUB
CONGRATULATIONS ON YOUR HATRICK AND FIVE
WICKETS GOOD LUCK FOR THE REST OF THE SERIES
REGARDS
KEITH TROTTER SECRETARY
WOODFORD WELLS

(G) ROWLAND NEILSON McCARTHY

DATE   6 December 1988
TO   MR MERV HUGHES: Bowler Extraordinaire
FAX NO   C/O W.A.C.A.
FROM   Anne-Marie Waters: KLEENEX PR

Dear Merv,
Congratulations!!!!!
    The early bird gets the wickets!!
    Must have been those radio drops we did that got you in training (or perhaps your hair cut).
    You might even get to make a McDonald's commercial now – not just appear on a poster!!
    See You When You Get Back.
        KIND REGARDS
        Anne-Marie Waters

MERV: Everyone has their own perspective. Kleenex, a division of Kimberly-Clark, is the major sponsor of Victorian cricket this season.

KIMBERLY-CLARK AUSTRALIA

RUSH
6 December 1988

SEND TO   Merv Hughes
           Australian Cricket Team

Congratulations on your outstanding performance in the Cricket Test.
   You even look good when you are taking wickets!
   Hope you are wearing your Kleenex Logo T-Shirt for all your interviews.
   All Kimberly-Clark Team proud of you.
           Greg Griffiths

 AUSTRALIAN CRICKET BOARD

TO   Merv Hughes
           C/- Ian McDonald, Aust. Team Manager
COMPANY C/- WACA
FROM   David Richards
DATE   6 December 1988

MESSAGE/COMMENTS
Congratulations on your inspirational bowling performances throughout the Test, but particularly yesterday in the difficult circumstances, following Geoff Lawson's injury.
   Best wishes from Malcolm Gray and all at the ACB.
           Regards,
           David L. Richards
           Chief Executive

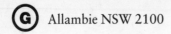 Allambie NSW 2100

6 December 1988

Mr Merv Hughes
IF NIA PLEASE LEAVE UNDER DOOR
Perth Cricket Ground
Perth WA 6000

Congratulations on your stamina, strength, to the Man of the Day.
From the Lindfield family, Allambie, NSW

MERV: I'm not sure which door they left it under, but it found me!

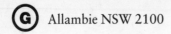 North Carlton VIC 3054

6 December 1988

Merv Hughes
C/o The Australian Dressing Rooms
WACA Oval
PERTH WA 6000

Man of the match stuff. Congratulations on a top effort.
Brian Wiggins

North Side Indoor Cricket Centre
North Geelong VIC 3215

6 December 1988

Merv Hughes
WACA Cricket Ground
Perth WA 6000

Well done Merv.
Magnificent performance. We are all proud of you. Glad to see
that you didn't bare your bum on the waca like you did here at
Northside ICC.
    Keep it up mate, and we will see you in the UK next May.
                    John and Joyce Holland

 North Footscray VIC 3011

6 December 1988

Merv Hughes
Australian Cricket Team
W A C A Ground
Perth WA 6000

Fantastic effort Merv. We are all thrilled and very proud of you.
Now for the Ashes tour next year.
                Love and Best Wishes
                Irene, Ian, Warren, Alan, Karen Dodemaide

Coburg VIC 3058

6 December 1988

Merv Hughes
WACA Ground
Perth WA 6000

Great effort big fella,
We love ya heaps, keep up the good work. Congratulations from
the entire Siddons family.

TO	Hyatt Regency Hotel
FOR	Merv Hughes
FROM	Warwick Burnham
DATE	6 December 1988

MESSAGE
Please deliver to Merv Hughes who is staying with Australian
Cricket Team.

Footscray Cricket Club

Merv,
Congratulations on your hat trick – a great achievement. All at
Footscray (and all Australia) are behind you and Tony as you
blast out the West Indies today.
    Regards
    Warwick

Belmont VIC 3216

7 December 1988

Congratulations Hilly on thirteen (13) of the best. So very pleased
for you on all your success. The hog was at attention when you
got Greenidge first ball for your broken hat trick.
            Peter and Gay Young

MERV: Peter was a state team-mate.

 Chelmer QLD 4068

8 December 1988

Merv Hughes
C/- Basha's Smash Repairs
112 Triholm Avenue
Laverton VIC 3028

CONGRATULATIONS ON HAT TRICK AND A GREAT TEST
MATCH
'MICKY REDDERS'
BRISBANE

 5 December 1988

Dear Swervin'-Curvin'-Weavin'-Wervin'-Unnerv'em-Mervyn,
Just a note to add to the initial congratulations. After your
brilliant display in Perth, rumour has it that the Mayor of
Werribee is going to name one of the town's round-a-bouts after
you . . . and then there's the inventor who has patented 'Merv-
Hughes Bottle Brushes'.

Jokes aside, it was great to see someone who is as committed (check that in the dictionary will you?) and as determined as yourself reap the rewards. I know that where that came from there is still a lot more in store.

Only yesterday I was going through some of my old assignments looking for some notes when I found a transcript of the interview you gave me back in 1985. Here are a few extracts:

'If I don't get anywhere this year I'll think about giving it away. If you haven't done a lot by the time you're 25 you are a last resort.'

'A lot of people told me I should change, settle down, change my attitude towards life . . . reckoned I was a bit of a rat-bag. I got there by being who I am, so why change? It's me.'

'You don't get negative criticism from anyone that counts.'

And then there was . . . 'Some days you get up and you feel good. You think: "Today's the day", you're jumping around and bopping. Other times you get up and you think: "Oh, shit – Here we go again." If you're waking up more days thinking "oh shit" you're obviously not enjoying what you are doing . . . so there's no point.'

My closing paragraph on the assignment (you never saw it) was: 'Merv was an interesting case. He continually said that he didn't set goals but his comments hinted to the contrary. He struck me as a sportsman who knows exactly what he wants and will do all in his power to achieve it.'

I thought those little snippets from the past might interest you. Rest up, rev up and look out for a scuff-stuff sign on an old sheet (amongst the other hundred) on Boxing Day.

Take care,
      love
      Trudy XX

MERV: Trudy interviewed me for an assignment she did at college. Trudy is Bluey's sister. She's a smart girl, too!

CITY OF WERRIBEE
12 December 1988

Dear Merv,
At the Ordinary Meeting of the Council of City of Werribee held on Monday, 5 December 1988, a resolution was passed that I forward to you a letter of congratulations for your magnificent bowling performance in taking a Hat Trick in the 2nd Test against the West Indies in Perth, Western Australia.

Council and the Werribee Community were particularly proud and pleased for you; it is indeed a rare and special honour.

We hope that you are able to maintain the excellent form you have recently captured and that the team can go on to bigger and better things throughout the course of the summer.

Congratulations again on a thoroughly well-deserved and distinguished honour.

> Yours sincerely,
> J.T. Kerr
> Town Clerk

G Werribee VIC 3030

12 December 1988

Dear Merv,
Congratulations mate on a great performance in Perth . . .

I don't know about you, but I wasn't too sure about all this early morning stuff throughout the winter, but I can see it has obviously done you a helluva lot more good than it's done me.

I think you better get some of those batsmen into the nets though mate and see whether or not you can't get them a bit more fired up. Hopefully as the summer wears on a little bit, some will run into a bit of form. It was good to see Deano hitting a few runs on Sunday.

The whole Council is genuinely pleased for you and you will receive a letter from the Town Clerk following a resolution in the

Open Council, which I thought was a pretty nice touch.

Now that you are in the 'big time' mate, you probably haven't got a lot of spare time, so I won't go on too long (unusual for me) – all the best for the rest of the summer, keep the head down and keep those Windies honest! I can see that it's going to be a long cold winter for me next year – I reckon you'll be in the Bahamas – I'm available to carry bags if necessary (I'm not proud!)

All the best Merv.

> Kind regards,
> Ross Tavener

MERV: Ross worked at Werribee Council and used the same gym as I did during the winter. We had lots of early morning sessions when we both wondered why we were doing it. I don't know what he got out of it!

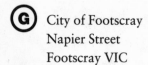

City of Footscray
Napier Street
Footscray VIC

15 December 1988

Mr Merv Hughes
Australian Cricket Team
C/- MCG Yarra Park
Jolimont VIC 3002

Hello Merv,
CONGRATULATIONS!! for your recent Hat trick. Was a great achievement in your cricket career.

> Best Wishes
> The Mayor Councillor Lynne Kosky, Councillors and
> Officers of The City of Footscray

 Euroa VIC

7 December 1988

Dear Merv,
My name is Karen Telford, you may not remember me. You
signed my scrap book of pictures on yourself when you came to
Euroa High School to do a coaching clinic.

This week I finished school so I have spent the week glued to
the T.V. Through your efforts I have almost filled another book.
There has been quite a bit about you. Every ball you bowled my
family and I sat there hoping that it would result favourably. By
the end of that five day Test we were so pleased for you.

I would just like to congratulate you on your fine effort. My
Dad seems to think that your amount of fans will have grown
considerably. Besides your Mum and Dad (who I can imagine are
very pleased) I am still your number one fan!!!

Congratulations and Good Luck for the rest of the season. I
will certainly be waiting for news items to collect. Please find
enclosed an article on your visit to Euroa, I thought it may interest
you. All the best for the rest of the season.
> Regards
> Karen Telford

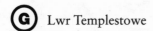 Lwr Templestowe

13 December 1988

Dear Merv,
I drove past Werribee the other day on the way to Torquay & I
thought that it really is time that I wrote & congratulated you on
your success in cricket. I have been following your career since
you won the Esso Scholarship & have never got around to
writing.

Its terrific to see the way you have persevered with your setbacks & finally reached the 'top'.

We used to be neighbours to Vinnie & Lyn Condon & we see them from time to time. I am always so pleased to see Werribee 'kids' doing well. Say hello to Rainer for me.

Max owns Glenroy Cellars so if you happen to be up that way when you break your drought in April, he would be happy to help you quench your thirst! (But watch your waistline!)

We wish you every success in the future & we know what its like to have bad times as well as good (enjoy the good!)

> Regards,
> Sue Crow (your old teacher Miss Howard in case you've forgotten!)

P.S. Werribee was truly on the nose the other day!

MERV: Sue Crow taught at Werribee High when Snappa and I were in Fifth Form. Sue was a recent teachers' college graduate, and so wasn't much older than Snappa and me. Snappa (dreamer) fancied her. He got as far as he did with Rana. Sue went on to be the Chief Executive of Women's Cricket Australia.

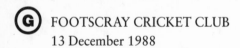

(G) FOOTSCRAY CRICKET CLUB
13 December 1988

Dear Merv,

On behalf of the Committee, Players and Supporters of Footscray Cricket Club I wish to firstly Congratulate you on your return to international cricket.

Your achievement on taking a hat-trick followed up by a 'bag' of 13 wickets to create a new record was a magnificent effort of which we all feel so proud particularly when placed under such pressure.

It is good to see that your dedications and determination have

reaped such wonderful results which no doubt will continue long
into the future.

> With Best Wishes and Good Cricket,
> Alec Boicos
> Hon. Secretary

Glenvale 4350
Queensland

Merv,
Hi, I am one of your fans, my name is Justin Lawrence. I was
wondering if you could send me some posters of yourself if you
don't mind. I play cricket for my shcool. I am a pace bowler. I like
your bowling and batting. I have got two hat tricks last year. My
Dad likes watching cricket. I have a few small pictures of you
(two bowling and one sitting down). [**And none eating?**]

> Justin

Prime Minister
Canberra

15 December 1988

Mr Merv Hughes
c/- VCA
86 Jolimont St
Jolimont VIC 3002

Dear Merv
I should like to thank you for agreeing to play for the Prime
Minister's XI in the match against the West Indies in Canberra
earlier this month. It was a great pity that the match could not be

played, especially as you had gone to so much trouble to come to Canberra, which I appreciated very much.

My best wishes for the rest of the season.

Yours sincerely

R.J.L. Hawke

Third Test v West Indies at MCG
(24, 26, 27, 28, 29 December 1988)
Australia 242 and 114 lost to
West Indies 280 and 9 dec. 361 by 285 runs.
M. Hughes 0/52 and 0/71.
First inns 21 not out, second inns 4.

MERV: My batting's improving. This is the first time I have played a Test and not taken a wicket . . .

Fourth Test v West Indies at SCG
(26, 27, 28, 29, 30 January 1989)
Australia 401 and 3 for 82 defeated
West Indies 224 and 256 by 7 wickets.
M. Hughes 0/28 and 1/29.
First inns 12, second inns dnb.

MERV: At least they played me at the SCG this summer.

Fifth Test v West Indies at Adelaide Oval
(3, 4, 5, 6, 7 February 1989)
Australia 515 and 4 dec. 224 drew with
West Indies 369 and 4 for 233.
M. Hughes 0/86 and 0/20.
First inns 72 not out, second inns dnb

MERV: I ran out of partners on the way to my first Test century! One wicket in three Tests, and now I have to wait until the middle of March to see if I'm in the seventeen players to tour England . . .

cherryBrook

Dear Mr. Hughes,

Thankyou for the
Photograph of you plaing
cricket. I am putting
it on my bedroom wall
and will show it to
all my friends
Thankyou
    from Jonathan

CHAPTER ELEVEN

The Struggle Continues

AUSTRALIAN CRICKET BOARD
16 March 1989

Dear Merv,
Congratulations on your selection for the 1989 Ashes Tour of
England. We leave from Melbourne on the 29th April.

 We have a huge task ahead of us – to *regain* the Ashes.
Australia has not won a full Test series in England since 1964, so
there is quite a challenge ahead for the 1989 team. We need to
start preparing for it now.

 I have asked our Coach, Bob Simpson and Physiotherapist,
Errol Alcott, to be in touch with you regarding preparation for the
tour. I urge you to give them both your total co-operation.

 You will soon be receiving from the Board Office a briefing
letter concerning the tour. Thereafter, please feel free to
communicate with Graham Halbish, Ron Steiner or myself about
any aspect of the tour.

 I look forward to seeing you *fit* and well on April 29th.
             Regards,
             Laurie Sawle
             Manager

---

 22 March 1989

Merv,
Dropping a line to a player is unusual in the selection business,
but then again I've always been a bit different. Your selection for
England has created some controversy. As with any Australian
sportsman who has any degree of success these days the knockers
have arrived on your doorstep. Hopefully you will go to England
with that firmly in your mind and determined to do something
about them.

 Some advice: You are a *fast* bowler. Very fast. You should never
lose sight of that. You also have *rare ability* to run through a
batting line-up, evidenced by your figures 7/81 (St. Kilda), 5/130

and 8/87 (Perth) and 6/36 (M.C.G.). In England, all tour, it will be very much to your advantage never to forget just how you achieved that success. I'm certain you didn't achieve it by bowling the sort of mindless crap Jim Higgs and I watched you bowl at Wayne Andrews and co. at the M.C.G. in March.

In England I hope you will continue to bowl fast. I hope you will see the advantage in using the seam and the shine. I hope you will be smart enough to use the bouncer only rarely no matter what temptations may be served up by the old English pros; the bouncer never frightened anyone, it's the one that drives into the rib cage that hurts, longest!

Finally I hope you come back to Australia established as a fine, very fast, thinking bowler. Bowl like you did at the M.C.G. that day and you'll come back a mug!

With very best wishes for the tour.

John Benaud

Merv – I would appreciate you keeping this letter confidential. As you know selection matters are traditionally private and this letter could be construed by some as an indication of my 'tour vote'. That would be unfortunate. Please accept my advice in the manner in which it is intended – to bring back the Ashes!

MERV: My first thought when I got this letter was, 'If I let anyone know about this letter, I'll never play for Australia again.' He's right, the knockers have arrived and now they're writing to me! But at least he's put me on the tour. I will use this as the framework for how I approach the Ashes Tour, and my bowling from here on. Knowing John and his fellow selectors have put me on the Tour gives me confidence that I have a legitimate place.

(G) AUSTRALIAN CRICKET BOARD
30 March 1989

Dear Merv,

1989 England Tour

I am pleased to confirm your conditional selection for this tour.

Please read the information provided below and note any items
which require follow up and give them your immediate attention.

1. Tour Party
Allan Border (Captain)
Geoff Marsh (Vice-Captain)
Terry Alderman
David Boon
Greg Campbell
Ian Healy
Trevor Hohns
Merv Hughes
Dean Jones
Geoff Lawson
Tim May
Tom Moody
Carl Rackemann
Mark Taylor
Michael Valetta
Steve Waugh
Tim Zoehrer

Laurie Sawle (Manager)	Bob Simpson (Coach)
Errol Alcott (Physiotherapist)	Mike Walsh (Scorer)

. . .

MERV: This touring party has been described by the English media as
the worst to ever leave the shores of Australia. We'll see.

31 March 1989

Dear Merv,

Obviously someone must have voted for you but I still haven't been able to find out who. No matter, congratulations – you have deserved your position in the team.

Since the end of the season I have spent a great deal of time thinking about why you didn't get more wickets in the last half of the season. I reckon I have gone through just about every possible reason but still can't get past fitness, concentration and patience, perhaps the last being the key.

I have said this before to you Merv and I will spell it out again. You have the talent to be a fine, if not even a great bowler. However, I also believe that you must want it more than you sometimes seem to display. I think I know you well enough to understand that you throw up a veneer to hide your true feelings and mask your own ambition and dare I say, keeness. This is fine and because I understand it I can more easily accept it.

However, many outsiders don't and criticise you for excessive weight, temperament and some of your 'antics'. I know we have discussed this before but I feel you must pay more attention to these matters.

I am as usual more than happy to spend whatever time is needed with you to assist you to fulfill your true ability. But in the end it comes down to you.

I should mention at this stage that we will be running a very tight ship in England and will be almost displaying tunnel vision in our endeavours to get the best out of the team. Winning is what it is all about and everything we do will be directed to this.

There will be a very strong emphasis on fitness and skills and I should warn you that everyone will undergo a fitness test on April 28 in Melbourne. Errol will run this and we will be particularly conscious of weight. In fact throughout the tour we will have a regular weigh-in with fines imposed to those who are slapping on extra pounds.

Enjoy your 'one week' drink in, but don't forget in the next few months you face your true test as to whether M. Hughes will be a Test cricketer or not. I have my money on you succeeding.

If you feel like discussing anything with me don't hesitate to phone.

Regards,
Bob Simpson

PS: Last season we had more problems with bad shoulders than usual so in England we will be working hard to avoid this. Don't forget to bring a baseball glove.

MERV: The message is getting louder: fit and thin gets me in, fit and fat means I can't take wickets so there is no place for me in the game. My manager David Emerson has found Ann Quinn, who is Pat Cash's fitness adviser, and she lives and works in Melbourne. Cashy won Wimbledon in 1987 and is currently ranked number four in the world. On the way out to have my first fitness assessment, Emmo asked me how I thought I'd go. 'I reckon she'll say I'm pretty fit but a bit overweight, Emmo.'

 MERV HUGHES
Activities to develop Cardiovascular and Speed Endurance

Horse trainers call it 'foundation', runners call it a 'base', baseball players call it 'legs', tennis players call it 'wind'. Whatever you call it, cardiovascular endurance is the ability to play hard and fast, recover from strenuous exertion quickly and still be at your peak for the last minute of the game. If one is not in top aerobic condition, then all other factors such as speed, agility, jumping ability, recovery and strength will be hindered. When fatigue sets in your mental processes are not as sharp and your whole game falls apart. Cardiovascular endurance is thus absolutely essential for cricket players.

Your cardiovascular endurance score of 55.25 ml/min/kg was very good Merv. There's a surprise package underneath that 22% body fat! – a cricketer with a great deal of endurance. In fact, you have the average endurance level of a VFL football player. That might sound good to you, but you are not about being average. A few kilograms off you, plus some more specific and varied training, will soon lift you to greater heights. More cardio-vascular endurance work and no take-aways, soft drinks or alcohol will help you achieve this!

I have also included some speed endurance work. This is an important component of fitness often neglected in many training programs. When you are batting or bowling, you are repeating bursts of speed throughout the match and it is especially important that you maintain such speed through to the last minute of the game. With a high level of endurance, the quality of such activity is maintained and the athlete is still fresh at the end of the final day.

The following activities are all different ways for you to increase your present levels and add variety to your training program. Select an activity according to how you feel, and you can adjust the intensity of the workout to your readiness (taking into account other training, heat, recovery, upcoming competition, and so forth). Most importantly you must enjoy what you are doing. As well as facilitating your performance Merv, an increased level of cardiovascular endurance will reduce the chance of injury, and increase your concentration span. It is thus considered to be essential . . .

MERV: Ten pages of different ways to exhaust myself follow.

In Conclusion
All of these methods are good ways to build up your endurance and add some variety to your program Merv. You should continually try to increase the length of the work periods, the speed at which work is done, and the distance over which it is done. The activity should be continued beyond the point of initial fatigue, and should be sustained until you are thoroughly tired. The heart rate is a good guide to pace. I recommend that you work out aerobically about 5 times per week, before you depart. Good luck.

Ann Quinn – Sport Science Consultant
9/4/89

MERV: I told, you, Emmo.

Ann is inspiring. She is so positive that I will be better off a bit lighter, and now that I have met her I just get the feeling that it will be impossible to escape: she'll track me down anywhere in the world if she thinks I'm not doing what she has advised. So it's time to put in.

I've never run so far for so long in my life. And I'm off beer. Apparently it can make you fat (as well as silly).

(G) AUSTRALIAN CRICKET BOARD
12 April 1989

Dear Merv,
Following your selection in the Australian Team to tour England this year, the Board has decided to increase the retainer payable under your Player Contract to the equivalent of $9,000 per annum, applicable from 1 April 1989.

You will therefore receive an additional $1,500.00 during the period from April to September 1989. This increase will be reflected in your usual monthly retainer payments, credited directly to your bank account.

Please don't hesitate to contact me if you have any queries. Any payment enquiries should be referred to Heather Waugh.

Yours sincerely,
Graham Halbish
General Manager

MERV: Of course, our exorbitant wages are paid for by the support of sponsors. Beer manufacturer XXXX is the team's tour sponsor.

AUSTRALIAN CRICKET BOARD
18 April 1989

1989 U.K. TOUR

XXXX Appearances

MAY	Tue 2	London – tour briefing; team photo; sign autograph bats; clothing issue.	
	Sat 6	London	P
	Sat 13	Worcester	P
	Wed 17	Somerset	P
	Thu 18	Somerset	P
	Sat 20	London	P
	Wed 31	Manchester or Birmingham	P
JUNE	Thu 1	Manchester or Birmingham	P
	Sat 3	Derby	P
	Sat 10	Leeds (1st Test)	P
	Sun 11	Leeds – Moortown Golf Day	T
	Wed 14	Birmingham or Manchester	P
	Thu 15	Birmingham or Manchester	P
	Sat 17	Northampton	P
	Tue 20	London	P
	Sat 24	London	P
	Wed 28	Oxford	P
JULY	Sat 1	Swansea	P
	Tue 4	Birmingham	P
	Sat 8	Birmingham	P
	Sun 9	Stratford – Golf Day	T
	Thu 13	Glasgow	P
	Fri 14	XXXX Highland Games – Glasgow	T
	Sat 15	Glasgow	P
	Wed 19	Southampton	P
	Thu 20	Southampton	P

	Sat 22	Bristol	P
	Tue 25	Manchester	P
	Sat 29	Manchester	P
AUG	Wed 2	Nottingham or London	P
	Thu 3	Nottingham or London	P
	Sat 5	Leicester	P
	Tue 8	Nottingham	P
	Sat 12	Nottingham	P
	Wed 16	Canterbury or Hove	P
	Thu 17	Canterbury or Hove	P
	Sat 19	Chelmsford	P
	Tue 22	London	P
	Sat 26	London	P
	Wed 30	London – end of tour lunch	T

P – Pub visits
T – Team appearances

MERV: I wonder if I can visit that many pubs and not drink for the entire tour? It's very important that we get behind our sponsor's product, and the team is more important than the individual.

---

 22 April 1989
1:21 pm

Dear Merv,
'G'day, My name is Melissa J. and I'm 15.
   I think that you are a cool bowler and you must have a lot of fans everywhere.
   I was wondering if I could have a photo of you please as I would be very greatful, Thanks!!!!
                Lots-a-Lubs
                Keep smilin'   MELISSA   Stay Cool!!!!

(**G**) FOOTSCRAY CRICKET CLUB
21 April 1989

Dear Merv,

On behalf of all the players, officials and members of the
Footscray Cricket Club I would like to congratulate you on your
selection for the 1989 England Tour.

To be selected to tour England is, in my opinion, the cricket
'ultimate' and is an honour that you thoroughly deserve.

Even though you are a great ambassador for cricket throughout
Australia, your success has been admired and followed most
intently by the sports lovers of the Western Suburbs. We are all
very proud of your achievements.

At this stage it is unfortunate that we have not been able to get
together to say farewell but I understand that at the moment you
must be the busiest man in Australia.

A presentation for you has been organised but as we have not
been able to organise a club farewell then it will make a good
excuse for a welcome home party.

May I take this opportunity to wish you a healthy, enjoyable
and most successful tour.

> Yours sincerely,
> Warwick Burnham
> President

(**G**) 24 April 1989

Dear Merv,

Thanks very much for ringing from Adelaide on Friday – it was
certainly appreciated.

I was most anxious to have a club farewell for you before you
left, but it was not possible because of your heavy commitments.
A few of the Footscray boys will probably catch up with you on
Thursday night. I apologise that I won't be there as I will be away
for a few days.

I have worked out that the only way to buy you a beer is to enclose a pound note. I trust that one cold, rainy night in England that you can buy yourself a beer on me!

On a personal note I really hope that you have a fantastic tour and that you pick up plenty of wickets.

> Regards
> Warwick

[Pound note pinned to the letter.]

MERV: I've still got the pound note. I'm off beer, Warwick! Ann Quinn has sent me a training, performance and diet diary. I'm in trouble now.

 MERV HUGHES TRAINING DIARY

ASHES TOUR – 1989

TODAY'S PREPARATION DETERMINES
TOMORROW'S ACHIEVEMENT

Dear Merv:

This journal is designed to provide you with an easy and scientifically accurate format for measuring and documenting all your activities. Diaries and journals are not new to serious athletes. In fact you would be hard pressed to find any world class athlete who does not carefully document workouts and biophysical data. Goal setting as well as an appreciation of personal progress, are often the primary motivators for keeping a training journal. We can use all this information to more accurately determine the conditions you require as an individual to perform at your best.

It's all very well to have your own diary, but it will only ever be as good as you want to make it Merv. And that all depends on how much you want to succeed. I can't do the work for you, neither can David, Bobby, Eril, your family or your friends. These people are behind you all the way, but the ball is in your court now Merv. We all know that you can make it and this diary is just one of those ways of making the road to success a little easier.

**SUCCESS IS NOT DETERMINED BY MERELY HAVING THE
'WILL TO SUCCEED' BUT RATHER, SUCCESS IS FOR THOSE WHO
HAVE 'THE WILL TO *PREPARE* TO SUCCEED'**

For you Merv, this means always putting in that little extra after your usual training sessions and playing days, as well as saying no to any tempting foods and drinks. I know you can do it and that dedication and perseverance is sure to pay off with improved performances in the months ahead. In fact, you're already half way there, Merv, because you have made the commitment to be the best you can be. Keep up the great efforts.

Good luck and best wishes always

Ann

 Hilton International Melbourne on the Park
Name: HUGHES, M MR (AUST)

GOOD LUCK FOR THE TOUR
KEITH STACKPOLE

MERV: A telephone message from Keith Stackpole reminds me of the depth of feeling Australian cricketers have for the Ashes Tour. Stacky was involved at Victoria when I first played Sheffield Shield cricket. It's great to hear from him.

CHAPTER TWELVE

The Ashes Tour, 1989

SYDNEY TO BANGKOK

Cocktails

DINNER

Poached Tasmanian Salmon
Supreme of Chicken Capricornia
with a filling of mango and roasted hazelnuts
or
Lobster Thermidor
in a white wine and mustard sauce finished with cheese
Pecan Pie
Fresh Seasonal Fruit
Coffee
Chocolates

SUPPER

King Prawns with Mango
Medallions of Veal Provencale
with a fresh tomato and herb sauce
or
Oriental Duck with Ginger
White Chocolate Mousse
with strawberries and palmiers
Coffee   Tea

BANGKOK TO LONDON

MIDNIGHT SNACK

Marinated Cucumber with Mint
Thai Beef with Fresh Basil
served with savoury rice
or
Vegetable Strudel
Cheese and Grapes
Coffee
Chocolates

REFRESHMENT

Cocktail Sandwiches
Fruit Tartelette with Rum Cream
Toblerone Chocolate
Coffee   Tea

BREAKFAST

Fresh Fruit Platter
Yoghurt with Cinnamon and Dates
Cheese Omelette
with grilled bacon, tomato and saute potatoes
or
Panfried Fillets of Local Fish in Parsley Butter
Hot Croissant
Coffee   Tea

Anniversary Dinner
and *Dinner to the*
Australian Touring Team

Wednesday, 3rd May, 1989

Field Marshal The Lord Bramall
G.C.B., O.B.E., M.C., J.P.
(President of M.C.C.)
in the Chair

Menu

Wines

Gascogne Blanc

Coteaux du Salaves
Rouge

Martell *** Cognac
or
Distinction Port

Seafood Trafalgar

Roast Sirloin of Beef Forestiere
Minted New Potatoes
Mixed Vegetables

Souffle Glace Grand Marnier

Stilton Cheese
with Celery and Biscuits

Coffee and Mints

Toast List

"Her Majesty The Queen"
Proposed by the President of M.C.C.

"The President Designate"
Proposed by the President of M.C.C.
Reply by the President Designate

"M.C.C., Cricket and the Australian Touring Team"
Proposed by Lord Deedes, M.C., P.C., D.L.
Reply by Mr. A. R. Border
Captain, Australian Touring Team

 Tullamarine

19 May 1989

Good Morning/Afternoon/Evening Mervyn, how the hell are you?
Sorry I didn't get to the airport, I thought the plane left at
11.30am, and at 11.30am I was in no state really for much at all.

Oh well, enough of the bullshit.

So you hate England. Well there you go.

Yes I have eaten all my chewies – thank you.

What have I been up to. Well I haven't been getting a bit lately,
bit of a worry when you don't know where your next Tammy is
coming from – eh Merv, you'd know all about this wouldn't you,
you little Cliff Richard You.

No only kidding, men are breaking down the f***ing doors.

Yes, I had an exciting night the other night, I went to a
clairvoyant. Mate, she was good. She reckons that I'm going to
get married. Marie is going to become pregnant . . . enough to
depress anyone eh . . . I can see it now . . .

Never mind . . . things could be worse . . . I wont say it . . . Yes I
will, I could be marrying you!!

Yes I also went to this party the other Saturday night, It was my
hairdressers 21st. Chrissy dominated. (for a change) – excuse me
I just have to open the mail. Back again.

Yes there were all these yuppies and mammas and uncles and
aunties and then there was me . . . hah, you've gotta laugh I
s'pose. But I have turned over a new leaf . . . no more excessive
drinking.

Falling, over, hanging shit, its so out of character (oops) for me.

Sheree is walking now.

Terry & Gail are fine.

Kaz is fine.

My ovaries haven't been better.

Work is giving me the shits. I need a holiday. I'm thinking
seriously about going to Fiji to work on a mission – don't laugh.

Or going to America next year. We'll just see . . .
Oh well, not much more news
Catch you
Chrissy

MERV: Chrissy Squires is sister of Marie and Terry Squires.

MERV: I am in England, trying hard but not getting a run. We have played the three One Day games and at the moment I don't look like making the First Test. I just have to bowl faster and shorter at the bowlers when they are batting.

 Melbourne

7 June 1989

Dear Merv,

BLOOD TEST RESULTS

	Your Results	Average
Hb	15.5	(13.0–18.0)
Wcc	10.75	(4.0–11.0)
Chol	5.32	(less than 5.5) – Dr Peter Brukner says less than 5.0
Trig	0.81	(0.5–2.0)
Feriston	1.28	(Greater than 100)

All the team tested except for David Boon, had cholesterol greater than 5, and you were the second best. Well done. As I said on the phone, its on the borderline of high. The usual acceptance is under 5.5 – but some say under 5. In any case you do need to watch it.

Just follow the guidelines we've discussed and you'll be right. Cut down on those FATS.

I forgot to ask you a few questions on the phone. Presumably you got the rubber (Hope no one else is censoring this letter!!) Have you tried those exercises? They won't take you long and will be time well spent. Have you been having your drink? – NOT beer! You haven't mentioned it, so I assume not. You could always take along a beer bottle full – like Pat did for you that night! – that will please 4X – and/or your English beer company!

All the comments should make sense on your nutritional sheets. How do your 'in between' weeks go? Do you binge on those weeks? Remember MODERATION is the key.

Sorry to hear you were a little down. It's a long trip and everyone will have those times along the way. Freezing cold Melbourne isn't all that good! This is actually my first time home since 1982 at this time of year.

I have photocopied another chapter of Rudi's book for you, with pertinent comments included along the way, relevant to you. He raises a lot of valid points, which may help you through the long months ahead. Please don't think, I think you're lacking in self-confidence – I don't think that's a concern for you! However, every athlete at some stage or another goes through lows and slumps and often gets the situation out of all proportion to what it really is. All your hard work, long hours and commitment to doing your best will be rewarded Merv. It just doesn't happen overnight. And you would not have been selected if the selectors didn't have faith in you and believe in your ability. So hang in there mate. Pat didn't win Wimbledon because of what he did a few weeks before – it was a result of the hard work and dedication over many, many years.

Hopefully by the time you read this letter, this will all be irrelevant. In any case, it's sometimes good to read these things on days when you're down. As I've said to you before 'it's today's preparation that determines tomorrows achievement'.

Good luck
Ann

P.S. How about a goal of 95kg – to keep and maintain – through to the end of the trip, i.e. gradually decrease to 95 – and keep it there.

First Test v England at Headingley, Leeds
(8, 9, 10, 12, 13 June 1989)
Australia 7 dec. 601 and 3 dec. 230 defeated
England 430 and 191 by 210 runs.
M. Hughes 1/92 and 3/36. First inns 71, second inns dnb.

MERV: After not playing in any of the three One Day Internationals, I was lucky to get a start in the First Test. Carl Rackemann is injured (not due to an injury in the nets) and the selectors played four quicks, so I got the nod and Greg Campbell played his first Test.

I'm lucky to have some wonderful people helping me out. I'm working a lot with Geoff Lawson and Terry Alderman, Bob Simpson is having a huge influence on every aspect of my game and Ann Quinn is constantly reminding me about the importance of preparation.

G TO   Merv Hughes
FROM   Ann Quinn
COMPANY Australian Cricket Team
            Leeds Broadford Post House Hotel
DATE   9 June 1989

COMMENTS
Congratulations
Hard work always pays off. Just make the next 5 days winners.
        Good luck
        Ann

MERV: Ann sent me this after the first day of the Test. We had batted and I was lucky enough to stay in long enough to make 71. A lot less bruises than after my 72 against the Windies in my previous Test.

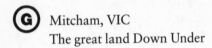

(G)   Mitcham, VIC
The great land Down Under

15 June 1989

Dear Merv:
First and foremost, a big CONGRATULATIONS. What a star, and not only as a bowler, but also as a batsman. 'Oddball Merv' was the big headlines on the front page of the Sun the other day. We are cutting out all your articles for you. My Dad doesn't miss a thing. By the time you get home, you'll have to hire a truck to come and get them.

I am sure the Merv Hughes I talk to next time, will sound a lot better than the one I talked to last week. As you will realise, when you finally get it, the letter I sent you will be a little meaningless, but there's lots of good little quotes and tips there to keep for later reference. Have you read all the concentration article yet? Too busy celebrating probably!! Don't forget, you're not supposed to break Marsh's record until Australia have won THE Ashes, not the first Ashes Test! We should have had a bet. I could have done well for myself. So much for not drinking at all until the end!!!! Did I not hear you correctly before you left Australia? I'll have to think up something for the rest of the tour re drinking. Talking of bets, Nicole (*Provis*) has lost five kilograms. That's quite an incredible feat for her. Do you still want to go out to dinner in London with Nicky and Pat? Let me know as I won't be there to organise everyone, but anything is possible. I speak to Nicky regularly and she always asks after you and says she see's you a lot on TV (she's now in Eastbourne – down South).

By the way, if you want to go to Wimbledon, just give Nicole a call, or Pat could set you up too, although he may have difficulty not being a competitor this year. Nicole will certainly look after you. I will fax you a phone number as soon as she gets one. (She rents a house for the two weeks). Also, another close friend, Julie Richardson, would look after you, Julie is the No 2 NZ player. . . . She'll be there for the week before and weeks of Wimbledon. She always stays with me each Oz Open. There's also Hana, although I know she has a lot of family she'll have to look after. Talking of tickets, Paul McNamee may give you a call to go to Lord's one day, and his Director of Oz Tennis (Paul's organization, he set up for under privileged kids) Susie Norton will more than likely call you. She's a darling, full of personality, and heaps of fun. Pat sends his apologies for not coming that day, but hoped to catch up with you soon. I spoke to him this morning, and he's really happy, and having a great time, which is the most important thing.

I am now wait-listed on July 22 and 23 to come to London, and will have to stay in London most of the first week as Pat will still be there. We have to do a lot of muscle testing as he'll have huge imbalances etc, and he should be right by then to get going a bit more. I figure I will probably come up for the Fourth Test for a few days. It looks as though it's a fair way away, so will probably just come up for about three days. After all it's not really far away when you're coming from Australia! One of my girlfriends in London may come up with me, as well as one of Pat's mates (Dean Barclay: you probably already met him). It will be good also to catch up with Simon, and I also have to go to the university in Birmingham for a government study.

By the way, don't worry about weights now that you are competing most of the time. However, the rubber band workouts should prove to be an efficient and effective way to get started on those weak legs of yours. I am dying to hear how they lasted during the Test.

That's about the latest this end. Let me know what you think of your new look diet analysis. This is all for your benefit only Merv, so tell me what you get more out of – ie more use to you. I am still waiting for more changes to occur, but you're headed in the right direction.

Once again, Congratulations. Keep up the great work, and I look forward to chatting with you soon.

Regards

Ann

P.S. Keep up those 'winning days' at Lords

PPS Let me know if you want any information about topics sent over, or other little things to help you. (eg relaxation, imagery: or let me know where you think you could improve)

Also, if you want anything brought over, just let me know.

Also, did you receive my fax? What is the fax number of the bus? Would it be better to send something to that fax?

 Hoppers Xing

18 June 1989

Dear Merv,
How in the heck are you? Just felt like saying gidday and letting you know how well the boys played (up) at Portland. You'll be too busy to read this I guess but I couldn't trust FOX FM to telling you so I thought I'd write anyway. [**I'm doing regular reports back to the Fox radio network in Australia while I'm on tour.**]
Congrat's on your half-century & your wickets. We all watched you from Portland Motel rooms. Actually you still had a strong influence on the men they didn't go to the Pub Fri night for fear of missing your batting efforts . . . Darren Watkins was very drunk & flashed his tally wacker to Boofy, Lyn Miles & Stretch and totally humiliated himself when some-one shit stirred him the next day. Boy he was upset with himself, he's still with Lisa Wyner I guess you know. Boofy & Trish had no-one. Naz swears he didn't miss you. Well CT & I bunked in with Stell & Jane & had heaps of laughs. Let Pete know Jane's fully recovered, she'll know what I'm on about.

So how's life with you, you big superstar? I've really missed you even though I never popped around much I was always thinking about you. I'm still here for you to talk to too. Don't ever forget or I'll break your other cheekbone. Say, do you socialise with Neil Foster, I do remember when we went Chinese with him that was a great night. I guess it's awkward when you're playing enemies.

Sorry I left out ↑ back up there that the Men's A grade won by 2 pts in the GF. They played so bad to start with then by freak of nature & the interceptor's return to form they up & won. Shane played well Steve was fast to break yet again & Terry hit some good long shots.

Rumour has it Ross & Josie are trying to make babies & in 6 mths Squiz should have no 2 started Deb & Rob's house is 3mths away from completion. They're sick of living in a van.

Gee your baby brother's growing up fast. He's keen on the basketball & footy. He's not too shy anymore either, gives cuddles & nurses just like his big brother does.

Clint & Sharon are well they thoroughly enjoyed themselves at Peta's send off night.

Anyway I got a wave out of (Gavin) [Snappa] the other day up the main st. He should be pleased with his house/garden. Looks ACE!! Are you in the wedding? Craig will be too I hope? He idolizes Gavin, always has done. Even if they don't talk he still loves him. So who do you love at the moment??? Must be hard to keep the women off. Met any wistful English women yet?? Lovely soft skin? Sorry just stirring.

Well I guess I've said enough. Love writing too much. Oh Collin Devereaux was 30 on June 11. Just to make you feel old. I bet that bugs you too! We're all getting on. But feeling young & doing whatever you want is better than anything. No restrictions. Great to talk to you.

Mervy hope you succeed just like Slabs. Take care of yourself, and for goodness sakes don't forget to wear protection. Your sunblock I mean.

> Love ya
> Kato XXX

FOOTSCRAY CRICKET CLUB
22 June 1989

Mr. M. Hughes
Australian Cricket Team
C/- Westbury Hotel
Conduit Street
London WIA4UH

By Fax:

Dear Merv,
Congratulations upon your achievements so far on Tour. You certainly showed them how to play the game with both bat and ball at Headingley.

All the best for the second Test from everybody at Footscray.
Regards,
Warwick Burnham

P.S. Try to win as quickly as possible so that I can get a decent night's sleep!

 Second Test v England at Lord's, London
(22, 23, 24, 26, 27 June 1989)
Australia 528 and 4 for 119 defeated
England 286 and 359 by six wickets.
M. Hughes 4/71 and 2/44. First inns 30, second inns dnb.

G

The High Commissioner for Australia
The Hon. Douglas MᶜClelland, AC
requests the pleasure of the company of

Mr M Hughes

at a reception in honour of
The Hon. Bob Hawke, AC, MP
Prime Minister of Australia
and Mʳˢ Hawke
at Australia House on Friday 23ʳᵈ June 1989

7.00 pm - 9.00 pm

R.S.V.P. Social Secretary
Australia House, Strand WC2B 4LA
01-438 8763

Please present this card on arrival

R Lara

4 July 1989

G'Day Merv

How the f*** are you? Played any cricket lately? Nothing shits me but waking up to your voice every morning on the radio comes close. Only joking.

I've been doing f***-all lately just working. Go to work in the dark come home in the dark what can you do. Went up to Mt. Beauty with Prissa and Barnsy on the long weekend. Had a good time, pretty pissy weekend. Met a few of the locals had a good laugh. Barnsys still as slow as ever.

Barnsy played his first game in the twos at Lara last week. I didn't see the game but they reckon he went all right. He hasn't changed, he got a blood nose before he got on, while he was on the bench. Typical.

Lara's not going too bad, they've won three games and only just lost a couple of close ones. Haven't seen many games because I work nearly every Saturday. What a wog hey. They've had a bad run with injuries. Glen Hearn, Waldo and Bomber have all had knee reconstructions in the past two months. They said Bomber won't play again. Russell Scott did his knee on Saturday but I don't know how bad it was.

Damage is playing for Anakie and a few other blokes have left. Its not the same as it used to be. Penguin and I go down on Thursday nights for a couple. Its good when the cricket's on. You've got a few backslappers down here.

The Adelaide boys came over last weekend and we went to the state of origin game. Fair crowd 92,000. Vic's gave them a hiding. And we gave the boys shit. They were big mouthing before the game but we soon shut them up. Took them to the wayside on Friday night after the hillbilly. We were on the piss all weekend. Thank Christ they went home so I can dry out.

Not for long. Got Chookas 21st on this Saturday and Sunday so it will be another big one this weekend. Must be getting old I can't even remember our 21sts.

Blue got a letter off Freda last week about the usual. I couldn't understand it. Probably like this one.

It sounds like they're all fighting fit down there. Gazza's playing truckloads of sport. Good on him. I bet Pop wishes he still was playing. Say G'day to Pete if she's still over there.

Geelongs kicking arse at the moment. Hope they keep it up. Keep giving Barnsy shit about it but he reckons they're all poofs down there and Footscray's a team of goers. I don't know about goers. I think they've gone.

Speaking of wigs, there's heeps around now, I've spotted about five in the last week without even trying. F***ing wankers – unless they wear em to keep there scones warm or something.

Sharyn and Stacey are going allright. Sharyn's farting around getting the wedding organised. There's only about 14 weeks to go so I've been told. We got two '54 Chevs for wedding cars. They look shit hot. Sharyn said to say hello. I better piss off now and get some sleep so you can wake me up in the morning. Keep up the good cricket. Knock a few pommy heads off. All the best.

SNAPPA

P.S. Sharyn wants to know if you can bring back a Paddington Bear for her. To sit on the bed. About a foot tall.

MERV: Sharyn is Snappa's fiancée.

MERV: Part of my arrangement with Ann Quinn was to write down everything I ate and fax it to her each week. This had a couple of effects. Every time I opened the bar fridge and looked at the chocolates, I knew if I had anything I'd have to write it down, and then I'd have to eat something good to make up for it, and then some time next week when I had forgotten the pleasure of eating whatever it was that I wanted to eat, I'd get a phone call or a fax from Ann and she'd go crook at me and I'd wonder if it was all worth it. So I wouldn't take anything out of the fridge.

Perhaps that was her strategy.

> Third Test v England at Edgbaston, Birmingham
> (6, 7, 8, 10, 11 July 1989)
> Australia 424 and 2/158 drew with England 242.
> M. Hughes 2/68. First inns 2, second inns dnb.
> It rained.

(**G**) MY FUEL FOR THE WEEK
Week Starting 10 July 1989

MONDAY 10th
Breakfast Rice Bubbles —*what kind of milk did you have with it?*
     Fruit Salad —*Vital or semi-skim or skim milk is what to have here.*
     Baked Beans
     1 Slice Toast – no butter ✓
     3 Glasses Orange Juice —*Drink natural. Fresh and natural is always best.*

Snacks/Drinks   3 Glasses Enduro Boost ✓

Lunch   3 Glasses Enduro Boost ✓
¼ chicken – no skin —*good*
1 bread roll —*I hope it was brown*
½ cup Beans ✓
3 boiled potatoes ✓ —*no butter ...?*

Dinner

Snacks/Drinks   1 Orange ✓
4 Bananas ✓
4 Glasses Enduro Boost ✓
3 bottles (sml) diet coke —*better than regular coke.*

TUESDAY
Breakfast   Rice Bubbles —*How much?*
Fruit Salad —*How much? What kind?*
  Baked Beans —*OK – not the greatest*
1 Slice Toast —*Any butter?*

Snacks/Drinks   2 Glasses orange juice —*I hope it was natural*
3 Glasses Enduro Boost ✓

Lunch   ¼ chicken no skin —*Good*
1 cup peas ✓
3 boiled potatoes ✓

Dinner

Snacks/Drinks   15 pints beer —*You're getting worse. I hate to think what you'll be drinking at the end of the tour. Marsh's record will be broken many times over. Don't destroy all that good hard work.*
1 pint = 250 calories That's 3,750 CALORIES This is not a substitute for dinner, and its even worse to drink on an empty stomach. That = a whole day's eating, and even more.
Did you starve the next day? or you could run 37.5 miles to run all that off. Its also more than a pound in body weight – sorry – FAT weight – and you know how hard that is to take off.

MERV: See what I mean? Lucky we only drew the Test match.

MERV: I have been going to church for ten years. We called it church, but it is really the Castle Hotel in North Melbourne, we call it church because everyone's there on Sundays. For five years I have been annoying the shit out of a young lady who is a regular. Mum was really impressed when I said I'd met a girl at church. But Sue didn't seem nearly as impressed with me as I'd hoped. She was always friendly, but that was about it. So I've given up on her . . .

 Prellipe
Yugoslavia

Sunday morning 16 July 1989

Hi Merv.
How are you and all the boys?
   Just finished my daily tobacco threading & heading out in the shed – now about to get into some yummy chocky cake & turkish caffe!
   I'm living with a Yugoslavian family in rural Prellipe – very poor – but a great education for me. Everyone is so content & at ease, busily working. Growing chillies and tobacco, baking bread, scrubbing clothes clean, pumping own water, hole in ground for toilet – I feel like I'm back in the 1920's. Have been here for five days. Heading off tomorrow for Greece. Prior to here we were in Dubrovnic for two wks staying there with a private family. Its fantastic when one gets the opportunity to stay in private dwellings, one really sees the true customs & ways of life in these amazing countries . . .
   Been in Yugoslavia now for about three wks & totally loved every moment.
   Prior to Yugoslavia, France, Spain, Switzerland & Italy – what a buzz. Each country so different & so much to offer. Got so much out of Italy & Switzerland. Switzerland is like a fairytale country with such wonderful people. Italy full of romance & red

wine and artwork, architecture so much history to take in. Zurich was party, party, party, with wine, hash, people, by the Zurich lake where everyone hangs out after work – a glorious place!

After there Greece & islands, Turkey, Israel, Egypt, back to Paris, London – I really would love to catch you – is it possible you might stay longer than the tour. Peta sent my mum your itinerary for me which I have now got, it says you fly out 1st September – shit! I don't know if I'll be there by then – really would love to see your beautiful face (Mumma just came up to me & planted a huge kiss on my face, patting my hair – she loves me! We can't understand each other – not a word, she's about 74 & an amazing worker!) Back to you my mate – please try & stay longer than the 1st of Sept . . .

Please write & tell me what your up too & all the news of the team & any world news that's happening – I have a Turkey address & if you write *now* I'll definitely get it – PLEASE! PLEASE! PLEASE!

Susan Kelly
Post Restante   I'll be there in approx. 3 wks
General Post Office   for a couple of days.
Adana
Turkey

Its two months since I left Aussie land for the second time, don't miss it much but I do miss the people especially Lizzy. Two days ago Jacinta & I were sitting in a tiny pub on the outskirts of Prellipe when all of a sudden amongst Yugoslavian music came Jason Donavan – both of us looked at each other & burst into tears & laughing at the same time – really couldn't believe what we were hearing – yes Melbourne was definitely still with us in a strong way.

Hows the team going? How many English ladies have you charmed off their feet with your smooth ways?

If you can you should make an effort to see the Melody Cords while in England – they are playing in the comedy festival in Edinburgh at the Carlton Studios from the 10 August for three wks. If you make it, to see them, please say hello to Jeremy for me (lead guitarist) – he's a wonderful person – would really love to see them also – I hope I make it back in time, time slips away so quickly with so much to do! . . .

Oh well my dear friend, I'll sign off now, missing you terribly & hope to see you. Hope all is going well for you. Remember me on the 28th July – big 26th my God baby we're getting on – still feel 18 though – loving every bit of life!

Love you & take care, God Bless,

Suzan (Sprite) Kelly

XXXX

P.S. Say gidday to Peta for me & give her my love X

Keep Smiling

Thinking of you in Yugoslavia

X

MERV: Start to ignore them and see what happens! I think I'll marry that girl one day.

---

 25 July 1989

Hilly,

How the f*** are ya? Firstly, I must apologise for not catching up with you in the three weeks or so before you left for England, but I realise you had a hectic schedule and were in demand plus I was extremely busy working on the house I bought.

I don't suppose you have missed much since you've been away as things have been *rolling* along quietly. Same old routine happening – working, going out, getting pissed, not getting a root, talking shit to dippy stinkers, then going home for a John Bull! Thank goodness for Robert Palmer's Mum and his four sisters!

Jason left the Wayside (which you probably already know) and had a farewell send off on Friday June 30. Great night! Sucked face with a *couple* of stinkers (no tanny though) and sat around

the piano singing songs until 6.30 am approx. Went to the Vic v
SA state of origin that afternoon, so it was a good weekend.

I've just got back from a few days in the snow at Falls Creek
and man what a good time! Skiing, going out, getting pissed, not
getting a root, talking shit to dippy stinkers, then going home for
a John Bull! A truly classical weekend, I went with 'Y' and a few
of her Sydney friends . . .

Sheilas!! AAAGH!! What a disaster that scene is. Meeting
many new and nice ones but nothing that sends shivers through
the foreskin. Met one that I'm pretty keen on but you know the
old story – the one you want is the one that doesn't want you. The
worst part is there's nothing that can be really done about it – or is
there? Do you Scotty Palmer and keep punching or do you Simon
Beasley and retire?

When you left for England I had just quit my job and I started
a new one on May 1. Well I've now quit that job and leave on
August 11. I'm going to work for a great new company. I'm
looking forward to it.

I've just recently rejoined the Gym at South Melbourne and
there's quite a few familiar faces – Richard, Johnno and Max all
say G'Day, just to name a few. Max (of MAX, MAX – Relax!
fame) is going to England on August 15 and mentioned that he
would like to catch up with you while he is over there – I've given
him the name of your Hotel but mentioned that you'll be busy
and may not have any free time available.

I've been going to see the Saints play most Saturdays and our
mate Sicko plays for them now. He's taken me into the players'
after match entertainment room and drank truckloads!! He passes
on his best wishes, as does Hawker, and both look forward to
having a mineral water with you on your return.

I'm off to New Zealand on September 9 for two weeks skiing
(snow). Looking forward to that as I have never been out of OZ
before. Just imagine two weeks over there skiing, going out,
getting pissed, not getting a root, talking shit to dippy stinkers,
then going home for a John Bull! Something different, hey!

A few people would like to send a cheerio but I told them to
f*** off and write their own letter! Seriously – Lisa, Ronnie,
Karen, Barnsey, 'Y' [name changed] (who has included a letter

of her own), Karen, Hobbsy, Kirk, Ivo, Karen, Jeff, Rod and not forgetting Karen.

Anyway, I've spoken enough about me and the happenings here but I've left this part to last on purpose. I think its absolutely wonderful that you are doing so well for yourself both on and off the field. I am really enjoying sitting up to 3 am each day of the Tests and watch you perform so well, and I believe the Promotions are going wonderfully well too. Keep up the good work. That's all – I'm not going to lick your arse anymore than that!

Gotta go Hilly, catch you soon, good luck and all that sort of stuff.

> Mr 'X' [**Name changed to protect identity, but I *can* tell you I played footy with him.**]

MERV: The following was in the same envelope, as X and Y were sharing a house at the time.

 31 July 1989 [**It must have taken X six days to write his letter.**]

Swervin Merv,
How the F— are you, doing alright by the sounds of things. Well nothing much has changed in Old Melbourne town. Boothie, Gaisey, Ange and myself are still single but there have been a few interests for some of us. Actually I don't get to see them very much these days probably because I've put the Castle on hold for a little while and I know that they still go every Sunday. I've just spent a week up at Falls Creek with Jenny (big Red), her boyfriend and a friend of his. It was a great laugh as Jen and I were learning to ski. As 'X' probably told you he came up for a day or two and we all celebrated my 27th birthday up there. Wasn't very exciting when you realise 30 is only three years away and as 'X' says only about five good breeding years left in me – nice hey. Haven't seen much of Danny but we still see a bit of Ron. I went to A Ball with him a few weeks ago it was a good night Ron had four beers and was gone – I ended up driving him home.

I am also going to New Zealand in September with a pommie girl from work. We are doing a Contiki tour – should be good fun as I did one around Europe which was great.

I'm trying to think of any juicy gossip but there has been a drastic fall of excitement, lust and just outright gossip since you left. Lisa is 'IN LOVE' and I wouldn't be surprised if they get hitched next year.

Well you sound as though you are doing alright in the girly stakes. 'X' and I heard on Fox one morning that you had a girl – we couldn't get in the car to go to work quick enough. We stopped at the first newsagent to get the SUN and to get the lowdown. Well she does have big tits doesn't she.

You Aussie boys have done us proud over in pommy land lets hope we can clinch the next two as well. I've even watched a bit of it on tele myself – very unusual.

Anyway just a short note to let you know we're thinking of you and if I must admit missing you too. Amigos just isn't the same without you and the conversation is so boring and sexless.

I do hope you have been having a great time. I know you have been, a girl I used to work with is in London and she has sent me a few tabloids from the newspapers over there. I also hope you are practising safe sex and using a condom. We don't want you to catch any English diseases I hear they are the worst kind. I ask the boys if they use condoms 'X' doesn't tell me and Ron says the need doesn't seem to arise that much. Oh well his time will come I'm sure.

I went out with 'X' and Ron on Saturday and Marie and Bernie were there. That was the first time I actually spoke to Marie and she's a very nice girly. She told us that you were coming home on 2nd September so we will catch up with you some time around then.

See you soon.
Love Ms 'Y'

Fourth Test v England at Old Trafford, Manchester
(27, 28, 29, 31 July and 1 August 1989)
Australia 447 and 1 for 81 defeated
England 260 and 264 by nine wickets.
M. Hughes 1/55 and 1/45. First inns 3, second inns dnb.
Australia regains the Ashes.

G AUSTRALIAN CRICKET BOARD
2 August 1989

Mr. M. Hughes
C/- The Albany
St. James Street
Nottinghamshire NG1 6BN
England

Dear Merv,
Congratulations on a magnificent Ashes victory.

From all of the reports received here in Australia and my brief
visit to Edgbaston, the professional manner in which the tour has
been approached and carried out by the whole of the Australian
touring party has been exemplary.

To be part of such a touring team that has been the first
Australian team for 25 years to win back the Ashes in England
when they have been held by England must give you a great sense
of pride and achievement that will endure for the rest of your life.

Well done – the victory will be extremely beneficial to cricket in
Australia.

Good luck for the remainder of the tour and your future cricket
career and thank you on behalf of the Australian Cricket Board
for such a wonderful achievement.

Kind Regards
Malcolm Gray
Chairman

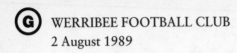

WERRIBEE FOOTBALL CLUB
2 August 1989

Merv Hughes
Australian Cricket Team
Albany Hotel

ON BEHALF OF THE PLAYERS, OFFICIALS AND MEMBERS
OF THE WERRIBEE FOOTBALL CLUB I CONGRATULATE
YOU ON THE MARVELLOUS ACHIEVEMENT OF BEING
PART OF THE HISTORY-MAKING TEST ELEVEN.
WE ARE PROUD OF YOU AND YOUR TEAMMATES.
CHAD RAVLICH
SECRETARY

CHAPTER THIRTEEN

London, Sydney, Hyderabad, Sharjah and Los Angeles

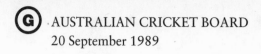

G AUSTRALIAN CRICKET BOARD

20 September 1989

Dear Merv,

Ashes '99 Victory Celebrations

I am pleased to confirm the arrangements in regard to the functions planned for Melbourne and Sydney next week.

Travel – attached is a schedule of flights booked with Ansett. In view of the uncertainty with the current pilots' dispute, there may be a change to your flight at short notice. If you are not going to be at your normal phone number on Monday, would you please ring Marie Stubbs at the Board office to double check your departure time for Melbourne. Flights from Perth and Tasmania are most likely to be affected.

Accommodation – Southern Cross Hotel Melbourne, arranged by North Melbourne Football Club as part of their original invitation; double rooms, bed and breakfast basis.

Dinner – enclosed are your official invitation and tickets. We are expecting about 800 people to attend, including several VIPs, ACB Directors and Selectors, representatives of all Board sponsors and the commercial world and over 250 members of the general public.

The evening will start at 6.30 p.m. with pre-dinner drinks for the touring party, Directors, Selectors, Board management and wives only, with other special guests joining us at 7.00 p.m. and the dinner commencing at 7.30 p.m.

Sydney – the touring party and wives are currently booked to Sydney on Thursday morning on AN 14 10.00 a.m. returning from Sydney on AN 27 at 5.00 p.m. Once in Sydney, the group will be taken to the Regent Hotel and from there the players will travel in a fleet of twelve open BMWs through city streets to the Darling Harbour Convention Centre, where the official lunch will be held – over 1,500 people have accepted.

VFL Grand Final – the North Melbourne Football Club Grand Final Breakfast will commence at 7.15 a.m., with the touring party being special guests of honor. This should conclude about 10.00 a.m.; lunch will be provided at the hotel and there will be bus transport to and from the MCG; seating will be outside the cricket dressing rooms. The players will do a lap of honor of the MCG in open cars as part of the pre-match entertainment which will be telecast to an estimated audience of eighty million people in the UK, France, Holland, Japan, USA, Canada and New Zealand.

Dress – for all official appearances and travel, please wear your team uniform, except for the VFL lap of honor for which you will need to bring white trousers and shirt, with the blazer to be worn also.

Mementos – there are a number of people who are giving freely of their skills and services to ensure that next week is a memorable time for you and your team mates. It would be fitting for the team to make presentations to these people and in that regard we are preparing ten stumps (similar to those presented to you in England) and fifteen bats for signature on Wednesday afternoon prior to the dinner.

Friday – despite a number of other invitations, including one from the Lord Mayor of Melbourne for the team to participate in a public parade, all have been declined so that Friday is a free day. I understand from Laurie Sawle that Ian Stanley is endeavouring to arrange access to Royal Melbourne for those who want to play golf.

If you have any queries please don't hesitate to ring me.

   With best wishes,
            Yours sincerely,
            D.L. Richards
            Chief Executive

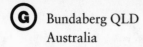 Bundaberg QLD
Australia

15 October 1989

Dear Merv Hughes,
I wish to congratulate you and the team for bringing home the
Ashes from the poms. You have showed Australia that you could
do it and do it extremely well. You and the team deserved all the
great success from the English Tour despite the doubts and lack of
support here in Australia. I must admit that you have fans here in
Bundy and that we admire your humour on the grounds.
 Well done, hope to see you in Bundy
   Sincerely,
   Daniel G.
   B.E., M.Sc.

 Glen Iris 3146

18 October 1989

Dear Merv,
Hearty congratulations on your splendid season with the
Australian Test Team in England.
 You bowled with admirable control and your occasional bull
dog bouncer had the moustaches of the English batsmen quivering
and the clean-shaven types ducking for cover without looking.
 From what I hear, your great team spirit and genuine interest in
the performances of your team mates also made an important
contribution to the memorable victory.
  Congratulations once again,
   Yours sincerely,
   L. H. S. T.

MERV: Lindsay Thompson is a former Premier of Victoria. I know when I get a personal note like this that the writer is a genuine fan of the game. That someone like him should take the time to write to me is quite an honour.

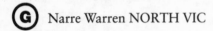

(G) Narre Warren NORTH VIC

19 August 1989

To Mr Hughes,
how are you? MY name's Brendan W. We've shifted into our new house on the 13th of August. How is cricket? I like cricket. Sometimes I watch the cricket on the T.V. My Dad plays cricket and he has a lot of trophies. Thanks for reading my letter.
                    'Brendan W.'

MERV: My pleasure, Brendan. Great to catch up with your news. I'm buggered if I know.

(G) AUSTRALIAN CRICKET BOARD
20 September 1989

Dear Merv,
The Board's decision to accept the revised invitation for the Nehru series was not an easy one and I want to explain our reasoning.
    On the one hand the Board would not normally agree to another overseas tour between an England tour and the start of the following home season. State Associations obviously want their best available players for the maximum number of matches and, after the Ashes win this year, good early season attendances would have been anticipated.
    On the other hand, the prosperity of cricket in Australia and

therefore your financial future as a cricketer, depends on our ability to stage International cricket successfully here each season. Because the home season of all other countries (excluding England) coincides to a greater or lesser extent with ours, the Board comes under pressure to have the Australian team tour overseas in November, December and January, in the same way that we seek to have overseas tours to Australia at that time.

I visited Calcutta in August for future tours negotiations and as a result, India has now agreed to a Test tour of Australia in 1991/92 and a One Day shorter tour in 1994/95. For our part, we have agreed to consider an invitation for a Test tour to India in late 1993 and have accepted the Nehru Cup invitation, but only after reaching agreement on a number of important matters affecting the Australian team. They are:

- the date of the series has been brought forward ten days to allow sufficient time between the Nehru final and our first home Test of 1989/90.
- the organising committee has agreed to provide business class travel in recognition of the short notice and unique timing of this tour.
- prize money and the daily meal allowance have been significantly increased.
- the tour guarantee has also been increased to provide for a special tour fee.
- Australia's matches are played in major centres with a minimum of travel including direct flights between match venues.
  Details are set out in the attached team letter.

Unfortunately I was unable to negotiate Charlie Pinto's services as liaison officer, as he has left Trade Wings. I met with Charlie and he sends his best wishes to the players who toured in 1986 and/or 1987. There will be a liaison officer appointed by Trade Wings, the official travel agents for the Indian Board.

I trust the above is helpful to you in understanding the Board's thinking regarding this particular tour and I extend our best wishes for another successful Australian visit to India.

Yours sincerely,

D.L. Richards

Chief Executive

MERV: Provision of Business Class seats is a special treat. That will make us want to go there. At least I can now say I have played cricket in the sub-continent.

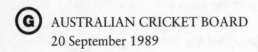

(G) AUSTRALIAN CRICKET BOARD
20 September 1989

Dear Merv,

1989 Tour to India, Nehru Series

I am pleased to confirm your conditional selection for this tour. The official title of the series is 'MRF World Series for the Jawaharlal Nehru Cup'.

Please read the information provided below; a further team letter will follow closer to the tour.

1. Tour Party

Allan Border (Captain)	Geoff Lawson
Geoff Marsh (V.C))	Tim May
Terry Alderman	Tom Moody
David Boon	Simon O'Donnell
Ian Healy	Mark Taylor
Merv Hughes	Peter Taylor
Dean Jones	Steve Waugh
Manager:	Alan Crompton (NSW Board Director)
Coach:	Bob Simpson
Physiotherapist:	Errol Alcott

2. **Tour Itinerary**
2.1. **Travel**

Oct 15   Departure for India via Singapore. Team
              members will leave directly from their home city
              to Singapore where the team will meet to join
              Air Canada flight AC889 to Bombay for transit
              and then on to Hyderabad.

Nov 3   Return to Australia; arriving Sunday 5
              November . . .

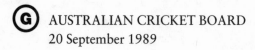

G AUSTRALIAN CRICKET BOARD
20 September 1989

Dear Merv,
Just when you thought you had got rid of me for a few weeks, I
am back to remind you that we have yet another important
challenge to meet.

The more success we have, the greater our responsibility
becomes. It would be easy to write off the Nehru Tournament as
unimportant. In fact, many years down the track it will most
likely be forgotten. Right now, however, it is important and vital
to our development.

As World Champions at One Day Cricket, and after a highly
acclaimed tour of England, we have now made a major shift up the
ladder in world cricket. We are still however, far from our true potential and until we fulfil that, we cannot afford to rest on our laurels.

The purpose of this letter is to remind you that we are now
embarking on another challenge and you are expected to arrive in
India in peak physical condition. Errol will have the scales with
him and I have replenished the 'BALL BAG'. Make a yard prior to
India and it will be easier in the heat of the sub-continent.

                    Yours sincerely,
                    Bob Simpson
                    Coach

MERV: When I caught up with Errol Alcott, I asked him what the dietary regime would be for our stay. He replied, 'No regime, Merv. No-one ever puts weight on in India.' Four weeks later I was eight kilograms heavier.

 WERRIBEE FOOTBALL CLUB
29 October 1989

Dear Merv,
On behalf of the Werribee Football Club I invite you to accept a Life Membership of this club. This Life membership has been awarded to you for your contribution to this club, on and off the field, and also for your wider involvement in sport which has brought the name of both this (town's) Football and Cricket (clubs) to national prominence.

Depending on your commitments, which must be time-consuming, and your ability to attend, we would like to present the Life membership to you at a function at the Sports Club. This function would be two fold, the presentation of the Award and also a thank you by the people of Werribee for your contribution to sport. I do not think that there has been a Werribee 'thank you' to you as yet.

If this function does get off the ground it will be a joint venture by the Werribee Football and Cricket clubs.

To enable pre-planning it would be better, if your commitments allow, to make the presentation early in the new year.

As I will be away for a few weeks during November could you contact Eddie Marriott or Kirk Norton with any decision on your part.

Thanking you in anticipation.
V.G. Ravlich
Secretary

MERV: I can't come to grips with honours like this. That I was lucky enough for them to have me while I was trying to make my way into VFL football was thanks enough. To be awarded a Life Membership for doing something I love is an honour indeed. Especially seeing as six months ago I was barred for life. No I'm not going into it, but it was a matter of honour and loyalty to my mates.

I wonder if it means free beer whenever I get down to watch a game?

 AUSTRALIAN CRICKET BOARD
20 November 1989

Dear Merv,

**RE: Benson and Hedges First Test – Australia v. New Zealand
Perth, 24–28 November 1989**

Congratulations on your selection for the above match. As you are aware, the conditions of your selection are set out in your Player Contract and in your 1989/90 Australian Players' Handbook and shall apply for all matches for which you are selected during the 1989/90 season. The selected team is:

Allan Border (Capt)	Merv Hughes
Geoff Marsh (V.Capt)	Dean Jones
Terry Alderman	Geoff Lawson
David Boon	Carl Rackemann
Greg Campbell	Mark Taylor
Ian Healy	Steve Waugh

. . .

 1989–90 Summer v New Zealand, Sri Lanka and Pakistan
Australia won 2, drew 4. M. Hughes 34 wickets,
169 runs and arthroscopic surgery on the knee.

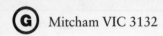 Mitcham VIC 3132

24 November 1989

Merv Hughes
Hyatt
99 Adelaide Terrace
Perth City WA 6000

Happy 28th, you're not getting older – you're thinning out! – and getting fitter faster and stronger (even the legs!) Hope you have a great day on Sunday, and the year ahead is a quintessential one – on and off the field.
Lots of Love Ann [Quinn] and Nicki [Provis] xxx

MERV: Nicole Provis, one of Australia's best female tennis players, also worked on fitness with Ann Quinn.

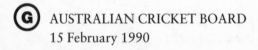

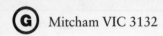 AUSTRALIAN CRICKET BOARD
15 February 1990

Dear Merv,

1990 New Zealand Tour

Congratulations on your conditional selection for this tour.
Please read the information provided below and note any items which require follow up and give them your immediate attention.

1. TOUR PARTY
Allan Border (Captain)
Geoff Marsh (Vice-Captain)
Terry Alderman
David Boon
Greg Campbell

Ian Healy
Merv Hughes
Dean Jones
Simon O'Donnell
Carl Rackemann
Mark Taylor
Peter Taylor
Steve Waugh

Dr. Cam Battersby	(Manager) Queensland, ACB Director
Bob Simpson	(Coach)
Errol Alcott	(Physiotherapist)

. . .

(G) February 1990

Dear Merv,

Well I was speaking to Ann a few hours ago and she told me you had your knee operated on you duffa, she said you were so bored? So I went down to the shops and bought you a card, so I hope the knee gets better very quickly.

The trip so far has been OK the only bad thing is the weather, its so cold over here. At the moment I'm in Chicago and yesterday they had a severe snow storm about 3 feet of snow something I'm not used to. My tennis well that's OK I've been hitting the ball really well I've just been stiff with my draws which is as usual?

Kansas City was OK not a very happening place but we stayed with a lovely family. Chicago is just like New York hectic.

Tomorrow we leave for Washington so I'm looking forward to that.

Ann said you would only be off your feet for two wks that's good. I suppose Ann has told you things have certainly happened with my sister and Todd she's too good and on Valentines day by the way where was my card? Todd gave Tash red roses. Too good. My Mum was telling me before the op you were playing fantastic

Keep it up. Well Merv get well quickly so you can get back on the fast legs. I'll write to you again soon so in the mean time look after yourself and no doubt I'll catch up with you when I get home.

Love
Nikki

 28 February 1990

Dear Merv,

I hope some of the words on this card will inspire you further. You have certainly been made to suffer an enormous amount these past few days. The fact that you went through such lows and depression just shows how much it all means to you. It's sometimes hard to be positive and think like a winner all the time, but everyone no matter what sport or what field of endeavour, experiences such lows.

We are all tested at many times throughout our lives – sometimes it helps us appreciate the good times and highs even more. I'm sure you'll look back on this period in years to come and laugh about it – when life was like a seagull and the jumbo jet!

But Life is great and you are a WINNER – so go and show those selectors and the rest of the team just how strong you are.

Every single leg raise, and lap of the pool, plus all your physio and your whingeing! will all be made worthwhile (Hard work pays off – remember).

So go and create those positive experiences, as now's the time the tough get going, and you're TOUGH and DEPENDABLE.

Good luck in your rehab in the next week or two and with your cricket.

I sure will be thinking of you and sending my positive thoughts across the miles.

With love
Ann

MERV: My knee was right after I missed the One Dayers. I wasn't selected for the Test match. Australia lost. What can I say?

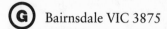 Bairnsdale VIC 3875

16 March 1990

Dear Merv,
Hi, how are you? I hope your knee gets better. Do you remember coming to Bairnsdale to the Basketball grandfinal because my team were runners up and I got my photo taken with you and you signed my shoe. I'll never forget it. I was wondering could I please have an autographed photo of you please. I would really like it.
> Love
> Brooke
> xx

(G) AUSTRALIAN CRICKET BOARD
26 March 1990

Dear Merv,

1990 Sharjah Tour

Congratulations on your conditional selection for this tour.
Please read the information provided below and note any items which require follow up and give them your immediate attention.

1. TOUR PARTY
Allan Border (Captain)
Geoff Marsh (Vice-Captain)
Terry Alderman
David Boon
Greg Campbell
Ian Healy
Merv Hughes
Dean Jones
Simon O'Donnell
Carl Rackemann
Mark Taylor
Peter Taylor
Steve Waugh

Ian McDonald   (Manager)
Bob Simpson   (Coach)
Errol Alcott   (Physiotherapist)
. . .

 AUSTRALIAN CRICKET BOARD
8 May 1990

Australia to the USA 1990

Congratulations on your conditional selection for this tour.

1. Tour Party
David Boon (Captain)
Terry Alderman (Vice Captain)
Ian Healy
Merv Hughes
Dean Jones
Darren Lehmann
Chris Matthews

Carl Rackemann
Jamie Siddons
Peter Taylor
Steve Waugh

Colin Egar (Manager)

2. Match Program

May 12   v Pakistan –   Downing Stadium, Randalls Island,
                                  New York City
                                  12 noon start (reserve day 13 May)

May 19   v Pakistan –   The Coliseum, Los Angeles
                                  4.00pm start (no reserve day)

Playing Conditions: 40 over matches; maximum 8 overs per
bowler . . .

MERV: I can't remember what happened, but I think we had a great
time.

G AUSTRALIAN CRICKET BOARD

MEMO TO Australian Team Members and Contract Players
SUBJECT   Preparation for Season 1990–91
DATE   25 June 1990

We all enjoyed the Ashes victory in 1989, now we must make sure
we retain the Ashes.

To do this we must go into the 1990–91 season with planned
preparation to make sure we reach a level of fitness, that will
enable us to play with the same determination to succeed as we
had in England.

England will be a tougher team to beat this time, so we've got
to be physically and mentally tougher.

Errol Alcott has worked out individual fitness programs for everyone, so its now up to you to follow his instructions.

In other words the holiday is over. Success doesn't come easy, so the better you prepare yourself the tougher it will be for the Poms.

Looking forward to seeing everyone fit and raring to go at the October training camp.

Regards,
Allan Border

MERV: I'm glad to see the off-season (of four weeks) is finally over.

Ⓖ AUSTRALIAN CRICKET BOARD

TO   Australian Team Members and Contract Players
FROM   Errol Alcott
RE   Fitness Program
DATE   21 June 1990

I am writing this letter with an enclosed programme of off-season conditioning, to let you know that the 1990–1991 cricket season is just around the corner. In fact there is only about 14 weeks in which to establish a reasonable level of fitness for the upcoming season.

As you are all aware the 90–91 season will be a long and arduous one especially with a three month tour to the West Indies. Preventable injuries are an unwelcome entity that can and have affected many cricketers at your level. . . .

The following programme of off-season conditioning is broken into two stages:

Stage 1 is to develop or build an endurance base of conditioning. It comprises 5–6 sessions a week for 6–7 weeks.

Stage 2 is to maintain your endurance factor but to really enhance your speed and power; facets of your game that are often required. It is also 5–6 sessions per week for 6–7 weeks.

If you follow this programme as outlined you will have reached a good level of conditioning by the end of September from which to launch into competitive cricket.

Fitness testing will take place in the first week of October, the details of which will be advised to you closer to the time.

The opening page of the programme has been designed to inform you of your past problems, recent problems and key areas to work on during the off season. . . .

MERVYN HUGHES

Previous History	Left knee cyst removal
	Right knee pain
	Cervico thoracic pain
	Right shoulder pain
Problem Areas	Left and right knees
	Thoracic area
Requirements	Leg strengthening
	Weight loss / control
	Abdominal strengthening
	Shoulder strengthening

Stage 1: Programme for Mid-June – July
3 sessions of endurance/speed training per week.
3 sessions of body conditioning (weights).

Endurance/speed

Session 1
4 reps x 200m (1 min rest)	3/4 pace
8 reps x 100m (1 min rest)	3/4 pace
2 sets 10 reps x 15m	full pace
1–2 min rest between sets.	

Session 2
4 reps x 150m (1 min rest)	3/4 pace
6 reps x 100m (1 min rest)	3/4–full pace
10 reps x 25m (walk back recovery)	full pace

Session 3

3 reps x 100m (1 min rest)	3/4 pace
8 reps x 25m (walk back recovery)	full pace
5 reps x 60m (1 min rest)	full pace
2 sets x 10 reps x 15m full pace	
1–2 min rest between sets	

. . .

Stage 2: Programme for August – September
3 sessions speed/maintenance training per week.
3 sessions power conditioning.

Speed

Session 1

5 reps x 200m	full pace
4 reps x 100m	full pace
5 reps x 50m	3/4 pace
4 reps x 60m	slow/fast/slow

Session 2

15 minutes	distance recorded
5 reps x 100m	full pace
5 reps x 30m	3/4 pace
5 reps x 20m	full pace

Session 3

4 reps x 200m	full pace
5 reps x 100m	full pace
5 reps x 20m	full pace
2 sets 10 reps x 15m	full pace

. . .

12 September 1990

Dear Merv,
My name is Quentin A.

   Can I please have a autographed photo of you. Is it true that
Victoria play England in a test in Ballarat at the City Oval if yes
are you in that Victorian team? Can you meet me in the rooms
after the day's finished on the Saturday if I am not there within 10
mins don't worry it's just because so I can get a photo of us.

   I would really like some hints on the game especially bowling.
Because I will be playing Outdoor as I just quit Indoor Cricket
because I believe it teaches you bad habits I will be playing with
Golden Point a Ballarat team.

>   Yours sincerely
>   Quentin A.

this is my Address
. . . Ballarat Vic 3350

Write back!

MERV: It is true, but it's not a Test match and I promise I won't worry,
Quentin.

---

 12 September 1990

Dearest Merv,
hi gorgeous, how's my favourite tequilla friend? I hear you've got
your body fat down to 13.85 – awesome effort!

   If you get down to single figures I'll take you out on an
unforgettable tequilla night but oh no, we can't do that because
we have to keep that body fat down, but I will reward you with a
pressie! I get my assignment back on sport motivation after my
holidays, so I will have to let you see it – only if I got a good mark

though!!! Oh well Uncle Mervin I hope everything is going well and the best of luck in achieving your goals, I know you can do it!! Say hi to Peta for me . . . Hope to see you soon.

> Lots of love
> little Provis (Natty)
> xxx
> xxx

MERV: Natalie is Nicole's younger sister, who I knew through all my fitness work with Ann Quinn.

(**G**) AUSTRALIAN CRICKET BOARD
19 November 1990

Dear Merv,

**RE: Benson and Hedges First Test – Australia v. England
Brisbane, 23–27 November 1990**

Congratulations on your selection for the above match. The conditions of your invitation to play are set out in your 1990/91 ACB Player Contract and in your 1990/91 Australian Players' Handbook and shall apply for all matches for which you are selected during the 1990/91 season.

The selected team is:

Allan Border (Capt)	Dean Jones
Geoff Marsh (V.Capt)	Greg Matthews
Terry Alderman	Carl Rackemann
David Boon	Bruce Reid
Ian Healy	Mark Taylor
Merv Hughes	Steve Waugh

Manager: Ian McDonald
Coach: Bob Simpson
Physiotherapist: Errol Alcott
Umpires: Tony Crafter (SA)
                         Peter McConnell (WA)

Twelfth man will be announced on the morning of the match.

The Australian Team practice schedule is attached, along with your authority to collect airline tickets.

Don't hesitate to contact either Ron Steiner or myself if you have any queries at any time.

            Yours sincerely,
            G. W. Halbish
            General Manager

First Test v England at the Gabba, Brisbane
(23, 24, 25 November 1990)
Australia 152 and 0 for 157 defeated England 194 and 114.
M. Hughes 3/39 and 2/17. First inns 9, second inns dnb.
Terry Alderman took eight wickets, Bruce Reid took
five wickets.

(G) VICTORIAN CRICKET ASSOCIATION
16 December 1990

Dear Merv,

Victoria v. England – Ballarat – 20–23 December 1990

You are invited to represent Victoria in the above match. The previously announced team is:-

Simon O'Donnell (C)	Dean Jones (VC)
Warren Ayres	Peter McIntyre
Darren Berry	Paul Jackson
Darren Lehmann	Paul Reiffel
Damien Fleming	Jamie Siddons
Merv Hughes	Gary Watts

12th man will be announced on the morning of the match . . .

MERV: And Quentin is nowhere to be seen.

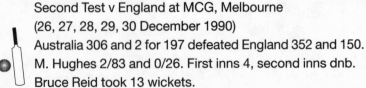

Second Test v England at MCG, Melbourne
(26, 27, 28, 29, 30 December 1990)
Australia 306 and 2 for 197 defeated England 352 and 150.
M. Hughes 2/83 and 0/26. First inns 4, second inns dnb.
Bruce Reid took 13 wickets.

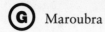 Maroubra

31 December 1990

Dear Merv,
Regarding the second test. The Media, for some reason, do not
realize that it was your softening-up of the 'Poms' that set the
stage for Bruce Reid and company to get right up them and they
certainly routed them or should I say rooted them.
    Good luck to you and the team for the New Year.
                    Regards
                    Reg S.

MERV: Thanks, Reg, I'm glad someone understood what I was doing.
The selectors replaced me with Carl Rackemann for the Third Test in
Sydney. Carl failed to take a wicket, so I was back for the Fourth and Fifth
Tests.

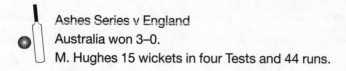

Ashes Series v England
Australia won 3–0.
M. Hughes 15 wickets in four Tests and 44 runs.

MERV: For the first time in a while, I don't need surgery at the end of
a series.

AUSTRALIAN CRICKET BOARD
25 January 1991

1991 West Indies Tour

I am pleased to confirm your conditional selection for this tour.
Please read the information provided below and note any items
which require follow up and give them your immediate attention.

1. Tour Party

G.R. Marsh	M.A. Taylor
D.C. Boon	M.E. Waugh
S.R. Waugh	M.R.J. Veletta
A.R. Border (Captain)	P.L. Taylor
M.G. Hughes	M.R. Whitney
T.M. Alderman	D.M. Jones
G.R.J. Matthews	I.A. Healy
C.J. McDermott	B.A. Reid

Refer attachment.

Laurie Sawle (Manager)
Bob Simpson (Coach)
Errol Alcott (Physiotherapist)

. . .

CHAPTER FOURTEEN

Life in Werribee,

epilogue

I was overseas in the West Indies, and telephones, which was how I kept up with mates during Australian summers, were not an option.

 Monday 25 February 1991

Hi Mervy,

How are you? Looks as though you've been able to dodge the BOUNCERS so far. Hope McDermott recovers from his nasty knock pretty soon. It, (his face), looked really awful on teli.

Here enclosed are some more clippings that you might be interested in. Uni def Richmond by 6 wickets in the one day final last Sunday week too, but that write up was cut into for your book clips.

Gary is going along well with his sport. The Rep Squad had their 1st win last Fri night at Albert Park. There were only 7 players, so Gary got a good run & did well. Of a Sat he starts at cricket at 8.45, then plays b/ball at the Rec Centre at 9.50 (*I'm* team manager this year) then he gets back to Bellbridge for the last hr of play . . .

The Hoppers Crossing batsmen continue to improve with the help of your father. Apparently the Mitchell boy is going back to Footscray next year. They asked your father to coach! (He's not interested) (at this stage anyway).

My tennis team are going well – we haven't been beaten on a Thurs yet (we play the top team this week though) & Tuesday's team wins when I *don't* play.

Today is very hot here, 38°, so the cooler is on & it's really lovely here in the kitchen. We thought your 'Merv' write-up this week (24/2/91) was really good – (Pop was most impressed).

Best go now – Gary's big romance is *off* (after giving that necklace with Together Forever on to Alisha). Since then he has given a new girl, Karen, a heart necklet!!

Love from us here
Fre

P.S. A couple of photos from the Naming Day plus a couple of clippings.

'Y and X, together with their parents, are pleased to announce their engagement to their family and friends. Love and congratulations for a happy life together.' [**Yes, that's Mr X and Ms Y from the 1989 Ashes tour, who had told me they were just sharing a house . . .**]

NSW are 0/70 at 2pm. They need another 80 in 4 hours to win outright (against Vic) & go to top of Shield ladder.
(3pm, 2/105, O'Donnell 2/28)
Mal Perry was thrilled with the book you signed for him.

MERV: Mum and Dad are back in Werribee, and life has moved forward since my mates were writing to me in Essex during 1983. Some of us have grown up.

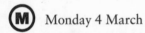

(M) Monday 4 March

Hi Mervy,
How's things?
Hope these letters get to you at some stage – it is very hard for me trying to work out just where to send them especially when I don't know how long it takes for a letter to get to the West Indies.

Yesterday at the Bellbridge BBQ and Presentation of Cricket trophies, Gary won the batting for the U'14s. That really pleased him & we thought it pretty good too, as he only played ½ a season. Just goes to show that his Dad (your dad too!) is a pretty good batting coach! Lots of the Hoppers Crossing cricketers (seniors) have improved heaps too, since he began coaching them at batting . . .

My Thursday tennis team had a win last week & now we are on top of the ladder. I'm to play with the Tues team this week too. Peta's friend Mick came back from W.A. at the weekend although Peta hasn't heard from him yet.

Your father has to have a test for an ulcer under anaesthetic on Wed; he won't be able to drive afterwards so Pete has taken an R.D.O. to drive him there and back.

Gary's team did well at b/ball Sat morning in W/Bee – they won 70 to 6. On Fri night they were beaten by 11 after a pretty close game for most of the night.

Next season, Bellbridge would like you to call at their practice night if at all possible. Because it is a Wed, I said you probably wouldn't have any hope of doing so, but I'd ask you anyway. They realize that oodles of teams must ask you, but, they thought, they *might* have a chance when your little brother plays there.

Cricket, I think, has got to Gaz – he's thinking of giving up B/Ball next season for cricket. Because he has to move up an age group, he doesn't think he'll do very well at B/Ball & may as well play cricket for a season.

Good to see Dodders back in the Vics team for their match against South Aust starting Thurs. I hope he does well, Lehmann suffered an eye injury at State practice (I think) and is to see about it today.

Because you weren't in the one dayer (1st one) I didn't watch the game. But this 1st Test, I'm sleeping on the couch, in the lounge room & watching *most* of the play. This morning it went off at 7, so we missed the last 2 hours, or so, of play. Their camera work isn't as good as here, but it's really good being able to see most of the play.

Thanks for ringing last Wed – it was good to know you weren't sick, as the papers said you had stomach pains and associated headaches. Lots of people asked about you when they read that; so it was good to be able to tell them you were quite o.k.

It was really sad to hear about Gus Logie's mother. Good, though, to hear of the Healy & Veletta babies. Kerry Wright had a baby daughter too & called her Amy Lousie. Last week I had a letter from Barb Jennings – Lindsays wife. Their daughter, Sarah, was born on Peta's b'day, 18th December.

Will go now Merv, hope you are having a great time & get lots more wickets. Congrats on your 4 in the 1st innings, First Test.

> Love from us here
> Fre

P.S. A couple of cuttings that might interest you : Shield team (Dodders in!) & Lehmanns eye injury & last district round write up & ladder.

MERV: Now that they have Dodders back in the team, they will go on to win the Sheffield Shield. I won't be there, but all of my mates in the Australian Team are going to wish I was.

First Test v West Indies at Sabina Park, Kingston, Jamaica
(1, 2, 3, 5, 6 March 1991)
Australia 371 drew with West Indies 264 and 3 for 334.
M. Hughes 4/67 and 0/79. First inns 0, second inns dnb.

(G) TO   Merv Hughes
               Australian Cricket Team
    FROM   Ann Quinn
               London
    DATE   5 April 1991

Dear Merv
Haven't talked to you in a while – so just faxing to wish you all the best for the next Test. We have been training very hard indeed here in London – & all is going great. Pat just left yesterday for Tokyo (also where Todd, Tash & Nick are too) – so I'm all by myself here in London! – but only for a few days before Cath arrives back.

   My Dad keeps me posted of all your results. In fact he just faxed through The Age article on your being low in confidence & bowling not going well – so I hope everything is ok – and you've sorted it all out. Think positively remember. I'm sure you'll correct it in no time.

Great news about the Vic team. I actually felt sorry for you not being there – unable to share the victory celebrations with all the boys. It sure was a fantastic achievement. Its amazing what a few extra nights training will do to a team! . . .

Not much news to report here. Pat's been really giving it everything & is ever so keen to do well – we'll keep our fingers crossed. Nick arrives here in 2 weeks & we're travelling around Europe for 6 weeks – we'll send my schedule when I know it. Let me know if you decide to come over (fare NY–London are only £100) so you should come & visit us all.

Well, good luck for the Test. We all miss you & your jokes (Pat & I rolled laughing the other day – when Pat told your story – about how many calories to deduct for a chuck!)

Work hard, believe, concentrate & have fun & success will return.

Good luck to all the Team.

Love Ann xxx

Third Test v West Indies at Queen's Park Oval, Port-of-Spain, Trinidad
(5, 6, 8, 9, 10 April 1991)
Australia 294 and 2 for 123 drew with West Indies 227.
M. Hughes 4/84. First inns 0, second inns dnb.

16 April 1991

Hi Mervy,

This is my last letter to you – it should reach you in Antigua on the 30th Apr.

Looks like you've seen plenty of rain this tour. What a shame it has spoilt so much of your cricket.

We had a great day at the wedding in Lancefield last Sat and I caught up with my cousins, Ian & David, and their families (Schneeberger). Gary also enjoyed his camping weekend at the Cumberland River. They got beaten by Dandenong before they left Fri night. That team hasn't been beaten this comp yet & over Easter won a tournament in Adelaide againast teams from all over Australia.

We took Peta to the airport Fri. arvo for her trip to W.A. We haven't heard from her yet (we *still* haven't received *your* post card yet and have just about given up hope of ever getting it).

Werribee def Box Hill over the weekend and Lara has had two wins so far. League teams are pretty up & down & there have been a lot of injuries and suspensions.

Sean isn't playing Baseball this season and hopes to go to see Libby and Alicia more often.

It's funny with Peta away – I miss her calling in & her phone calls.

We hope to go to Warrnambool and up to the Grampians next week for a couple of days. (It's not the right time of the year to go to Mildura – so your father says.)

The Herald-Sun people have been on strike so there has been trouble getting papers for a few days. They are back working again now. Your column wasn't in on Sunday, nor was Stacky's.

Best go now, enjoy the rest of your trip – looking forward to seeing you again.

Lots of love from us here

Fre

30 April 1991

TO   Merv Hughes
           Australian Cricket Team
           Royal Antiguan Hotel

FROM   Ann Quinn & Pat Cash

Merv,
Well done on taking four wickets yesterday. Hope all is going
well. We are still hard at work in London . . . Here's Em.
     How ya doing you old so-n-so? Wish you the best – love Em X.
     So what's news? Hope you've been getting my messages. Are
you coming over to see us all? You had better call us and fill us in
on everything. A few setbacks this end – you'll no doubt read
about them in the papers – but all will be OK . . .
     Hope this finds you well, look forward to hearing from you
VERY SOON.
                    Lots of Love
                    Ann

Piss off ya poof. Hope you like the cutout I found in a magazine.
Thought you might appreciate it and need it.
                    Love and kisses
                    Pat

P.S. Say hi to Peta for me next time you talk to her (Ann).

 Fifth Test v West Indies at Recreation Ground, Antigua,
St John's
(27, 28, 29 April and 1, 2 May 1991)
Australia 403 and 265 defeated West Indies 227.
M. Hughes 4/65 and 2/49. First inns 1, second inns 13.

3 May 1991

Hi Mervy,

How's things? [**This can't be from Mum, she's already written her last letter.**]

Great last Test – I stayed up and saw all of the last day's play! Congrats on your game – fancy all of those dropped catches. I really enjoyed watching – BUT – after no sleep for 24 hours I had to go & play tennis. We were one short too, which meant we all had to play an extra set. We won easily & after tennis I was able to come home & sleep (and sleep & sleep & sleep).

Gary is anxiously waiting for you – he wants to go with you & get his hair cut. (He is also disappointed that he hasn't been mentioned in your cricket column) (when the rest of us have).

We finally got your post card – six weeks after you wrote it. Thanks for it.

Ian is feeling the best today that he has been in ages. (I think all the cricket got to him a bit as I liked to watch as much as I could & that then disturbed his sleep.)

Peta enjoyed her holiday in WA with Helen. She has been out and about this week too & hopes to go to Warrnambool before returning to work.

Gary got a really good report at school – we went over Wed & met his form teacher who reported on all of his subjects. His b/ball is going well too. They have only been beaten once on Sat's in W'Bee. Friday night is harder tho & they have only won a few there.

Best go now – have a great holiday – hope the weather is good & that you & Sue enjoy yourselves. See you in a couple of weeks.

Love from us here

Fre

(PG) May 1991

P.S. I bought you a present – Teenage Mutant Ninja Turtle bandaids. [I think there is something seriously wrong when your sister knows that a gift like that will be appreciated.]

Dear Mervie
I'll keep this short & sweet (cos I know you'll have more exciting things to do than read this!!!)

The F'cray boys are going to Hobart (not Adelaide) this weekend – Gav, Sharyn & Stacey are fine. Sharyn is 4mths pregnant. She was crook the 1st 3mths but is OK now. Gav is hanging out to see you. Shazz got put off at work & things have been slow for Gav – as in one day's work last week. Pris has been giving him days at Sands & Macs here & there. Stacey had to do a project on a famous Aussie & did you. All the other kids did explorers etc. She got an excellent for it.

Haven't seen Pris & Shazz for a few weeks but they are fine. Brent came around to show you his kinder photos. He knocked on the door & asked 'Is Merffie home?' Cute.

Michelle & Paul have moved into new home (so we have lost video & microwave). She is 3mths pregnant.

Lisa Foote is too (about 1½ mths).

Kato is due to have her baby at any time. Tricia has moved out of home to house in Wyndomvale.

Marie sent her uniform booklet with you on front cover. It looks grouse.

My knee is OK. The two weeks in Perth & the week I didn't play gave it a good rest & I'm back playing everything.

Ma, Pa, Gazza, Nanna, Kate, Seanie, Tracey are all fine. Sean said to say hello & we passed on all your messages & they all said get rooted back!

Can hardly wait to see you. Have the best holiday & a good rest before you get home.

Lots & lots of love
Peta XXX

P.S. Congrats on winning last Test & doing so well.

P.S. Grant Burns is going over to Canada for at least five weeks 27 May (so he hopes to catch up with you before he goes). Kath & Burnsie got the house about one mth ago on 90 day settlement – so won't move in for a few mths.

MERV: I think life has changed again. Snappa's about to become a father, most of my mates are settling down, Sue (the girl from 'church' who was in Yugoslavia last time you heard from her) is on her way to holiday with me in the US and the house that I share with Peta no longer has a microwave or a video. Time for some serious life decisions.

CHAPTER FIFTEEN

Everybody's Mate

Over the years of my career, the tone of the letters I received didn't change much. They were nearly always encouraging, and most of them were friendly. The thing I found interesting was that once I had established myself in the team, many people wrote to me as though I was a mate of theirs, but I had no idea who they were. And being mates, they didn't hesitate to offer advice when I needed it.

Merv G. Hughes
(Victorian Cricketers)
Adelaide Hilton International
Victoria Square
Adelaide 5000

A Guide Too Being Very Cool
A MUST FOR EVERY CRICKETER

Dear Mr Hughes and Victorian Cricketers,
Being the national heroes that, to me, you are, I thought that I'd write you a list on how to be very very cool.

These rules and regulations are mostly for South Australian reference (as conditions vary from state to state) unless written otherwise.

Read On:

The Rules

1) always, when in SA, listen to the radio station 5A.FM. 107.1, 91.1 on your dial. Never under any circumstances should you listen to: KA.FM (used to be called 5kA) Tripple (sic) FM 5AA or 5AD. Extremely uncool.

2) Always use the world 'Ryeballed'. It means anything you want e.g.
    5A is so Ryeballed (5A is so dumb)
    5A.FM is so Ryeballed (5A.FM is so cool)
    It can mean good or bad. It'll take a while to get used to.

3) Always be friendly when someone asks for an autograph. Most of you are very friendly but some of the Australian players have proved to be mean and horrible and that sticks in the autograph askers mind forever.

4) Try to avoid being near David Hookes. It completely ruins the precious image. he's not respected in SA.

5) Always drink XXXX beer, none of this SA shit. It sucks.

6) Never listen to cricket commentators on T.V. because they sometimes are okay but mostly are very bad. Too Ryballed for words.

7) Never be seen drunk. Very uncool. Ruins the image.

8) Never go anywhere at night but:
   St Leonards, Glenelg
   The Casino
   'McMahons', Jonsley
   'The Botanic' near the Adelaide Hospital
   and the 'Avoca Hotel' South Rd Edwardstown.
   Ring the SA.FM community switchboard for cool places to hang out. Ph . . .

9) When being interviewed try to talk more to the guys from National Nine News because Greg Rees, the sports presenter is very cool.

10) Watch National Nine News.

11) Listen always to 'The Morning Zoo' on SA.FM every week morning from 6.00 – 9.00am. Always listen to 'Chicken Man' at around 6.45 every week morning because that's a series that is very funny. A must.

12) Never listen to or sing any Rita MacNeil songs very very uncool. Very very very very uncool. Never in public should you sing Rita MacNeil songs, just pretend she doesn't exist.
   For Gods Sake You Mustn't hear Rita MacNeil.

13) Try and avoid watching television. Everything on T.V. is very uncool. Get a video or go out. Avoid Rita MacNeil, Beaumont Tiles, Meadow Lea and Poly decorator commercials.

14) BE SEEN singing 'John Lennon' songs.
BE SEEN singing 'Beatles' songs.
BE SEEN singing 'Who' songs.
BE SEEN singing 'The Kinks' songs
BE SEEN wearing Bryan Ferry T-shirts.
(I wear these – like me!! very cool Bryan Ferry T-shirts)
BE SEEN wearing Kleenex Tissue T-shirts.

If you need any more help in whats cool ring 5A.FM community switchboard on . . .

I hope you all found this helpful and remember be proud to show off your new found coolness.

P.S. Remember always go to the BUTTON DELICATESSEN
. . . Thebarton 5031
PH . . .

always go to the Thebarton Library

[P.P.S.] Merv,
My dad girlfriends cousin really likes you, and I sort of told her that we were really good friends and every thing. and she wants to meet you she's 26, blonde hair, blue eyes
          Julie Whittford
          . . . SA   Ph . . .

Could you ring her, she wants you to ring her.
Thanks Buddy

MERV: It looks like it's not easy being cool.

Burnside SA 5066

February 1990

Dear Merv,

Hi! You are most likely to be the most popular player in Australia,
and I guess you get heaps of fan mail, well, sorry but here's more!

I have been a fan of yours for simply ages! Even when you had
long hair! And I consider you to be one of the best fast bowlers in
the world, I'm *sure* you agree!! You are exceptionally talented,
and I envy you!

This year I went to the Adelaide Test, for three days out of five,
and I had a great time watching you bowl, field and have lunch! [**And
don't we all know which of those three I'm best at!**] We took three 24
films of photos, and I've enclosed the good ones of you in my
opinion. Hope you like them, and if you don't want to keep them,
you can always send them back autographed, but it's up to you!!

I know heaps of people who think you are wonderful, and I am
sure you are aware of your popularity. I'm pretty sure you're
going to win the 'Most popular player' competition, I voted for
you three times! Personally I hope I win the holiday, if I do, would
you come with me? [**I can't find a photo of you in the letter, so
you won't mind if I tell you later, will you?**]

Well, anyway I'll ask you when and if I win – I think all this is
just wishful thinking unfortunately!

I think I'm getting off the track, (this must be a most confusing
letter, that is *if* you ever get to read it!!) back to what I was saying
about when I saw you at the cricket. You were going down the
stairs to lunch, and I felt so sorry for you, because of your knee.
You hopped down, and were then swamped by autograph
hunters, it must be a most annoying job! Actually I think it's today
that you are having your knee operation, hope *all* is going well!

On the last day of the Test, you were going onto the field, and
you called up to Geoff Marsh (who was injured at the time, and
unfortunately still is!) for your zinc. He came down and gave you
the zinc, and then you said to get the helmet. So as Geoff ran up for
the helmet, I ran over to you, right by the fence, and took a photo
as you looked into the camera! I said thanks and went back to my

seat, as you started whistling some tune I didn't recognize (no offence there!) and when Geoff came back you pointed over to us and said something like 'it's them again . . .', the rest of it I couldn't recognise, but we were thrilled thank you! All I know is, Geoff ran off chuckling away, it must have been pretty funny! (It was probably something like: 'it's them again, what idiots' etc. etc.)

I read somewhere, oh that's right, in this years W.S.C. magazine, that you are a fan of 'Mental as Anything? So am I!! I bought 'Cyclone Raymond' back last year, and am still loving it. I think they have great music, especially the most recent of it. Martin Plaza has the best voice in Australia, in my opinion, and he's really talented at writing music too. Have you got 'Cyclone Raymond'? I suppose you don't have much time to listen to music, because you're not home all that much! But I do hope you've at least heard 'Monster on the Playground'? It's brilliant!

I read in the 'Ashes Glory' that the team listened to Cold Chisel, or a bit of Roy Orbison, but now, Merv, you can take the 'Mental as Anything' music, and introduce the whole team to their marvellous music!

Finally, I'd like to thank you for reading this letter, and I understand that you are an exceptionally busy man, but I can't help hoping for a reply, but I'll try not to!

Good luck for your bowling in the future, and I also hope the operation went very well! Thank you for entertaining me and others for all these years, both on and off the field. I saw you on 'Hey Hey It's Saturday', 'Sale of the Century' and 'the Comedy Company' and you were brilliant in all of them, especially your punchline 'Nice meeting you, Mr. Lillee' was extra good!!

Thanks again and good luck.

   Love

   Marina L. xxx

PS Say 'hi' to Tony Dodemaide from me when you see him next, thanks! xx

PPS Whenever you're in Adelaide, PLEASE drop in sometimes and I'd adore to see you and the rest of the team.

(G) Woodhouse ...
Glenthompson
Australia

23 February 1990

Dear best cricketer of the world (Merv Hughes),
[I like an understated opening, always leaves you with something to say for a big finish. Good luck.]
    Hope your knee is much better. I heard it is improving. Your going to play against New Zealand aren't you, because if you are, Great! Because I think you are great.
    It's a pity that Border didn't get his fifty isn't it but you won anyway. I went to the M.C.G. and saw Australia beat Pakistan and did you see Jones hit that six! I think that if you were there Pakistan would be all out for zero runs.
    My name is ALEX C . . . and I live in Australia our property name is 'B . . . h' our farm name is 'F . . . h' I am 11 years old. Please write back and can I Please have your Autograph!
                    Yours sincerely
                    Alex C.

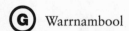

(G) Warrnambool

February 1990

To Mr Hughes,
I am a freak at cricket and you are my favorite player. **[See what I mean by an understated opening.]** I am more a bowler than a batsman and hope to play for Victoria and maybe even Australia. I am almost in Grassmere U14's and my best friend is almost in too.
    I have admired your progress in the last year or so and I hope your knee recovers fully I heard the commentators say in the 2nd test against Sri Lanka that you bowled just over 450 deliveries in

England and about 495 bowls back here in Australia.

Hope you get some good figures in the next year.

Signed

Matthew W.

MERV: Confidence is very important in the development of sports people.

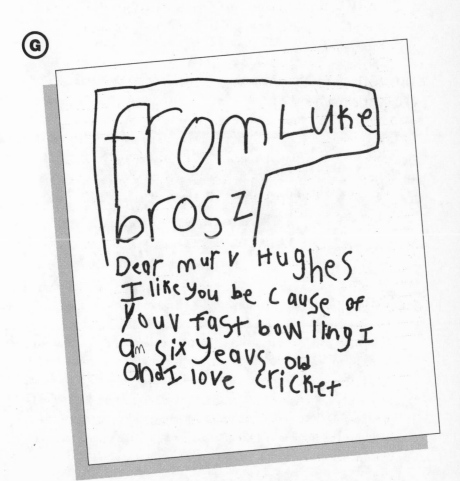

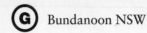 Bundanoon NSW

February 1990

Dear Merv,
I am a 12 year old Boy who admires you greatly, you are to me the Best cricketer in Australian cricket today I have enclosed a picture of you walking back to your run up. If it is not to much trouble could you please send it back to me with your Autograph and could you Also please send me a photo of you
                    Yours sincerely
                    James N.

MERV: This is what I like: modesty, flattery, and James has paid for his own photograph. Good lad.

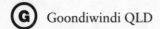 Goondiwindi QLD

19 February 1991

Dear Merv,
How are you? My name is Tyson C . . . I love playing cricket, and I play for a team in Goondiwindi Queensland called Pathers.
    I like bowling and my best performance is 4/2.
    I enjoy your exercises and your tongue. [**Now I don't think we need to go any further, Tyson, thank you. I will deny everything.**] I like your moustache and I like watching you bowl your bouncers.
    I am also going to write to Dean Jones. Please could you and Dean come out to Goondiwindi to give me and the team some fielding, batting, and bowling tips?
                    YOUR FAN:-
                    Tyson

P.S.; Please Reply.

 Footscray

18 March 1991

Merv Hughes
Footscray Cricket Club
Western Oval
Pavilion Footscray Oval
Footscray 3011

Dear Merv,

G'day Merv. I have been wanting to write to you since that fantastic day on the 12th of November 1990, when you won some prizes for me on 'Sale of the Century'. I would like to take this opportunity to thank you because you did not only make my day, you made my year also. You see I was *consistently* having a very bad year, as I had just finished school in 1989 and from January 1990, to November/December 1990, I was unemployed and had a very difficult time finding employment. My degree didn't seem to matter to employers. But you my fellow Western Suburbs friend, took the darkness out of my misery and depression and shed some light for me.

After winning, I thought, 'Well there is some light at the end of the tunnel'. Thank you Merv . . .

I tried desperately to get hold of your address but to no avail. No one would give it to me, your privacy is well respected. However, I do hope you get this letter either way. The address I have sent it to is the only one I could think of sending it at.

Once again thank you very, very much on giving me some good news, as my life has changed since then. I have had good fortune since my win. Today I am employed and $4500 richer. Thank you Merv, you are wonderful. I always said you were my favourite cricketer but, now you have just confirmed that you are my favourite Western Suburbs Neighbour. Good-bye from me and one day I might bump into you and say hello and thank you in person.

Yours sincerely,
MALLY M.

MERV: Not only am I a genius, I'm a lucky charm as well. Can't see you carrying me around on your keyring, though.

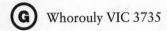

(G) Whorouly VIC 3735

3 July 1991

Dear Mervyn,
I am an avid cricket enthusiast and watch all the matches on TV, even sitting up all night to see the West Indies Tests.

Congratulations on your performances in the West Indies, it was a shame not to win the series, but everyone did their best.

I would like your autograph for my grandchildren please, they would be thrilled to bits.

Best of luck,
Audrey F.
(MRS A. F.)

(G) Parkholme SA

8 October 1991

Dear Mr Hughes,
I sincerely hope you will not be offended by enclosed, it is my own design.

Being a 75¾ yrs old chook Aussie who has been a cricket fan from way back, I lived in Melbourne then! and went to Test matches in the 1930's.

I have tried when you have played here in Adelaide to get your autograph also the rest of the time so far I have only been lucky enough to obtain Steve Waugh & Carl Rackemann still there is always this coming season. Do you think Allan Border would like a look alike.

My eldest grandson Robert P. (nickname Spender) is Captain of Mt. Lofty A Grade Cricket team and has been for the last two seasons. My hobby is knitting dolls. I also have a 'Swag man' called Bill.

Once again I hope you will accept this in the spirit it is given.

Belated and sincere congratulations on your engagement.

Sincerely

Gladys B.

MERV: Gladys has sent me a knitted doll. Enough to scare a baby from ten paces. They won't catch on. Perhaps I should put Gladys in touch with Mally.

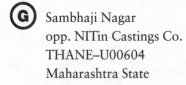 Sambhaji Nagar

opp. NITin Castings Co.

THANE–U00604

Maharashtra State

India

December 1991

To Mr. Merv Hughes

Respected Sir,

I wish you Happy Christmas & A Happy New Year.

Sir, I am happy to receive your Autographed photoes & Autograph.

Sir, Thank you very much for obliging me the Autographs.

Sir, I hope you will accept this letter with my sincere thanks.

Once again I wish you Happy Christmas & A Happy New Year.

Thanks again

Best wishes

Regards

Yours sincerely

Anil Karkhanis

MERV: The Indians are great fans and students of the game. It always gives me such a kick to get requests from other countries. I'm happy to send an autograph, I've just got my doubts about the address.

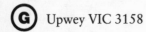 Upwey VIC 3158

3 January 1992

Dear Merv Hughes
Hi!! My name is Michelle and I'm a collector of cricket photo's. I was wondering if you could tell me where I can get an autographed photo of yourself and a photo of yourself & your wife on your wedding day? What's your wife's name? Also could you please tell me where I can get an autographed medium size T-shirt of yourself? I'm trying to get this whole set. I only need 3 more shirts and I'll have the set. I collect all kinds of stuff, such as autographed hats, photo's, posters, T-Shirts, books, etc. If I bought a cricket ball and sent it to you could you please get Victorian side to autograph it for me. Would you mind? What interests do you have besides cricket? Does Victoria bring out a year book? Could you please tell me anything on the history of the Victorian Cricket Association. Mr Hughes I would appreciate any help that you can give me.
　　　　　Thanks
　　　　　Michelle P.

Rangeway WA 6530

20 Februay 1992

Dear Merv I to watch you play cricket espiecisly when you clean bowl the other Batsman that is facing you. My name is Daniel W. and I go to S.t. Johns school in Geraldton and I play cricket for S.t. Johns school. We have two wicket keepers one is me and the other is Luke H. We both have fifteen overs each our games are thirty overs long.

My highest score is Nineteen. I made four fours a quick single then I Hit two runs and got out. I got caught weve played 8 games and weve got 3 games to go.

I hope you make a century in your next game see you when you play your next game.

P.S. Don't forget to wright back, please Merv!!! and can you please give me your autograph.

MERV: Autograph no worries, but don't hold your breath for the century, Daniel. And can I give you another tip. Don't write to Ian Healey – ex-school teacher, red pen, smart arse – spare yourself some grief.

 Deception Bay QLD 4508

March 1992

Dear Mr Hughes

Hello, my name is Scott. I am 11 year old. I have a very exciting hobby and I am writing to you because I would be really happy if you would be a part of it.

I collect letters and autographs from famous people. I have been doing it for 17 months and I have just my 127st reply today. I hope that one day I will be famous myself for having the biggest and best autograph collection in the world. I hope I haven't written when you are too busy. I was really hoping that you would be able to spare a couple of minutes to answer my letter.

If it's possible could I have an autographed photo of you please. It would make me very proud if you would give me your autograph for my collection. So far I don't have a lot of famous sporting people in my collection. I have autographs from Wally Lewis, Leroy Loggins and the Brisbane Bullets. Allan Border, Grant Kenny and Lisa Curry Kenny. I hope that this year I will be able to contact a lot more sporting people.

I love to watch cricket. I play it at school though I don't play for the school. My sport is Ten Pin Bowling. I think I'm pretty good at it. I've been bowling for about 7 months and I have 6 trophies so far. I even have a 1st 2nd and 3rd place trophy for different competitions. I am going to Canberra this year to play for my bowling centre. If I play really well I might bring home a medal. Anyway in case you are very busy I wont hold you up for too much longer. If you don't have a photo spare would you please still reply.

Your autograph on a piece of paper would be just as good. It doesn't matter what you send but it would mean the world to me to have you reply. Thank you for reading my letter. All the best to you.
> Sincerely
> Scott R.

MERV: I hope your address is not an indication of your motives, Scott.

(**G**) FOOTSCRAY FOOTBALL CLUB
26 March 1992

Dear Merv,

RE: CELEBRITY MEMBER
I am writing to advise you the Board of the Footscray Football Club has unanimously appointed you as the Club's Number 1 Celebrity Member.

The Board believes that you have brought great credit and distinction to Footscray, having played with the Footscray District

Cricket Club, and then of course on to State Cricket and International stardom.

We trust that you will accept this appointment as our Number 1 Celebrity Member and the Board looks forward to you and your friends being our guests for the match against St. Kilda next Sunday.

Once again congratulations for a wonderful Cricket season and being our Number 1 Celebrity Member.

> Kind Regards,
> Graeme Pearce
> Chief Executive

MERV: What greater honour can be bestowed than to be invited to be a Celebrity Member of the greatest football club in the history of inflated pig bladders.

In July 1992 I finally got around to visiting Trish Cockrem's class. They had been studying famous Australians, and they conducted a mini 'Press Conference', then had to write a report about it.

 24 July 1992

Merv,
Just a note to send some of the write ups. Remember they are 11 & 12 year olds. One is hilarious I think you'll love it. Thanks again for a great morning. I'll reimburse you if you were out of pocket with cab fares. I forgot when you turned up, I was in shock! and excitement!! My forgetfulness is getting worse in my old age.

Anyway, thanks, train hard, get fit. (I hear you were one of the fittest at Aussie training.) Good luck for the rest of the season. You can do it.

> See you in Brissie soon.
> Trish

24 July 1992
Merve Hughes
My eyes bulged, excitement bubbled up inside me. It couldn't be.
It is . . . Merv Hughes has walked down the steps of my grade
seven classroom. I could feel myself smiling at him. Our teacher
Trish Cockrem walked up to him casually and said hello.
I couldn't believe it. Miss Cockrem knew Merv personally,
well I knew Miss Cockrem was famous, but not that famous. Not
famous enough to know the best bowler for Australia in all time.
I needed his autograph right then and there.

Miss Cockrem told us to go upstairs into Mrs Stulzel's
classroom, where Merv would talk to us about his life, this is
what I found out: Merv has played 63 matches getting 144
wickets including 2 hatrics. Merv has played cricket ever since he
could stand up! He was encouraged to play by his father who was
sports crazy. Merv's best game would have been his 1989 Ashes
Tour, his funniest moment on field would have been when the
captain thought Merv game him a wake up call (he didn't) and
put Hill not Hughes on the score book. Before cricket Merv
played Aussie Rules Football, Golf and Basketball (NOT VERY
WELL).

Merv Hughes is a great Man with many talents and if you are
wondering how long he has had his moustache he has had it for 8
years. Merv if you ever read this thanks for coming you are a
great guy.

Written by Emma-Lee C.

24 July 1992
Merv Hughes visits school children
St Peters Lutheran College
I met Merv Hughes when our class was working in our classroom
when someone came to the door. I recognised him straight away.
(even though I forgot his name and thought he was Don
Bradman)

Merv Hughes is a very well known cricket legend. He was born
in a little town called Euroa, and loved to play cricket in the

backyard with his father. He played cricket within his school and
trained in Melbourne for five years until he made the Australian
team. Merv is now also known for his moustache.

During Merv Hughes time as an Australian cricketer, he has
travelled to many places to play games such as America, Bermuda,
Sharjah, Canada, India, West Indies, New Zealand and England.
He has played 37 tests and 26 one day games in his career, and
even though he has been playing cricket for 27 years, he has
played Aussie Rules for a long time too.

Merv's favourite grounds are the grounds in South Australia
and the W.A.C.A. in Perth.

Even though Merv missed out on playing in Sri Lanka, he
hopes to get to South Africa to play.

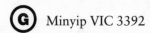

Minyip VIC 3392

30 November 1992

Dear Merv,
I like it when you stir up the crowd and do stretches on the oval. I
think you are the best bowler on the Australian team. I like it
when you hit a big six. [**How do you think I feel?**] I don't play
cricket match, I only play it at school or with my brother.
Cameron, my brother, always hits me for a six or a four. [**That'd
be why you don't play much.**] I am 11 years old and in grade 5.
Could you send me somethings please?
                    From Andrew S.

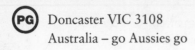

Doncaster VIC 3108
Australia – go Aussies go

7 May 1993

Dear Merv,

Rumor has it that you are 'frustrated'. Well, seven months ago I
was hit by a car, ⇒ comatose, life support etc. Man, there is
something about near death experiences that gives you the most
phenomenally appreciative outlook on life. That's why I'm
writing, because I want to talk you out of this 'frustration'
because not only is it a waste of energy and thinking time that
would be better spent on positive thinking or talking up your
young teammates (Chill man, I'm not saying you are old) Brendan
Julian and Wayne Holdsworth but . . .

Merv, it means that you have forgotten your roots. You hail
from Footscray, and are essentially what I'd call the 'working
man's cricketer.' You were a bloke who really enjoyed a beer or
two (or three or four or . . .), and had what everyone thought was
a 'weight problem'. I say 'weight problem' as everyone in
Australia is under the bullshit philosophy that to be a cricketer
you must be an athlete (this part is true) and to be an athlete you
have to look like an Olympian (this part is bullshit). As I'm sure
you are quite aware, Merv, you are you, and need not change the
essential you, part of which is your natural physique.

But getting back to your roots, how's your wife? Only kidding.

You've come a hell of a long way since those Footscray days.
And I know that inside you, when you take away all the publicity
hype and bull that would make a normal man's head swell, you
are still a 'Footscray Boy'. So Don't Sweat it Man. Next time you
are thinking to yourself how aggravating it is to not be able to
play just remember how absolutely fantastic it is that you are
touring England, with a great Australian team and playing in the
'Ashes' the series that puts the 'icket' in cricket.

I suppose I should tell you that the reason I can empathise so
easily is (and I'm not telling you this for sympathy) because I am
never allowed to play Australian Rules football again after my

accident. If I do, I could die, or get far more serious brain damage than I've got now.

My response has been to hopefully be assistant coach of my club's U-19's team this year, and help them win the premiership that we couldn't win last year. (We made the grand-final, and lost to the team that we beat convincingly in the 2nd-semi final and had beaten by 133 points the last time we played them in home-and-away. Why did we lose the g.f. then? The ground was under 10cm of water as it had rained every day for four days leading up to the g.f. and for 2 hours solid on the day of the g.f., and the ground had no sandbase and was flat i.e. not exactly superabsorbent.)

What I'm trying to say (and believe me, not being able to play footy would 'frustrate' the hell out of me if I LET IT) is that involvement and positive action by you in helping all your teammates, but especially Brendon Julian and Wayne Holdsworth, is best for everyone. I hope you don't mind me saying that they are a big part of the future of Australian cricket. Your role is to act as father to these younger cricketers. You better do your job well, because the future of Australian cricket is resting in your hands . . . and I'm counting on you.

Finally, I guess I better explain why my style of writing seems to presume that we are old mates. Merv, we read about you in the paper and see you on T.V. $\Rightarrow$ Merv the larrikin. That is just you and I respect the fact that you don't bow to the society's pressures and act like the average Australian cricketer in front of the cameras, or in fact in any part of your life. So I think that the Merv that comes through the media is just a slightly distorted version of the real you.

So although we've never met, and you've never heard of me. I know you.

Please write back, or if you don't get the opportunity, call me on your return to Australia.

My home phone number is . . .

Good luck in the series. May you bring home the Ashes,

> Your mate,
> Daniel

MERV: This was an uplifting letter. I had expressed some frustration as I tried to recover from a knee operation in time for the 1993 Ashes Tour and to get a letter like this tells me a couple of things. One is that I should just shut up and stop feeling sorry for myself. The other is that playing for Australia is not a personal thing: a lot of Australians are wishing me well, but the team, and its future, are more important. And I reckon Daniel is exactly right about my weight.

First Test v England at Old Trafford, Manchester
(3, 4, 5, 6, 7 June 1993)
Australia 289 and 5 dec. 432 defeated
England 210 and 332.
M. Hughes 4/59 and 4/92. First inns 2, second inns dnb.

(G) PUMA AUSTRALIA PTY. LTD.
10 June 1993

Dear Merv,
You've done it again.

Just as the press get off your back and leave you alone, you go and turn yourself into a superstar once more!

All of us in the Puma Australian team feel proud of your performance in the First Test.

Congratulations.

Yours sincerely,
Herb Elliott
Managing Director

Ashes Series v England
Australia won 4–1.
M. Hughes 31 wickets, 76 runs and a piece of dead bone
in the leg above the knee requiring surgery.

 Gainsborough
Lincolnshire DN21 1AP

18 August 1993

Dear Mervyn,

Just a note to say a big 'thank you' for all the enjoyment you have
given me this summer. I am sorry that I am having to type this, but
my joints are a bit seized up, so I have difficulty in holding a pen.
I hope you don't mind.

I watched your television interview during the Test at Leeds
and thought what a great character you are. It just confirmed
what I had suspected whilst watching your performances on the
field, as there was always something happening whether you were
bowling, batting or fielding.

I was also sorry to hear that you had received a few critical
letters and I only hope that you can ignore them, as evidently
some people don't appreciate a bloke who can combine good
cricket with a nice bit of showmanship thrown in. It has been a
real pleasure watching you and the rest of the team this year, even
if I am an Englishman.

Finally, Mervyn, I wish you all the good luck and good health
that is going in the future. I can tell that you have been suffering a
bit with a strain at times but, all credit to you, you have soldiered
on for the sake of the team.

Thanks for a lot of entertainment and may you carry on giving
us pleasure for a few more years yet.

Yours sincerely
Basil W. G.

MERV: You're right, Basil. I'm just about buggered, but if I can make you smile while I'm giving it to your team, then I'm happy, too.

 Walton
Liverpool L9 1BX

21 August 1993

Dear Mervyn,
I'm writing to say how much I've enjoyed watching you play in the Ashes Series.

It's saddened me to see you sometimes receiving a poor reception from the English spectators. British sport in general is badly in need of strong competitors like yourself instead of the wishy washy 'Mr Nice Guy' attitude we see so often. Just as many English supporters appreciate your strength and character which has brought a touch of colour to our cricket grounds. Long may you continue.

What, with your character and Brendon Julian's good looks it's been a great Test series for women! **[So what you're saying here is that if BJ and I were out together, I'd be the one who's a 'really nice person'. Thanks for nothing.]**

If you're ever in Liverpool and in need of a good drinking session please call at the above address where this young lady will be happy to show you around!

> With very best wishes
> for your future career
> Geraldine R. (Miss) xx

MERV: You're on, Geraldine, as long as it's not a round of English beer.

G Old Bonalbo 2470

Dear Mr Hughes,
I hope you do not mind me writing to you.

I am an avid supporter of Cricket (I played when I was young & against England too & we won). I am wheelchair bound & I do lots of Crafts.

I set about making a cricketer Doll in softsculpture & I enclose photo of the result!!!

I would like your permission to let my few friends to have a 'MERV HUGHES' doll too. Would you mind?

I do hope your knee is soon perfect again. The team is not the same without your fun & entertainment.

Yours sincerely
Valerie M. N.

P.S. I must be the oldest Merv Hughes fan (73 years young).

G West Didsbury
Manchester M20 2WW
England, UK

Dear Merv,
I have followed your career ever since I first saw you play in 1989, on the 'Ashes' tour. In my opinion you were a great bowler, and a lovely bloke off the field. Thank you for all of the pleasure which you gave to me, and to many other cricket followers. I remember meeting you in 1993, you made me laugh, and it really cheered me up! I would like to wish you every happiness in the future.

If possible, please could you give me your signature, it would be much appreciated. I have enclosed an international reply coupon for your attention.

Best Wishes
AHMER K.

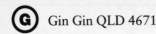

Gin Gin QLD 4671

3 March 1993

Dear Merv,

You have inspired my ten year old grandson John to such an extent that he tries to emulate you when playing cricket either at home or on the playing field at school. Last week during an inter-school game on the home ground he bowled a double hat trick and when in batting scored 1 six 3 fours and two singles. He was elated, we his family proud. Now Merv I hope that you too feel a certain pride in having inspired a little boy to play so well. I know how busy you must be but a brief acknowledgement to John would really make his day. Possible?

Congratulations too on your usual strong play and sense of humour.

Yours sincerely
Merle W.
John W.
. . . Gin Gin Q 4671

Mr Merve HUGHES,

My name is Margaret S., I am 67 years old and have 8 grandchildren. My late husband who passed away earlier this year collected autographs for his sons and our grandchildren. I am now trying to write to famous cricketers in an attempt to continue my husband's hobby.

I have enclosed some pictures and cards and would be honoured if you would autograph them for my grandchildren. You were one of my husband's favourite players.

Thankyou for your valuable time.

Thankyou,
Mrs M.S.

... Merewether
New South Wales 2291

Mr Hughes,
Could you please return my pen thankyou

God bless

MERV: I'm still a hit with the old ladies at least.

(G) FOOTSCRAY CRICKET CLUB
7 September 1993

Dear Sue and Merv,
On behalf of everybody involved at the Footscray Cricket Club
we are very proud to honour your contribution not only to
Australian cricket but to international cricket.

I know that you are both well aware of the function scheduled
for October 3rd. However, I would now like to formally invite
you both for what I am sure will be a most enjoyable evening. The
function commences at 7pm at the Western Oval and it is planned
to finish at 11pm.

Separate invitations have been forwarded to Freda, Ian, Peta
and Gary so if they are reluctant to attend I would appreciate it if
you could use a little persistence. We will have a number of guests
who will be invited to speak but if there is anybody else you
consider should be invited either on a complimentary or non-
complimentary basis then please advise either Geoff Collinson or
myself.

Looking forward to a most successful evening.
                    Yours faithfully,
                    Warwick Burnham
                    President

CHAPTER SIXTEEN

Merv Hughes
Personals

Sometimes, letters arrive that require no explanation.

G 14 October 1986

Dear Merv (Walrus),
We have met before, sort of. Well we have spoken to each other, sort of. Yes, we were the ones that made you get up at the Adelaide Oval to get us Allan Border and Greg Matthews autograph. We were very grateful.

We got your autograph at this match when you were fielding at third man.

We play cricket ourselves for a club in Adelaide.

Our names are Beth and Jo (Joanne). Beth is a batsman and I am a spin bowler. We won the 'A' grade premiership two seasons in a row. We are saving up money to go to the cricket. We hope to see you there.

> All our love
> Jo and Beth
> xxxx

P.S. Please reply to this letter as soon as possible. We look forward to hearing from you.

Our addresses are: Beth P.
                       . . . St. Agnes,
                       S.Aust. 5097

                       Joanne P.
                       . . . Valley View,
                       S.Aust, 5093.

G Aspley QLD 4034

Dear Mr Hughes,
I hope you don't mind my writing to you like this but I just
wanted you to know what an attractive, sexy guy I think you are.
Never in a million years would I have dreamed of writing a letter
to someone like you but I noticed someone asking for the address
to write to one of the other guys and thought 'what the heck – it
can't hurt' so here it is. I've never been a big Cricket fan – it
always seemed so boring and dull – especially the series games but
recently I have found myself watching it. I think there must be
hundreds of other females here that feel the same; its great to see a
great looking guy strutting around the field and in your case one
who has such a brilliant sense of humour and love of life.

I have no idea when or even if you'll ever get this but I just
wanted to write anyway to say thanks for making cricket so much
more interesting to watch. If you get a chance and if it's not a
hassle I would appreciate your autograph. Oh by the way you've
got a great backside. Keep up the good work.

       Take care
       Debby H.

G Mt Druitt NSW 2770

Dear Merv
Although I'm not a sports person, in fact far from it, over the
years whenever your face has appeared on TV or in the
newspapers there has always been something about you that
appealed to me, maybe it's the roguish glint in your eyes, or the
fact you seem to be a rough diamond with a heart of gold.

I really don't know for sure, but your appearance on The Ray
Martin show with your sister prompted me to write. I was going
to sooner but I had no idea where to send the letter and probably
this letter won't reach you anyway.

I don't know if you were having a piece of Ray, and the viewing audience when you said you were not yet 30, but I've always thought you were older (not very complimentary). Well I have the opposite problem. I'm way over that but only look around 30.

But as we all know, age is a state of mind, as long as you look after yourself (especially if you're a woman) you can look great at any age.

So Merv if by some chance you do receive my letter, I hope one day we could meet that would be great, but seeing as I'm only 5'2" it would really be a case of the long and the short of it. But if you don't want this, could you please acknowledge receiving my letter.

> Sincerely
> Eileen

(P.S. I've enclosed a photograph)
The touch up on the photo was a double chin I used to have Ha!

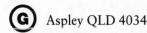

Aspley QLD 4034

Dear Merv,
I hope you don't mind my writing to you. This probably seems really crazy to you but then I'm always doing something crazy. Although this is the first time I've ever been silly enough to write to anyone famous. I did write to you a couple of months ago requesting an autograph but as I wasn't sure where to send it you may not have got it. I feel like a fool but as I'll never get to meet you in person it doesn't matter.

Congratulations on winning the one day series in the West Indies. It was just unlucky you didn't get to beat them in the five-day games. It was great to watch anyway. The Australians did an excellent job. Personally, I think you are the sexiest looking guy in the team. Not an attractive, handsome guy but you do have a certain appeal, especially to females plus a great arse.

Well I'd better finish this and get ready for work. I would appreciate an autograph when you get a few minutes.

Thanks from a Merv Hughes fan.

Debby H.

 Kyneton

21 March 1988

Dear Merv,

Hi! How are you? I hope that your back is not giving you too much pain and I hope that you aren't feeling too uncomfortable at the moment. I was very sorry to hear that you won't be going to England after all, you must be very disappointed – although I am quite happy to see you stay in Australia!

I read in the newspaper that you were going to try and 'become fitter' and lose some weight – well, I've said it before and I'll say it again, I think you're lovely just the way you are! Of course if you want to keep your place in the Australian side you'll have to do something about it, but I think Allan Border is simply having a 'whinge' for the sake of it! He isn't exactly 'slim' himself and there are a few others in the team who could be classed as pudgy – David Boon for example. Don't get me wrong, I think he's great, but you are definitely not the only guy in the team who needs to watch his weight!

I'm just sorry that you have injured yourself because you deserve to have a bit of good luck come your way. I am sure you would have made good use of your time in England and you can only hope that the chance arises again soon. One good thing about your predicament is that you'll have lots of time on your hands to write letters (that is if you can write!). I realise that a guy of your gorgeous, totally wonderful status would be bombarded with letters, but just remember that I'm waiting and that I'm willing to take whatever comes my way if it is even remotely connected with you! Naturally, I'd be willing to take you in person but obviously with your injury, your exercise is limited and that puts an end to what I'd have in mind if I ever got within 10 ft. of you!

Anyway, I had better be going, once again I'm sorry to hear about your injury, but remember if you want your back rubbed or anything like that . . . although on second thoughts, a letter would be fine! Take care of yourself and I hope to hear from you very soon!

> Lots of Love,
> Diane E.
> xxx

 18 January 1992

Merv
Hi I didn't know how I should've started this letter because I don't want it to sound too formal and say To Mr Mervin Hughes and just saying Merv sounds very Australian. At the moment I'm watching Australia play India in the first final and the score is 0/18.

Well I better introduce myself. Hi my name is Clare W . . . and I'm a great Tasmanian (you know the small state off Victoria). Anyway I'm a 13 y.o. girl who has loved to watch you play ever since I could understand the play of cricket which was a few years ago.

As soon as your book MERV MY LIFE AND OTHER FUNNY STORIES came out in 1990 I had to go and buy it.

I was just wondering if it was possible for you to write back and would it be possible to get your home address because I only got to write to you through the Board because there was an article in Star magazine about Simon O'Donnell.

If you do decide to write here's my address:

Miss Clare W.

. . . Newstead TAS

7250

        lots a luv & kisses

        Clare

P.S. Are the rumours I've heard about you getting married are they true?

P.P.S. If they are I'm expecting an invitation!

P.P.P.S. Only joking about the other P.P.S!

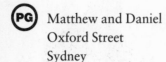 Matthew and Daniel

Oxford Street

Sydney

24 January 1991

Dear Merv

We think you are a fantastic cricketer. You really remind us of the Village People, do you remember them?

    Keep up the good work.

        Love

        Matthew and Daniel

PS We are gay too.

CHAPTER SEVENTEEN

The End

(G) AUSTRALIAN CRICKET BOARD
26 January 1994

Dear Merv,

1994 Coca-Cola Australian Tour to South Africa

Congratulations on your conditional selection for this tour.

Please read the information provided below and note any items which require follow up and give them your immediate attention.

1. Tour Party

Allan Border	(Qld)	Captain
Mark Taylor	(NSW)	Vice-Captain
David Boon	(Tas)	
Matthew Hayden	(Qld)	
Ian Healy	(Qld)	
Merv Hughes	(Vic)	
Dean Jones	(Vic)	
Craig McDermott	(Qld)	
Glenn McGrath	(NSW)	
Tim May	(SA)	
Paul Reiffel	(Vic)	
Michael Slater	(NSW)	
Shane Warne	(Vic)	
Mark Waugh	(NSW)	
Steve Waugh	(NSW)	

Manager:	Dr Cameron Battersby (Qld)
Coach:	Bob Simpson (NSW)
Physiotherapist:	Errol Alcott (NSW)

. . .

MERV: I'm back. I haven't played a Test in Australia this summer because I had a piece of dead bone the size of a 50-cent piece taken from the end of my femur when I got back from last winter's Ashes tour. So I missed three Tests against New Zealand and three against South Africa.

First Test v South Africa at New Wanderers,
Johannesburg (4, 5, 6, 7 and 8 March 1994)
Australia 248 and 256 lost to
South Africa 251 and 9 dec. 450.
M. Hughes 3/59 and 1/86.
First inns 7, second inns 26 not out.

MERV: Despite a rear-guard action where Tim May and I tried to keep the South African bowlers at bay for three hours, we got rolled. I gave Gary Kirsten some advice, he got out and I got fined 1000 Rand by the match referee. I also got involved in a full and frank exchange of views with a spectator. The ACB fined me an additional $4000 for the Kirsten incident and gave me a $2000 suspended fine for not hitting the spectator. The hearing was held in Sydney while I was asleep in Johannesburg. The message was clear: Australia's tactics had changed and it was time to pull my head in. Shane Warne was also fined $4000 by the Board for an on-field incident.

G Shane Warne & Merv Hughes

A.C.B. Alan Crompton, with two kilos of plumbs in his gob spat out the greatest dribble I have ever heard.

You two had already been fined etc. As a fair dinkum Aussie that was that as far as I concerned.

If I was Captain of Australia there would be no $4000.00 fine for the simple reason there would be no Aussie's over there (we would be on the plane home).

In 1964 I was in that dreadful place called South Africa. You would not send your mother-in-law there with a sick dog. The Yarpies are going to get there come-upperance because the blacks have been waiting a long time to repay them their dues.

The bottom line is obvious, in that, if Warne & Hughes where just ordinary cricketers no problem. Or a pair of silver tails with Uni degrees.

All the best

Sender: Once a jolly swagman . . .

Second Test v South Africa at Newlands, Cape Town
(17, 18, 19, 20 and 21 March 1994)
Australia 435 and 1/92 defeated
South Africa 361 and 164.
M. Hughes 0/80 and 0/12. First inns 0, second inns dnb.

MERV: I did not play Test cricket again.

M. Hughes
53 Tests, 212 Test wickets, 1032 Test runs.
33 One Day Internationals, 39 wickets, 100 runs.

MERV: Eventually it dawned on me that I was not going to make my way back into the Australian side. Throughout a player's First Class career, the ACB contributes to a provident fund. However, to claim the money from the fund the player must be formally retired for two years. So, at the end of every career, a cricketer needs to admit to himself and the world that his time in cricket is over. I was forced to put my feelings into words.

23 April 1997

Richard Watson
Acting Chief Executive Officer
Australian Cricket Board

Dear Richard,

It is with great regret and overwhelming disappointment that I write these words.

Since my last appearance for Australia in 1994, I have been working extremely hard (And hoping for several other rival fast bowlers to retire gracefully, injure themselves or burn out) in my aim of securing a third Ashes tour in 1997.

However, after being consistently overlooked by the Victorian selectors, it dismays me greatly to have been similarly overlooked by the national selectors.

It is obvious that with the departure of Lawrie Sawle (chairman) and Bob Simpson (coach) from the selection panel, two of my greatest supporters, that my time is up.

This decision by the national selectors to overlook me has hurt and embarrassed me deeply.

I had felt that the new panel's decision to name Mark Taylor as captain offered me some hope but the recent demise of another fat boy in David Boon has indicated there are limited positions available for overweight cricketers.

With great regret (and overwhelming relief), I must announce that I have now officially retired from international cricket, unless you need me in the next month.

Yours sincerely
Merv Hughes

9 October 1998

Mr Ken Jacobs
Chief Executive
Victorian Cricket Association

Dear Ken

Perceived Reality

Selectors' Version	My Version
Selection for Victoria is not something given lightly	Representing Victoria is a privilege and an honour
Practical jokes are good for morale	I have always given 100% effort in everything I have done for the Victorian Cricket Team both on and off the field
Practical jokes can be counter-productive if taken to excess	Dead Ants wasn't my idea
The Victorian Team must have an extensive pre-season training program to ensure maximum levels of fitness	I like to go into a season mentally fresh
All players must show high levels of achievement in the beep test	Show me a bowler who can score highly on the beep test and I'll show you one who can't but still took 212 Test wickets for Australia
Fast bowlers must be fit and capable of multiple spells	I would have thought with a coach named Barrel and a Captain who lives on chocolate milkshakes and toasted sandwiches, I'd be a chance for selection
Your pre-season training is often disrupted by your commercial obligations	A man has to eat

We had bad luck on the day	I played for the Canberra Comets in the Mercantile Mutual Cup last year and we beat Victoria!!!!
When fielding, if the ball comes to you along the ground, once it gets within two metres of your feet, you can't see it.	I'm a great catch close to the wicket
We think you have a great deal to offer Victorian Cricket in some form of coaching capacity	A man has to eat
By formally announcing your retirement, you can have access to the Players' Provident Fund	A man has to eat

Given what seems to be irreconcilable differences between the selectors and me, it is with regret that I formally announce my resignation from First Class cricket.

I am sure you, the Victorian Cricket Association Board and the Victorian cricket community understand what a great honour I consider it has been to play for Victoria.

> Yours sincerely
> Merv Hughes

Just as I was preparing this book, a letter arrived that brought memories flooding back.

 Bangalore 560050
India

22 April 2001

Dear Sir,

As one of your most ardent admirers, I am very happy to write to you and wish you all the best in life.

The other day I re-read an article 'A typical Aussie Paceman' published in THE HINDU newspaper (Madras) dated 21 May 1994. I enjoyed it thoroughly and it prompted me to write to you. Here are some excerpts from it:

'Perhaps the significance of Merv Hughes in the Australian new ball attack is yet to be comprehended. What's vivid to the cricket fans is the Victorian's massive build and thick and drooping "Walrus" moustache. Surely Hughes does not enter the field to amuse the public but to instil fear in the batsmen. You need to ask only the batsmen the world over as to how Hughes has tormented, teased and sorted them out.

'Hughes is perhaps the only player in the present squad in whom is manifest a true and typical Aussie fast bowler's trait . . . spitting fire and demonstrating fulsome "aggro". He has an attitude and approach which suggest his contempt for batsmen.'

The write-up also quotes you:

'That's the way I was brought up as a junior. The environment I was brought up in stressed on playing to win. On the ground you play within the rules of the game to win. You play tough . . . you play hard.'

Well, sir, you played the game real tough and hard and made wonderful contributions to the game. And you became one of the biggest names in Victorian and Australian cricket. Like me, your fans everywhere recall with great pleasure your innumerable splendid performances.

May I seek a kind favour from you?

I am a serious collector of autographs of Test cricketers and my collection *is 50 years old*. It covers many great legends like m/s Bradman, O'Reilly, Larwood, Miller, Worrell, Soberes, Hutton, Compton, etc.

But YOUR autograph is missing.

May I request you to kindly send me 7 or 8 of your *autographs* and an *autographed photo* (preferably an action picture).

If possible, will you kindly also write me a brief letter?

I have enclosed sheets of paper and self-addressed envelope.

I would deem it a *SPECIAL PRIVILEGE* to add your autograph and letter to my collection. I am sure you will oblige me.

Thanking you and with all best wishes to you and your family for good health and happiness ALWAYS and with Kind regards,

> Yours sincerely,
> D.N. Raghavendra Rao

P.S. Please do send me the autographs. Kindly do not disappoint me, Sir.

> Many thanks. DNR

MERV: Sometimes the effort put into a letter by its writer is magnified in the eyes of the recipient.

At the end of 1995, Peta decided I needed a bit of a rev up, so she contacted thirty of my friends and asked them to write down a memory involving me that she could present me for Christmas. Surprisingly, people responded.

G November 1995

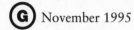

Dear Merv

Two things occurred to me when Dan & I were first contacted by Peta about this project. The first was that you have a one-in-a-million sister and a fantastic, supportive family. Her idea was borne out of the thought that the following collection of notes and memories would serve to give you a boost after a particularly difficult period of injuries and other general frustrations associated with your cricketing endeavours. A fantastic gesture and one that I know will mean a lot to you. (Whether you will admit it or not!)

The second notion came to me when I considered the range of people that were to contribute. No doubt you will pick up this booklet in years to come when cricket has become a series of fond memories and be able to track the progress of your (now) 34 years, not through wickets and runs, but through laughs and friendships (and quite possibly alcohol). Many have come to know you through cricket just as I have. Few are happy to leave it at that. All of us in these pages are linked by a common denominator. (Sorry, I know maths was never a strong point of yours!) All have come to know and love Merv the person, whatever you happened to be doing at the time.

Personally, I always struggle when I'm asked to describe what you're about or to recount a favourite story that involves yourself. After so many years and countless times doubled over, pissing myself laughing at another spontaneous antic, maybe I've come to expect it as normal. For instance, I would defy anyone playing in your group to maintain concentration for a full 18 holes of golf, particularly if you're a couple of strokes behind! I find myself surprised that people meeting you for the first time are taken aback, perhaps expecting a shallow veneer of the usual 'personalities' who play by the accepted rules and take themselves far too seriously. In that way your greatest strength is that you have achieved what you have without compromising anything of yourself or the people around you.

Since I have known you we have both experienced a few ups and downs, on and off the park. No matter who you are, you still need people around who you can trust to call and talk to about anything, anytime. I value our friendship enormously and was rapt to be chosen as godfather to your gorgeous daughter Madeline. I look forward to many more years of laughs and beers.

So read on, safe in the knowledge that, at one stage or another, you have successfully pestered and annoyed the living shit out of each and every one of these contributors!

And we wouldn't have it any other way.

> Love ya.
> Dod

MERV: Tony Dodemaide and I spent our cricket lives together as team-mates at Footscray and playing for Victoria and Australia. There is no better way to know a man.

Acknowledgements

It is often said that the production of a book is like the birth of a child. Well I've been involved in both in the last few months and there are no similarities. All of my thanks and love go to the four most important people in my life: my wonderful wife Sue, and my three marvellous children, Madeline, Timothy and Scott.

Ian Cover has been a great support throughout my career and its afterlife. He suggested that the letters I have received over twenty years would contain a few laughs, and gave birth to the idea behind this book. I hope he was right. Thanks Ian.

Sue Hines was brave enough to buy me lunch and listen to Thommo and me tell stories, and then agree to publish *Dear Merv*. Thanks Sue. Thanks also to everyone else involved in the production of the book: Jacqui Thompson, who laughed at all the right spots; Andrew Cunningham, design genius; Rachel Lawson, the smiling editor with the soft touch; and Peter Thompson, who polished the idea.

Thank you to those thousands of people who have written to me over many years. Your interest in me was always an encouragement. Thank you to all those who have let me use their letters in *Dear Merv*, and a special thank you to Mum and Dad, Peta, Gary, Snappa and Katie Toohey.

The author wishes to thank the following for their kind permission to use their letters:

> Australian Cricket Board, Rob & Deb Barker, John Benaud,
> Diane Borserio, Luke Brosz, Timothy Burges, Warwick Burnham,
> Pat Cash, Geoff Collinson, Ian Cook, Elsie Crampton,
> Tyson Cross, Susan Crow, Alex Cuming, Karen Dethomas,
> Tony Dodemaide, Herb Elliott, John Forbes, Jenny Gavrilovic,
> Basil Godley, Darren Goodwin, Daniel Gorza, Graham Halbish,
> Hon. Bob Hawke A.C., Graham Hill, Andrew Holland, Freda
> Hughes, Ian Hughes, Peta Hughes, Ken Jacobs, Melissa Jarmey,
> Anil Karkhanis, Ahmer Khokhar, Justin Lawrence, Michelle
> Maloney, Graham May, Joanne Perry, Ann Quinn, Mally
> Rebuffo, David Richards, Lawrie Sawle, Reginald Seeney, Bob

Simpson, Richard Smith, Snappa, Keith Stackpole, Andrew
Stewart, Joanne Stoios, Helen Sutherland, L.H.S. Thompson,
Daniel Tofler, Katie Toohey, John Townsend, Victorian Cricket
Association, Mark Wakelin, Don Wigan, Brian Wiggins, Sean
Wiggins, K.M. Wijesuriya, Matthew Wood.